The Self-Help Guide for
Special Kids and Their Parents

The Self-Help Guide for Special Kids and Their Parents

Joan Matthews and James Williams

Jessica Kingsley Publishers
London and Philadelphia

First published in the United Kingdom in 2000 by
Jessica Kingsley Publishers Ltd,
116 Pentonville Road,
London N1 9JB, England
and
325 Chestnut Street,
Philadelphia, PA 19106, USA.

www.jkp.com

Copyright © 2000 Joan Matthews and James Williams

Library of Congress Cataloging in Publication Data
Matthews, Joan Lord.
The self-help guide for special kids and their parents / Joan Matthews and James Williams.
p.cm.
Includes bibliographical references and index.
ISBN 1 85302 1-85302-914-9 (pbk : alk. paper)
1. Autism in children 2. Autistic children 3. Parents of autistic children. 4. Self-help techniques. I. Williams, James, 1988– II. Title.
RJ506.A9.M38 2000
618.92'8982--dc21   00-030212

British Library Cataloguing in Publication Data
A CIP catalogue record for this book is available from the British Library

ISBN 1 85302 914 9

Printed and Bound in Great Britain by
Athenaeum Press, Gateshead, Tyne and Wear

To Doug

Dedicated, loving, patient husband and father, who has put up with our endless projects and schemes, who has endured the constant invasion of his office, and even provided the computers, paper, software, and expertise we needed to keep the creative processes going.

Abbreviations

My mom and I are sometimes lazy, and we didn't want to write the same thing over and over again, so you'll see some abbreviations in this book. This is what they stand for:

NP = normal person

SP = special person (anyone who suffers from a developmental disability, an autistic-spectrum disorder, a sensory disorder, or who has special neurological needs that average people do not have)

NPs = more than one normal person

SPs = more than one special person

NK = normal kid

SK = special kid

NKs = normal kids

SKs = special kids

NFs = normal feet

NB = normal baby

SB = special baby

NBs = more than one normal baby

SBs = more than one special baby

Contents

Preface to the Revised Edition

Imagine an ordinary classroom full of ordinary eight-year-olds engaged in ordinary activities. Suddenly the teacher announces that it is time for the 'Finding Game.' All heads turn to the back of the room and stare at a strange-looking boy who is rolling the hem of his shirt and humming to himself. The teacher tells this boy to stand and face the back wall. As soon as he complies, the other kids jump up from their desks and rearrange themselves, giggling in anticipation of the fun they are about to have.

When the kids are seated at different desks, the boy at the back of the room is told to turn around and identify all the students by their first name. He turns, struggles to refocus his eyes after having closed them, and stares out at the sea of eager faces. He feels panic rising from the tips of his toes to the top of his head.

To him, everyone looks alike. He can hardly tell the difference between a girl and a boy. As he stutters out the names, trying to remember that boys have short hair and girls have long hair, the kids in the class laugh and whoop with delight. He is apparently reciting names at random. The fear is so intense now that the boy starts gnawing on his tongue. His teacher tells him to stop. Then he grabs his shirt and starts to roll the hem upward. The kids titter as they see his soft belly, the result of low muscle tone. The teacher again tells him to stop. Next, he starts rotating from side to side in a maneuver the class has dubbed the 'washing machine'. Again, he is told to stop.

After it is all over, the boy has identified only five faces correctly. But the teacher praises him, because the day before, it was only four.

Now, let's skip ahead to another day, about three months in the future. The strange little boy is once more standing in front of the class. He now knows the name of every student in the room, but has stubbornly refused to acknowledge or work with any of them. To help him interact with the students, the teacher has devised the 'Question Game,' whereby the boy has to pick one student per day and ask him or her a question in front of the class. The boy has been given a class list, and each day he crosses off the student he 'interacted' with.

Again he stares out at the sea of faces, and while they still all look alike, he can now attach a name to each face. He opens his mouth to ask his question, but his mind goes blank. He has forgotten how to speak. His mouth stays open and he begins to bite his tongue. The teacher tells him to stop. He repeats all his inappropriate behaviors – from rolling sideways to falling over on one of the desks. Every eye is on him as he struggles to remember his question. Finally he hears himself announce the person of the day and ask a question, but it is not the question he'd rehearsed. He repeats it under his breath to make sure he heard himself correctly. The audience titters with laughter.

Fortunately the person of the day is a compassionate boy, who gives a brief but sincere reply. The questioner sits back down at his desk, trying now to cope with the pounding pain that has suddenly developed in his head.

As barbaric as these scenes seem, they provided the impetus for the book you are now reading. The little boy, as you've probably guessed, was James, the co-author of this book, and the ordinary classroom was his second grade. I had the opportunity to witness James's public deterioration during the 'Question Game.' The look on his face was of a condemned man facing a firing squad. Within a week, I had pulled him out of mainstream education entirely. Like his former classmates, he was eight years old at the time.

At first, we simply needed to get over the experience of mainstreaming before we took the next step. We began taking walks, all the while talking about James and his life. If we encountered anyone we knew, James would usually tune out and play 'frozen.' I would nudge him on the back and prompt him to 'say hello.' On one occasion after that had happened, I asked him, 'Why do I always have to remind you to say hello? What's so *hard* about saying hello? Why can't you just say it?'

His response surprised me, and as we discussed the complexities of saying hello from his point of view, I realized that his thoughts on the subject were valuable, and maybe could help other parents and the children themselves understand what was going on.

We went home and wrote an essay called *The Fear of Saying Hello*, and that's how this book was born.

Our first topic naturally led into another and another, until we set ourselves a goal of two chapters a day for two weeks. That number proved woefully inadequate so we kept on writing. In this initial phase, I did all the typing based on James's ideas and my interpretations of these ideas. Finally I burned out, wrote our intended final chapter – Saying Goodbye – and got up from the computer. I needed a break from the trials and tribulations of our misunderstood SP – special person. But James slipped into my chair and started typing on his own. Every time I called for him, it seemed, he was sitting there clacking away. His topics became increasingly exotic and funny, but when I sat down to read some of them, I was shocked and impressed at how insightful he was on subjects I had no knowledge of. All in all, he wrote about 35 chapters, many of which are included in this book. In the first edition, all his writing was in a block, but we re-organized the chapters for this revised edition, so his work got scattered around. Be on the lookout for his by-line. He also snuck in new problems within chapters, many of which I only just discovered, and recently added several new chapters (see Chapters 12 and 25) for this revised edition.

When the first edition was completed, we sent it to an e-mail acquaintance over the Internet. She reviewed it on several bulletin boards, and parents wrote to us asking for a copy. As the word got out, reviews of it started appearing in various places, and more requests came in. Distribution was a snap: James simply sent out the computer file of the book as an e-mail attachment. We got requests from all over the world, and we were introduced to the awesome power and convenience of our global communication system.

James returned to school at age 10 and, at the time of this writing, is a fully mainstreamed fifth-grader without special services. He has friends and a full social life. He has had the great fortune to have been born in the era of computers and e-mail, which have given him a way to communicate without the terrors of eye contact, loud voices, and people who are standing too close, demanding a reply. He has also been blessed with a father who buys every new electronic machine that comes on the market, and it is his father's patience and willingness to teach his son how to type, learn through computerized instruction, send e-mail, and set up a website that have made all the difference in this formerly alienated, speech-impaired child. Without Dad, this book would certainly have never been written.

J.M.
2000

Imagine the boy has grown-up a little more and is three years older. He is now in fifth-grade and is doing well in school. There are no more barbaric scenes. His teacher sees how well he is doing and is caring and nice. No bad kids are in his class. In fact, many things have happened in his life at school.

For example, his class dissected sheep's hearts and looked at chicken bones under a microscope. The little boy played 'Father Time' in his fifth-grade play and chased Dick Clark around the stage, but didn't catch him!

Now he has had many *good* experiences in school, and is starting to like it. Of course, the boy is me, James, and everything I have said is true.

J.W.
2000

Disclaimer

When the original version of this book was distributed over the Internet, we received some harsh criticism about the dismal way our special person's life was depicted, and about the tendency of the mother to 'hit' her child on the back whenever she wanted him to do something. Also, both parents in our book seemed to be unstable 'rage-aholics', ranting and screaming at their special-needs child for the tiniest infractions of the household rules. We were asked by a number of people to state that the evil mother is a fictional character, or better yet, to change the whole tone of the book.

We are not suggesting that this is how we or other real parents behave, but that often this is how a special-needs child perceives the adults around him. A special-needs child, remember, is generally denied a normal childhood, and goes from one therapist to another, where he is poked and prodded and forced to do things normal kids aren't even aware of. In my experience with experts and therapists and certainly with adult bystanders, few adults take a special- needs child's feelings of distress seriously, nor do they even attempt to get into the child's world or to listen to the child's claims that something hurts when it wouldn't hurt a normal kid.

This book was written to give those kids a voice, to help you get into their heads, to give you a new understanding that a light tap on the back can be experienced as a hard whack by an overly sensitive child, and that a slightly raised voice can seem unbearably loud to a child with sound sensitivities.

We purposely exaggerated reality to make a point, therefore, but some of the scenarios are so outlandish that we hope you will find them funny. James and I actually had a great time coming up with the predicaments faced by our poor SP, and though we want the reader to learn from them, we hope you regard them more as satire than actual fact. In reality, I sometimes place my hand on James's back in a protective, supportive fashion when I know he is terrified. This protective gesture turned into a 'hit on the back' in our discussions, as a way of demonstrating how terror overstimulates James's nervous system to such a degree that he cannot tolerate any physical contact with anyone, not even the gentlest touch.

I still admit that the imperfect, impatient mother is in me, and part of our book's purpose was to present Mom in other than glowing, heroic terms. Mom is only human, and we believe those selfless moms who sit on the floor with their special child for 12 hours a day 7 days a week are as fictitious as the mother in our story, who is constantly on the phone complaining about her child.

Reality lies somewhere in between, and though our book is not intended to be taken as literal reality, we hope that you will come away with a better appreciation of the complexity of your child's world, and most importantly, the depth of his feelings. In almost all other books, it is adults who speak for the children. In our book, the child speaks for himself.

He deserves to be heard.

This is a purely illustrative text and any derogatory reference to particular individuals or professional groups was our perception and is not meant to offend.

'He' is used in reference to SPs throughout the text, as our own main reference is of course, James. We appreciate many of your SPs will be 'She's'. Please bear with us.

Thank you

Joan

1

Saying Hello

Problem

When one normal person comes up to another normal person and says 'Hello,' the first NP expects the second NP to make eye contact, smile, feel good that someone is talking to him, then say hello back.

But a special person can't do all that. When an NP comes up to an SP and says 'Hello,' the SP freezes, looks down out of sheer terror, feels fear in his entire body, and forgets how to talk. He just wishes the NP would go away.

Usually, the NP will repeat himself. 'Hello,' he'll say, more loudly this time. But the special person has forgotten how to speak. Sometimes the SP's mother will hit him on the back and command, 'Say Hello.' The special person, out of fear, may echo 'Hello' quickly but then become frozen again. Often, though, the mother's message gets scrambled, and the SP may hear, 'Say yellow' or 'Sail low,' or something that makes no sense.

A very thoughtless NP may shout 'HELLO!' a third time, which hurts the special person's ears (see Chapter 2: Noise Sensitivity). Now the SP might shout 'Hello' back, out of fear that the other person will say a fourth hello even louder. Other times, the person who said 'Hello' gives up and goes away.

Solution

The special person needs to practice saying hello over and over with a mom or a sister or a nice aunt. He needs to videotape himself saying hello, so it becomes a familiar situation, and he can do it without having to think. It might help if you let him watch excerpts from movies in which people are greeting each other appropriately, though you run the risk of having him fixate on a particular scene and then repeating it endlessly. (See Chapter 24: Having an Urge to Quote.) You might want to write up short skits in which people are saying hello in various ways, then have the SP try out all the parts. After he has practiced hello in this formal fashion, you may want to start saying hello to him at random during the day, so he gets used to a spontaneous need to respond. Your familiar voice is not the same as a stranger's coming out of the blue, but if you throw out a dozen hellos every day, eventually the terror of having to greet someone may lessen.

One of the main problems with mastering the art of saying hello is that, down deep, the SP doesn't really understand *why* he has to say hello. After all, what does that weird word mean? It doesn't convey any information other than to say 'I'm here,' but to the SP's way of reasoning, it is obvious that he is here because you can see him. After all, most SPs use their eyes, not their ears, to take in environmental information (see Chapter 23: Auditory Processing Delays), so an auditory signal that someone is present seems irrelevant in the face of a visual one. And even if the SP isn't terrified by having to interact with a new person and deal with a change in his life (see Chapter 9: Change), he wants simply to launch into his topic of interest without a useless preamble that only wastes time (see Chapter 29: Being Obsessed with Time).

In short, there isn't any good reason for saying hello, and that may trouble your SP. You may have to concede that this is one more of those silly NP requirements that every NP follows and no NP questions. You can throw up your hands, laugh, and say, 'Well, you know how it is with NPs. They need at least two different reminders for every one thing that happens.' Try not to use the 'Stupid NP' defense too often, but with something as irrational as saying hello, you may have no better explanation.

2

Noise Sensitivity

Problem

When one NP talks to another NP, nobody is bothered by the noise. The first NP knows instinctively how loud to speak, and he automatically adjusts his volume to the conditions of the environment or the condition of the listener (if the listener is very old, for example, the NP may talk louder). NPs generally have well-functioning feedback systems, and unless they are wearing earmuffs, they can usually tell how loud they are speaking by listening to themselves.

When an NP talks to an SP, the NP talks the same way he talks with another NP – in other words, too loud. The noise is often like a swarm of bees or like a drill bit whirring in the SP's ear. The SP often looks down or turns his head away from the noise. The NP, noticing that he has lost the SP's attention, often talks louder, hoping the SP will hear him. The mother may hit the SP on the back and say, 'Someone is speaking to you.'

The SP knows this, but is defending himself from the pain. He either tunes the NP out, or plays frozen (see Chapter 49: Playing Frozen) so that he becomes oblivious to everything around him. This makes the NP angry, and he might talk even louder and louder. Or he might just give up and walk away, deciding that the SP is a jerk and not worth the trouble.

The mother of the SP may force the SP to answer back, and the SP, in terror, will reply using his loudest voice, since he is not threatened by his own noise. The mother will then say, 'SHH! You're talking too loud.' But the SP doesn't understand this, because EVERYBODY talks too loud to him, and nobody tells NPs to be quiet.

This is very confusing to the SP.

Solution

SPs, for noise sensitivity, try to wear ear plugs as much as possible. Wear them all the time in the house and when you are talking on the phone. If you spend a lot of your time in the quiet, you will not be as afraid of noises as you once were. If someone is talking very loud, remember that this is how you are experiencing it, not the other NPs. You might try to reply in a very very soft voice, to alert the NP that he is talking too loud.

You might also try auditory integration training (AIT). For a complete description of AIT, see Appendix I.

3

Eye Contact

Problem

When one NP talks to another NP, they both look into each other's eyes. That is how it is done – looking helps an NP understand what someone else is saying. It also gives a non-verbal message that the listener is paying attention. Besides, NPs like to look into each other's eyes; it makes them feel connected and validated by each other.

When an NP talks to an SP, the NP expects the SP to look at him. However, at the first word, the SP goes into a state of shock, as mentioned above. Since the SP just wishes the person will go away, he is, of course, afraid of eye contact, because making eye contact will acknowledge that the SP *knows* the NP is speaking. And looking into someone's eyes only makes the terror of his presence worse.

The SP experiences another person's eyes as if they were two bright suns blinding him. The eyes glare at him like enormous spotlights. They slice through him like giant bolts of lightning. They remind him of those swinging lights in the ceiling that cops shine into your eyes when they're giving you the third degree. The SP experiences a terror so horrible that he feels he is shrivelling up under the intense heat of the NP's glare. The NP, however, thinks the SP is just rude and ill-mannered when he looks away. Sometimes the SP's mother hits him on the back and commands, 'Look at someone when they talk to you!' The SP now has to do it out of fear and terror of his mother as well as of the stupid NP. So the SP looks up, goes into shock, gets blinded, and wants to go home. And at this point, it becomes absolutely impossible for the SP to hear, let alone understand, what the NP is saying.

Solution

Don't make the SP look and listen at the same time. If he turns his head, he is trying to listen to you in his own way. He can hear you better if he is not (a) being struck by lightning bolts of terror, (b) filled with an intense desire to go home, and (c) overwhelmed by the visual images in a person's face. Sometimes an SP's brain can process only one sort of sensory information at a time. If he's looking, he's unable to listen, and vice versa. Don't ask a lot of questions of the SP. He does not want to talk to you if you are a new person. He is having enough trouble just looking at you without having to remember how to speak. So instead, why don't you talk to the SP's mother, who undoubtedly is dying to talk to someone after having spent the day with her weird child, and when the SP is ready to talk to you, he will speak. He is not being rude or inappropriate; you would not do any better if you had to deal with his terror.

Help the SP practice eye contact at home, where he is not terrified. *SPs,* first look at a person's nose. Noses are not as scary as eyes because they do not change their expression or convey a person's feelings. They also are not the sensory organ that acknowledges understanding and identification. In other words, the nose does not say, 'Aha! I see you standing there!' The other person will probably not know that you are looking at his nose, so you can fool him into thinking you have good manners.

However, if it is absolutely impossible for you to look and listen at the same time, keep turning your head, but frequently say, 'I'm listening,' to let the speaker know that you are paying attention in your own way. *Mothers,* you can help your SP by simply explaining to a new person that your child can understand better when he is not making eye contact. If the new person thinks this is weird, chances are he/she won't accept your child no matter how much explaining you do.

4
Recognizing Faces

Problem

When an NP is born, he is programmed to seek out his mother's face. As she sings and coos to him, he studies her features, learning the physical details of the benevolent giant that he apparently has wrapped around his little finger. As a normal baby grows, he goes through a stage called 'falling in love with the world.' He seeks out faces whenever he can and smiles at them, delighting in the massive expressions of delight and affection that he receives in return. Every time this happens, he is learning a little more about the human face, and a brain center that is solely responsible for facial recognition gets stimulated. As the young NP develops, so does his facial recognition center, until he can easily recognize lots of different people in his world.

When an SP develops, he fears eye contact, as you know, so he turns away from faces. Hence, his facial recognition center is understimulated and doesn't develop properly. As he grows up, even when he is ready to make eye contact and interact with other people, they all look the same to him, because his brain hasn't been trained to recognize the subtle differences between people. James, for example, thought all Asian women were his babysitter, Holly Kim, and he'd shout, 'There's Holly!' every time an Oriental woman of any age walked by. Even when he finally had a best friend, he had a hard time telling the difference between the friend and the friend's younger brother. Sometimes he'd look at one of these brothers and say, 'Which one are you?' His 'best' friend, of course, would be irritated. And people would often pass by and say, 'Hi, James,' and James would say, 'Who are you?' Stroke victims who lose that part of their brain talk about how terrifying it is not to be able to recognize anyone and to have a supposed stranger greet them as an old friend.

It makes them fear all social contact, they say. Is it any wonder, then, that our children are afraid of other people?

Solution

The best way to develop an ability to recognize faces is to look at them, thereby stimulating the face center of the brain. However, if an SP is terrified of eye contact, looking at real people is simply too stressful. Therefore, have your child look at lots and lots of photographs of faces. Photographs are not scary because they do not say hello to you and do not expect you to talk to them. James has a computer CD of old movies that has dozens and dozens of photos of actors. He figured out a way to tap directly into the photo files so he could view them apart from the commentary.

Actors' faces are good because they tend to be posed and display exaggerated emotions. Photos can be viewed in the privacy of one's computer room and can be looked at over and over. Pretty soon your SP will experience the joy of familiarity and recognition when he brings up the same photo repeatedly, and of course, he'll be able to study the facial features slowly so that he can learn from them. We also study videos and sometimes we freeze a single frame at a time and analyze what the person is feeling. The key here is the slow pace and the ability to repeat. Real life whizzes by at a pace that is simply too fast for the SP to process, and there is no going back. Often I've wished for an instant replay capability in real life so James could have some extra processing time. If possible, I make James redo an interaction that went badly, so we can re-write reality.

The important thing in teaching an SP is to get the necessary information into the brain in *any* way possible. A face on a photograph will stimulate your SP's brain the same way a real face will, often much better, if he routinely blocks out real people. Learning to identify people will go a long way in beginning to solve the other terrors associated with social contact.

5
Eye Sensitivity

Problem 1

When a normal kid goes into a large store, or a mall, or a park, or a new house, he thinks, 'Oh boy! Look at all this great stuff!' Then he/she goes from one thing to another, deciding what to investigate and what to pass by. This gives him/her great pleasure and satisfying visual stimulation. Normal kids (NKs) like to look at all kinds of new things, picking and choosing what they will look at more closely.

When an SP walks into a large store or other place with too many things to look at, he immediately goes into overload. Probably this is because his eyes process things very fast and he goes crazy from all the images he sees. They are like darts or bullets shooting into his eyes. He covers his eyes, just like you would if you were being attacked.

When the NP looks at something new, it takes him a while to process the new thing. However, when an SP sees something, he understands and processes it immediately. He is all-finished looking at something in a second! That's why he looks at something briefly, then turns his head away to rest. Sometimes his mother hits him on the back and says, 'LOOK! LOOK at this.' But the SP has ALREADY looked and doesn't want to keep looking at the same thing, which bothers his nerves. This is just like the NP's annoyance when the SP chants something over and over (see Chapter 47: Mouth Control). The SP loves to hear the same sounds over and over, because he tends to be a slow *auditory* processor, as opposed to his being a rapid *visual* processor. This is the first major principle for understanding your SP, and it will help you go a long way towards understanding what your SP avoids and what he fixates on.

He does not know he is annoying you when he chants and doesn't understand *why* you are annoyed. Well, when you make the

SP look at something for a long time, that is the same kind of annoyance to him as his chanting is to you.

Solution 1

Don't make the SP go into large malls or superstores. Let him sit in the car, or stay home, or wear sunglasses. The world has too many things in it anyway, and for the SP, the world has twice the too many things that you think it has!

Until James was seven, he used to hide his face in the seat of the car when it was time to enter a supermarket, or he'd lie on the floor whenever we went into a large department store. Finally I asked him what the problem was, and he said, 'There are too many things to look at.'

I said, 'Don't look at them.'

He said, 'I *have* to look at them.'

'Why?'

'Because they are *there*.'

This is not the world that I live in – where things lunge at me, demanding my attention – but I imagine I'd be hiding my head in the upholstery, too, if that was how my sensory system worked.

Mothers, don't use your own experience of how many things you chose to look at or how long you wish to look at them as a measuring stick of appropriateness for your child. If your SP processes something after looking at it for a second, this doesn't mean that he has ADD or a short attention span. He should be allowed to look at things just as long (or as short) as he wants.

Problem 2

When a normal person looks at his dinner, he thinks, 'Oh boy! Something good to eat.' If the person next to him is eating something weird, the NP simply looks the other way and continues eating his own food. Even if his neighbor is eating fried tree bark with raccoon sauce and boiled ants, the NP will just ignore it.

The SP's sensitive eyes, however, get sick at the sight of weird food. It makes him want to throw up. He cannot eat if someone next to him is feasting on, for example, salmon sandwiches, clam chowder, or anything having a weird color and/or smell (see

Chapter 10: Nose Sensitivity). Since his eyes are generally his dominant sense, he may judge a food's taste by what it looks like, and if it's visually repulsive, his mind may react to it as if it were last year's green eggs and ham.

Solution 2

If you are eating something weird, let the SP eat at another table, or let him barricade himself with cereal boxes. Or better yet, put two or three cereal boxes around your weird food. Don't make him eat at the table if seeing your food makes him feel like throwing up. This is especially important at holidays, when he is already miserable because of all the people invading his house. (See Chapter 26: Special Occasions.)

Problem 3

When an NP has his picture taken, he smiles, says 'Cheese,' and looks into the camera. He often loves having his picture taken so he can see how handsome he is.

When an SP has his picture taken, the flashbulb blinds him, hurts his eyes, and makes afterimages in his mind for up to an hour later. This drives the SP crazy, and thus he fears cameras as if they were instruments of torture. Even the sound of the camera bothers him, because he knows the flash is coming.

Solution 3

Don't make the SP have his picture taken. This is very important. His frown or closed eyes will only spoil your picture anyway. Videotape him instead, or let him look down during a group photograph. We have an amusing family picture in which the only part of James that can he seen is his hand waving from behind the couch. I also have a summer camp picture consisting of three rows of beautiful little smiling faces and James standing off to the side, obviously saying something negative. (He was actually chanting to reduce his fear of the flashbulbs.)

When James was older, he revealed to me that the flashbulbs no longer hurt his eyes but he still feared cameras and photographs.

They made him feel very weird. As we were talking, I remembered a movie scene in which a tribesman grabs a camera and dashes it to pieces, because he believes that having his picture taken would 'steal his soul.' When I related this story to James, his eyes lit up in recognition and he said, 'That's what it's like. That's how I feel. It's stealing my soul.' This discussion impressed me in two ways: First, that James would apparently understand a difficult concept such as his 'soul' even though he had a hard time understanding basic ideas. Conversely, I realized once more that James's worldview was seemingly that of a primitive human being. Like the tribesman, James probably experienced all the terrors felt by ancient people who were unable to control their world. Because of his language deficits and neurological delay, James's brain might have still been in the hunter-gatherer era, particularly since they experienced life as an 'eat or be eaten' proposition.

In this regard, it was easier for me to understand the terror James always displayed when a camera was produced. It wasn't just a flashbulb he was facing; it was annihilation. And interestingly, after our discussion, James stopped fearing cameras and now loves to have his picture taken.

6

Eye Teaming*

Problem

Because an SP has overly developed peripheral vision and has badly developed head-on vision, his eyes go in different directions, and can't team properly. The reason why an SP has overly developed peripheral vision is because, since he is in a state of fear all the time, he is afraid a predator is going to attack him. As you all know, predators do not attack you from the front, they attack you from the side. So the SP must stay alert, and use his peripheral vision to defend himself! This fear stands in the way of learning eye teaming. Hence, his eyes can't work together properly, so SPs see differently from an NP.

But this also tells you why he cannot aim. Since he cannot see properly, and sees in a criss-cross, he sees things in a different place, rather than where they are in real life. That's why he's always dropping things and bumping things and cannot catch a ball. The mother, finally, will hit the SP on the back and scream, 'Use your eyes, like everybody ELSE!'

Solution

Tell your SP that no predator will attack him. Then get him vision therapy.

[*By Mom*]: Vision therapy helps not only with eye teaming but with focusing and other aspects of vision. A developmental optometrist can do a complete evaluation of how your child sees. If the hemispheres of his brain are not working together normally, chances are his eyes aren't either. By helping the eyes to work as a

---

* By James, age 8

team, you're encouraging parts of the brain to work as a team as well. Ironically, this will cut down on some of the visual hyperacuity and overload your child suffers from. If his eyes work as a team, then they won't be sending so many random images into the brain. The left hemisphere, which screens and filters, will be able to establish some control over what visual information makes it into the brain, and visual overload (the kind that James suffered every time we walked into a large store) may be reduced.

7
Touch Sensitivity

Problem 1

When one NP touches another NP, a warm exchange of feeling takes place. NPs like to touch each other and be touched. It is what NPs do. Mothers touch their kids; kids hold on to their mothers. This is one of the basic ways that NPs interact and bond with one another.

When an NP touches an SP, the SP feels an unpleasant sensation on his skin and sometimes throughout his whole body. He might feel itchy or have a burning sensation. If he can get away, he usually does. Or he flinches, or plays frozen. An SP kid often doesn't know how to get away, so he turns off all his feelings as someone touches him. The SP's mother hits him on the back and says angrily, 'Aunt Bertha is hugging you. Smile or something.' So the SP smiles in fear that someone might start yelling at him, which will hurt his ears (see Chapter 2: Noise Sensitivity) and further compound the discomfort.

The SP sometimes lives in great fear that someone will touch him and that nobody will understand how awful it is to be touched. He might want to wear heavy clothes in the summer, or put a hood up over his head, or walk around people. The touch Problem is made worse by the fact that the SP sometimes has balance and space problems and often doesn't know how to walk around another person without colliding into that person (see Chapter 19: Space Problems). Often after a bump with an NP, the NP will complain or yell and make the SP feel even worse.

Solution 1

Be respectful of the SP's personal space. Do not touch him unless he wants to be touched. Hug him if he is in a hugging mood, but make sure that it is his mood, not yours. Remember, the SP has learned to put up with a lot of suffering, and he will simply suffer your touch the way he suffers a loud piece of rock music or a light that is too bright. He will wait for your touch to be over, as if he were being tortured. That is not the reason you are touching him, is it?

If the SP bumps into you, remember that he probably did not see you. He is not doing it because he is daydreaming or clumsy, but only because he did not process your image in his mind.

Problem 2

When an NP gets his hair washed, combed, or cut, he thinks, 'Oh boy! How good this feels. Mmm, so soft and refreshing.' After a haircut, he feels clean and neat and cool. He loves hearing the scissors go snip, snip, snip as his long locks of hair fall on the floor. When he goes home and washes his short hair, he loves the feel of the water and soap on his scalp.

When an SP gets his hair washed, combed, or cut, he thinks he is being tortured. He is in intense pain. His scalp hurts. His hair hurts. The feel of fingers digging into his scalp is horrible. The fingers scratch him, like high-nailed demons, no matter how gentle the NP tries to wash his hair.

A haircut is worse. His hair hurts as it is being cut. Yes, it *hurts*. The SP wants to cry in pain except that hair cutters are usually mean and unsympathetic and they tell him to shut up and be still. Haircuts are humiliating, too, because everyone else just sits there calmly and lets their hair fall around their chair. It doesn't occur to the SP that those other people are not experiencing *any* pain. He just assumes that they are coping with the agony better than he is, which makes him feel like a failure.

Hair washing, if it comes in the morning, makes the SP afraid to get out of bed, because pain awaits him. He does anything to avoid having his hair washed.

Solution 2

Offer the SP a large bribe, such as ten lottery tickets, to have his hair cut without a fuss. Make it large enough so the SP will be fixated on his reward and thus better able to endure the pain. During a hair washing, let the SP listen to music or sing to him. You might let him chant or kiss the walls or do echolalia, or quote from movies that have otherwise been banned from your house. Let him indulge all those forbidden impulses, and he may forget about the pain on the top of his head.

Problem 3

When an NP gets new clothes, he thinks, 'Oh boy! A new shirt! New pants! I'll look great!'

When an SP gets new clothes, he immediately rejects them because they are new (see Chapter 9: Change) and they feel different. But even if they are just like the pair he wore out, the SP will have to get used to the feel and shade of the new pants. It is very hard for an SP to get used to a different style of clothes. If he has worn sweat pants all winter, it is difficult for him to start wearing shorts all of a sudden, and feel the air on his legs, etc. When the summer if over, it is hard for him to start wearing pants again, since they put pressure on different parts of his legs. He dislikes tight things, and so hates tight shirts or pants.

Solution 3

Let the SP wear what he wants. Don't make him go places where he has to dress in good clothes that he is not used to. Limit his social contact to events that are casual. Don't make him go to his cousin's wedding, for example. He will not have a good time, and nobody will want him around anyway. Hire a babysitter and let him stay home in his favorite clothes.

Problem 4

[*By James, age 8*]: When an NB (normal baby) is born, he starts mouthing toys, to experience them and see how they feel. This gives the NB chewing experience, which will help him as an NK and NP at mealtimes. He loves the feeling of toys.

When an SB (special baby) is born, sometimes he is filled with touch sensitivity. He will want to get away from objects touching him. Hence, the SB has no interest in mouthing toys, so he does not mouth anything at the appropriate time. If you make him mouth anything, he may scream. He just wants to get away from touch, since to an SB, touch feels like somebody stabbing or hurting him.

Solution 4

Start slowly. If the SB is simply trying to escape from your touch, he is not ready to be touched yet. Don't force him. The SP must get used to the feeling of toys in his mouth, too. He might be eight years old when he is ready, but that's fine because an SP is different from an NP. Start with a flat toy. Flat toys are not as scary; they do not scrape his mouth because they are not bumpy.

Do not force him to mouth toys. Then he will scream because somebody is forcing him and yelling at him. At some point, the SP will get in the mood for mouthing toys, and he'll do it! Be patient and do not force him!

[By Mom]: Try putting your finger into his mouth and pressing on the upper palate. This helps because you are flattening out and desensitizing the surface of the mouth so that bumpy things will not feel like thumbtacks scraping him.

8

Shaking or Holding Hands

Problem 1

When one NP greets another NP, sometimes they shake hands. The first NP extends his right hand to the second NP, who extends his right hand, and they shake across their bodies. NPs like to make contact in this way, and it is a form of introduction and connection to them.

When an NP greets an SP, you know what happens – the SP goes into shock, or plays frozen, or has his own variation of a panic attack. At any rate, his ability to process information or make judgments becomes severely hampered by his anxiety.

Therefore, if the NP is thoughtless enough to extend his hand, the SP will either tune the hand out, or will respond with a tactile version of echolalia, i.e. he will extend the hand that looks like the hand that is being extended toward him. (Echolalia, you remember, is an indication that input has been received but not processed. Thus, output will remain unprocessed; the outputter will simply regurgitate what went in.) In other words, when the NP extends his right hand, the SP will extend his left hand, since both of those hands are on the same side of the room. The same brain problem that made it hard for the SP to figure out how to use 'I' and 'you' (see Chapter 43: The Rules of Language) will make it difficult for the SP to figure out which hand to extend when someone else's right hand is thrust at him. If he's frozen, his mother may prompt him, 'Shake this person's hand,' and then the SP raises his left hand. But the mother may say, 'Use your right hand!' This is an added stress, since the SP doesn't understand why it matters.

Finally, as a right-hemisphere processor, the SP may be left-handed, and thus it would be natural for him to extend his left hand, making it ever more confusing.

Solution 1

Practice shaking hands repeatedly at home. Train the SP to extend his right hand as a reflex. Do it over and over, hundreds of times. If he panics when he has to shake a real stranger's hand, you can prompt him to extend his right hand and shake. But don't hit him on the back!

Problem 2

[*By James, age 8*]: Since there is not much internal activity going on in an NP's mind, he can process more than one thing at the same time. So he can process the sights and sounds and concentrate on holding hands at the same time. This is an important task to learn – holding somebody's hand in a public place, especially if your mother wants to protect you from cars that are in very dangerous places. This is the way people have always survived on busy streets in the NP world.

But since there is tons of internal activity going on in an SP's mind (because there are so many sights and sounds that must be processed), the mind slows down like an overloaded machine. Also, since an SP cannot process more than one incoming sensory channel at a time, his mind is clogged up with many thoughts and the only way to get rid of them completely is to process a MILLION things at the same time, which he cannot do. So he becomes overwhelmed by the sights and sounds of the NP world, and cannot concentrate on holding on to somebody's hand, too. So he often lets go of his mother's hand and runs into the street.

In addition, the sensation of the other person's hand may feel like something stabbing him (see Chapter 7: Touch Sensitivity). And he may not understand how a car can sometimes be dangerous because it is not dangerous when he rides in it. He will only learn about how risky things are if he tries them himself (which means that he will have to do a dangerous thing like run in front of the car before he KNOWS it is dangerous), because he does not have future judgment. (See Chapter 78: Future Judgment.) So he might stop holding the person's hand, just so it can be a little easier to process all the stuff he has to process in his head, or so he can more easily run in front of a moving car to see for himself if it is dangerous. His mother hits him on the back and screams, 'Hold my hand! You're slowing me down.

We're going to be late.' The SP may then turn out into the road, not noticing that any cars are coming, because he is too busy processing other things. His mother can't hit him on the back since the SP is not in her reach, so she screeches at him, 'You're going to get killed! Cars are dangerous! COME BACK! You're not safe!' But the SP was only freeing himself from a huge confusion in his head, so he could manage it better. He couldn't concentrate on where he was going and other things, too, so he did not see the cars.

Solution 2

[*By Mom*]: Normalize the tactile sensations on his hands so that he can hold somebody's hand in enjoyment, and it does not feel like a person stabbing him. Have him touch lots of objects of various sorts, so his hands won't be so sensitive.

Then you can give him left-brain exercises, so he is not overwhelmed by all the sights and sounds at once, and he can concentrate on holding hands and process things at the same time. If he is chanting while you are walking down the street, let him do so if he is not bothering anybody. Chanting actually cuts down the amount of input, so there isn't as much activity going on in the SP's brain and he can focus on what you want him to do.

9
Change

Problem 1

When a normal person gets a present or a new thing, he feels happy. He looks forward to his birthday and to Christmas because of the great new stuff. When he makes a new friend or goes to a new place, he feels excited, too. This is what makes his life interesting.

When a special person gets a present, he is filled with the same terror he feels when a new person says hello to him. A present represents a *change*, and *change is the most terrifying thing in the world to an SP*. He spends his whole life trying to avoid change. You probably already know this, but if not, it is the second major principle that will help you understand your SP.

Fear of change causes all kinds of behavior problems in the SP. For example, the SP is always under a terrible amount of stress and dread because NPs are constantly changing their mind. The SP learns to distrust the world and other people because they are always modifying their schedule or throwing things out or buying new things. They don't understand that change affects the SP like an earthquake or a volcano. Everything gets disrupted. The SP lives in a very fragile world, like a house of cards. One slight alteration can cause the whole house to fall down.

Solution 1

The easiest solution for the SP is to live alone and not to have anything to do with other people. This will only work if the SP can do his own laundry, make his own bed, prepare his own food, and hold down a job to pay for his life. Mothers can start training their special kids early in self-help, so they don't have to have roommates who are constantly rearranging the furniture, taking the scissors out of the drawer and not putting them back, leaving the remote on the couch rather than in its proper place, and behaving in an unpredictable and disorganized fashion.

If the SP cannot get away from people because he is young or in school or living at home, he can try to have special chants that make him feel safe. Sometimes reciting the alphabet or counting to ten can help relax him enough so he can deal with the change.

The people who live with the SP must learn that when the SP freaks out because they buy a new toy, for example, he is only reacting to the extreme fear that he feels. He has just endured an earthquake or a typhoon inside, and he has to recover.

Problem 2

When an NP sees a movie, he understands the movie just by seeing it once, and he says to himself, 'What a nice movie,' and resumes his life. He will see a different movie the next week, because he likes new things.

When an SP sees a movie for the first time, chances are he is too scared to understand anything, since the movie is new and hence a change. So he has to see it two or three times before he overcomes his fear. But then, even though he is no longer afraid of the movie, he understands and processes *auditory* things very slowly. It may take him ten times as long as it takes for an NP to understand something he has heard. Since he wants to understand, the SP may go to the same movie over and over again.

NPs get driven crazy by this type of repetition, but this is how an SP learns. Unfortunately, the SP may become so used to a given movie that he is unable to watch anything else. NPs say that he is 'fixated' on a certain movie, and they try to get him to stop watching it. They don't understand that the predictability of an old movie is soothing to an SP, who is constantly terrified by the unpredictability and changeability of real life.

Also, in a movie that he is has seen repeatedly, the SP does not need to fear change and the future, because he knows what will happen. This is a way of escaping the fear the SP has of his own future and the constant changes in his life.

Solution 2

Let the SP see a movie as many times as it takes for him to understand it. If ticket money is an issue, make him wait until the movie comes out on video. If he has a hard time waiting, chances are there is some other movie already released on video that you can interest him in for the next month or so. He is not acting 'autistic'; he is merely trying to ameliorate his terror of the changes of everyday life.

10

Nose Sensitivity

Problem

When one NP eats with another NP, they usually don't notice if the food stinks. If the first NP is eating, for example, a salmon sandwich, the second NP can usually ignore the smell by concentrating on his own food. If they are both eating salmon sandwiches, then neither one is bothered by the smell.

If an SP eats with an NP, often the NP's food stinks and makes the SP want to throw up. The SP can often smell the stink even if he goes into another room. The stink might linger in the house for hours afterwards, making the SP want to throw up every time he goes into the kitchen. The NPs don't understand, or they laugh at the SP, which is cruel. If the NP had to sit at the table with someone eating a swamp sandwich, he would get sick, too, and no one would laugh at him. Sometimes the mother of the SP hits him on the back and says, 'Don't leave the table. That's rude.' So the SP has to sit and suffer, since it is hard for an SP to block out a smell. Usually he will stop eating so he doesn't throw up. Then the mother of the SP hits him on the back again and says, 'You're not eating your dinner. And I went to the trouble to make you your favorite noodles and sauce. You drive me crazy. I don't know what's wrong with you.' Then the SP has to (1) sit and suffer the smell, (2) starve in silence, and (3) feel miserable because his mother yelled at him yet again.

Sooner or later, all that hitting is going to give the SP a sore back. So he has to go to the chiropractor (see Chapter 58: The Chiropractor).

Solution

Let the SP eat by himself if you are serving something that has a strong smell. Don't make him join you at a dinner party if you are serving, for example, Chinese food. Let him eat his white rice in his own room. Don't make him try new foods. New foods are new; and anything new is terrifying to the SP. He experiences it like a hurricane (see Chapter 9: Change), and nobody is in the mood to eat when they are in the middle of a hurricane. If the SP wants to leave the table, let him. He is not trying to be rude. He is defending himself because of his own sensitivity. You would not be able to eat a nail polish remover sandwich or a swamp sandwich. So why do you continually force your SP to eat things that are obnoxious to him?

11

Food Sensitivity

Note: This is a separate problem from that in Chapter 10.

Problem 1

When an NP gets a nutty bar, for example, he says, 'Oh, boy! I love nuts.' And he chomps away. When he is given a piece of peanut brittle or almond bark or corn, for example, he digs right in. He loves to try new and exotic foods and to go to fancy restaurants and pay lots of money for things with fat and sugar and spices.

When an SP sits down to a meal, he wants to eat the same thing every day. That is because he is afraid of new things (see Chapter 9: Change). But he is also afraid of things that feel bumpy or sticky or hard in his mouth. He wants his food to be smooth, requiring as little chewing as possible (see Chapter 13: Chewing and Swallowing). He remembers how easy it was to drink his food when he was a baby, and he feels like throwing up when rough things are in his mouth. He is also afraid that his teeth don't work, or that they will fall out if he uses them. Most SPs like mashed potatoes, well-cooked spaghetti (with non-lumpy sauce), and vanilla ice cream. Pizza is also OK, as long as it's plain. Sometimes pepperoni is OK, too, because it does not have things which scratch his mouth.

Rough, chewy foods are like fingernails scraping against the roof of his mouth. He cannot stand the feeling. As a toddler, the SP often starves rather than eat a rough, scary food.

Going out to dinner at a new place, or going over to someone else's house for dinner, is difficult because other people don't understand and they think that if you just starve the SP, he will learn to like NP food. He would rather starve. His mother hits him on the back and says, 'Look at all that *w-o-n-d-e-r-f-u-l* food. Aren't you hungry?' Of course, he is hungry, but he can't bear the thought of thumbtacks scraping his mouth. So he starves. Pretty soon the entire group of NPs is talking about how weird the SP is and how difficult he is to raise. The SP wants to leave the table, but the NPs won't let him. They want him to be present when they humiliate him.

Hence, the SP has a hard time going to the bathroom (see Chapter 15: Toilet Training, and Chapter 16: Going to the Bathroom). And he dislikes foods which make it harder to go (for example, meat) and likes to eat nonchewy foods which help him go (for example, spaghetti). Also, spaghetti makes him calmer, because of the serotonin release caused by the carbohydrates, which is why he likes it.

Solution 1

Don't make the SP eat a whole meal filled with new foods. He will get sick. He has to get used to a food visually before he can even think about eating it. Let him eat what he wants. Chances are he has a lot of food allergies, and is allergic to most NP food anyway. Introduce new foods SLOWLY. Add a bite at a time, and respect the SP's claim that a given food makes him want to throw up. He's not making it up!

When going to someone else's house, particularly that of an older family member who believes that starving the SP is the best treatment, bring his food along with you. Let him eat an entire package of macaroni and cheese, or spaghetti. It will calm him down so he can endure the rest of the gathering. Your SP is not trying to be rude; probably he is just trying to tell you that he is allergic or is afraid of the food.

[By James, age 9]: Mom once heard Temple Grandin describe her own fear of minute changes, and of tiny little things being altered in the environment. Temple said that autistic kids had to get used to change in tiny little bits. Therefore, in our house, we have a thing called a 'Temple Grandin.' When Mom puts my juice in a new glass or gives me a bigger bowl or the cheese is cut funny, the change is called a 'Temple Grandin.' Sometimes Mom doesn't notice the Temple Grandin, and when I say, 'You just gave me a Temple Grandin, didn't you?' she often laughs when she realizes what she did, then apologizes and removes the TG. Every so often, though, she flies into a rage and screams, 'I can't stand all this SP stuff! You have to get used to things being different! If you were in the desert during a war, you'd NEVER survive! Do you hear me? You'd starve!' Then I quickly apologize and accept the new thing so she'll stop yelling at me. Sometimes I wonder how she can have so much understanding of SPs on paper, but still yell like a normal NP mother.

Problem 2

When an NP eats, he knows when he is full, and he stops eating when he is full. This is so he will not get sick by overeating. Since he can regulate other things, he can also regulate how much he eats.

When SPs start eating foods that they like, they do not know how to detect when they are full so they just keep eating and eating and eating, and they overeat. After all, if an SP cannot regulate other things, how can he regulate eating? Actually he is not so different from a dieter who has been starving and suddenly is allowed to eat. When an SP is finally given a food he likes, he gorges and binges just like you or I do when we come off a diet.

However, the SP's mother gets worried since he is eating a lot and not exercising (see Chapter 51: Exercise) and is sitting around watching TV and doing his computer all day. After all, he has enough trouble being socially accepted, and being fat and grotesque will not help him. So she hits her SP on the back and screams, 'Don't eat too much! You're going to get fat!'

Solution 2

The easiest solution is to tell the SP when he is full (he cannot tell himself if he is full), or if he has to pee, for that matter, or when he is tired. You must tell him everything relating to his body. You must treat him like a baby.

And treating him like a baby also means stop hitting him on the back!

12

Food Allergies*

Problem

When an NP starts eating, he just eats until he is full and is calm. He does not worry whether he has an allergy to any food he eats, or whether he has a pounding headache (see Chapter 55: Headaches) a few days after he eats what he is eating. He just eats and does whatever he wants to do.

When an SP starts eating, though, many problems arise. First, he is worried that the food stinks or looks bad. He is also afraid that he is allergic to the food. So he will not eat the food and perhaps starve because he is afraid of getting a pounding headache (see Chapter 55: Headaches) a few days after he eats. Normally while he is starving, his mother may walk by, hit him on the back, and say, 'WHY AREN'T YOU EATING YOUR LUNCH LIKE YOU ARE SUPPOSED TO BE DOING!' She may call up the grandmother, who then tells her that kids don't starve themselves, and the grandmother won't believe it when she is told that THIS kid will.

Allergies possibly attract teasing. (See Chapter 40: Teasing.) When the SP is eating lunch at school, his classmates are probably going to tease him about not being able to eat the wheat entree and how he always has to bring a sack lunch every day because of his 'allergies.' If this happens, this will make him not want to go eat lunch anymore, and the SP will possibly not even want to go to school (see Chapter 39: Going to School) anymore. So he just sits and suffers, waiting for the school dismissal bell to ring. Then, when he talks to his mother about it, his mother may hit him on the back

* By James, age 11

and say, 'Who cares about teasing! That's what happens to everyone and you'll just have to learn how to cope with it!'

This also makes going out to dinner a stress for an SP. After all, he may not know whether there is food that he can eat that he is not allergic to. Often he plays frozen (see Chapter 49: Playing Frozen). His mother may hit him on the back again and say, 'WHAT DO YOU WANT TO ORDER! NOW MAKE A DECISION SO YOU WON'T KEEP THE WAITRESS WAITING!' So then the SP may be sneaky and purposely order a thing he is allergic to just to teach the mother a lesson. However, this always fails, and he always gets punished by getting a headache to boot (see Chapter 55: Headaches).

Solution

Do not yell at your SP just because he has wheat allergies, or any allergy. Your SP is not telling a lie (see Chapter 45: Telling Lies and Keeping Secrets), he is telling the truth. Try to find special health foods if possible for your SP. Don't make him starve. It is common for SPs to have food allergies, especially wheat allergies. For example, I have wheat allergies. And an autistic kid we know can only eat white food because she is allergic to colors in food. When I was little, I ate only white food.

There is no guessing what may happen in an allergy. You must keep trying until the allergy is solved. You must not give up until you have solved the mystery. It will only be then that your SP won't always be suffering in pain by how he eats. So, experiment by taking some foods out of his diet, and seeing if it takes his pain away. If it does, then you've figured out the mystery.

13

Chewing and Swallowing

Problem 1

When an NP eats a crispy, crunchy food, he says, 'Oh boy! Crispy! Crunchy!' And he eats with great pleasure. He loves the feel of his jaw going up and down and his teeth smashing and mashing the food. He loves the feel of the food going down his throat and into his stomach. *'Mmm, satisfying,'* he thinks.

When an SP eats solid food, several uncomfortable things happen. First of all, he has to open his jaw, and this can be painful, particularly if he grinds his teeth at night. Then he has to put something foreign into his mouth, which is a new thing and a change, and he hates changes (see Chapter 9: Change). So he immediately gets afraid of the new food. Then when it's in his mouth, he has to *do* something to it, and he hates doing things in general. The new food hurts the roof of his mouth and it feels funny. And usually it tastes weird, too, because even the same old thing tastes different in a new batch. Some SPs dislike the feeling of the food going down their throat; it makes them want to throw up. They often spit things out. Their mother hits them on the back and says angrily, 'Don't spit out your food! Food is valuable! Some kids have to eat from garbage cans.'

Solution 1

Respect the SP's need to eat only a few foods, but gradually try to get him to eat a wider variety of nutritious things, since malnutrition will make his SP-ness worse. If you want to introduce a new taste into the SP's diet, mash it up so he can familiarize himself with the taste, without having to think about the texture and the unpleasantness of a new thing in his mouth. It took me (Mom) a long time to realize that James can't stand any kind of chunkiness in his mouth. It activates his gag reflex. He didn't eat beans, for example, until he was eleven and discovered refried beans at a Mexican restaurant. He had adamantly refused them previously, not because of the taste but because beans are discrete little chunks that caused him to wretch. But in the mashed state, he accepted them. And perhaps more important, because James's orientation to the world was primarily visual, if something looked different, that immediately meant danger. When he told me something tasted bad, what he really meant was that it *looked* bad. I doubt if taste was ever the main consideration in his food choices, since he'd eat raw mushrooms and steamed mussels with gusto, but refuse chocolate.

[*By James*]: One thing my mom did when I was a toddler was to cut my food into alphabet letters and geometric shapes, because they were familiar and I loved them (see Chapter 28: Being Obsessed with the Alphabet). Then I wasn't so afraid.

Problem 2

Sometimes an NP mother tries to sneak a new food into her SP by disguising it, so that it looks like a food that the SP likes. Other times she puts something horrible into the middle of his peanut butter sandwich, for example, some new pill or perhaps even canned salmon, hoping the SP will get used to it or not notice it in the middle of his favorite stuff. So he eats it, but suddenly his mouth is full of horrible-tasting, horrible-feeling garbage. He can detect a new anything, even if it is disguised, just like the princess could detect the pea under 50 mattresses! So he spits out the salmon all over the table. The mother, in a rage for his bad behavior, hits him on the back and screams, 'Why can't you eat normal food, like everybody ELSE???'

Solution 2

Who are you trying to fool? Do you think your SP, with his advanced sensory capabilities is not going to notice the fact that you hid POISON in his food? He can tell what kind of water you used to mix his apple juice with! He can tell what kind of milk you put in his oatmeal (that is, what brand and percent of fat). He has the supersensitive sensory organs of an animal, which will die unless it's extra-vigilant about taste and smell. So if you are trying to get your SP to eat a new thing, be honest about it. Say, 'This is new today, but I want you to eat a tiny, tiny bit. Tomorrow it won't be new, and you won't have to be so afraid.'

14
Hating Water*

Problem

When an NP feels thirsty, he gets up from what he is doing, because he is not obsessed with time (see Chapter 29: Being Obsessed with Time), and he is not worried that he will not be able to do his work if he just stops for a little while. So he gets up and has a drink of water and goes back to his work. This is how it has always been with NPs.

When an SP feels thirsty, he does not get up from what he is doing, for the following reasons: (1) he is obsessed about wasting time (see Chapter 29: Being Obsessed with Time), and (2) he is afraid he will not go back to his work if he stops for a little while. Also, since he hates water, chances are he will suffer being thirsty and will hold out for something else rather than water. (When my mom asked me why I hated water, I said that when it is cold, it tastes like an acid, and when it is hot, it tastes like fire. Probably that was not true, just something I thought was true. I always rejected water when my mother tried to give it to me. I didn't drink water for the first seven years of my life, I hated it so much.)

Another reason why the SP suffers from thirst is because he has learned to ignore and fear his body's signals. So when the mother finds the SP working and suffering from thirst, she will hit him on the back and scream at the SP, 'Why are you suffering! Why don't you go get a drink of water? Why are you like this! What is WRONG with you?'

Now the SP now feels sad and rejected. Since he is so sad and in terror, he immediately forgets how to talk and he cannot tell his mother that he is afraid of having a drink because he will have to

* By James, age 8

change what he is doing, and he fears change (see Chapter 9: Change).

Solution

Our solution was to train me to swallow pills. I started drinking water then because it was the only thing I could use to take those pills. I didn't drink water for the first seven years of my life. I survived, but I was lucky! The doctor said I was severely dehydrated because juice and flavored drinks do not give the body as much liquid as plain water does.

After your SP is used to swallowing pills with water, than you can gradually get him to drink water by itself. This may also help the SP's headaches (see Chapter 55: Headaches). You could also offer him a reward – a dollar, for example – for every cup of water he drinks. In my case, my mom bought all the different kinds of bottled waters until I found one that I liked. Then she kept buying that kind for me. Eventually, she started filling the empty bottles with water that she filtered in our house, but because the bottle was familiar, I could drink the water inside.

Now I can drink all types of water, and my skin is smooth and not dehydrated anymore.

15

Toilet Training*

Problem

When my sister was sixteen months old, she attempted to use the toilet by herself. It didn't work, because the lid was closed (to prevent me from unrolling all the toilet paper into the toilet), but she managed to pee on the closed lid, then she slid down a waterslide of pee and landed in a puddle of it. When my mother found her howling in frustration, Mom still picked her up and praised her over and over for her desire to grow up. My sister quickly mastered the art of using the toilet by herself, and by the time she was two, she no longer wore diapers. She is an NK (normal kid).

When I was sixteen months, I was still nursing like a baby. I didn't have the tiniest interest in using the toilet. By the time I was two, then two-and-a-half, then three, I still thought the toilet was a place in which you threw things to see them float or a place to stuff the toilet paper after you'd unrolled it. If my parents took my diaper off, I simply behaved like the birds and the beasts – letting everything just fall out of me.

By the time I was three-and-a-half, I had a little control. I was able to use the potty now and again. There is even a videotape of me using the potty. However, I still wore diapers and was unaware of the need to stop wearing them.

When we moved to Northbrook, Illinois, and my parents enrolled me in preschool, it was necessary to toilet train me. That was very difficult for everyone, especially me.

* By Mom, pretending to be James

Solution

Parents, please be patient with your SK. He does not understand you, and he doesn't understand the message that his body is trying to tell him. He does not understand when the poop is coming, or when the pee is coming until he is ready to burst. Sometimes he has to use a strange bathroom, and this makes him afraid, because it is new (see Chapter 9: Change). Also, something is leaving his body (the poop or the pee), and this makes him afraid. He wants all the pieces of himself to stay together.

You can try to point out the advantages of not walking around in a stinky diaper, particularly if your SK is four years old and weighs 50 pounds. You can also take him to the toilet every fifteen minutes and have him see if anything comes out.

Please do not yell at him. This will only confuse him (see Chapter 41: Verbal Confusion), since he has an even harder time understanding you when you yell.

16

Going to the Bathroom

Problem 1

When an NP has to poop or pee, he says, 'Oh boy! I have to go to the bathroom.' Most NPs enjoy going to the bathroom, since it means that something yucky is leaving their body, and they feel light and clean afterwards. Most NPs enjoy all the things their bodies do, since they enjoy their bodies.

When an SP is first learning how to use the bathroom (see Chapter 15: Toilet Training), he is confronted with an impossible task. He has to (1) figure out what his parents want from him, and (2) figure out what is going on in his body. This puts him under a lot of stress, and he wants to play frozen. Sometimes his body plays frozen, too, and the pee and poop get stuck, which is painful to the SP. After a while, going to the bathroom is a terrifying and stressful task for the SP, and he tries to avoid it.

In time, he gets so that he can go if he uses the same old bathroom, the same number of wipes, the same hand motions, etc. However, that means that going in someone else's bathroom is an impossible task. Often an SP will simply hold it all in and wait till he gets home, which means he has to suffer for hours and hours. Sometimes he is afraid that if he goes in the strange bathroom, he will not be able to wipe himself well and therefore have to be itchy for hours and hours. As a result, he does not like to go anywhere for a long period of time (see Chapter 26: Special Occasions). If he goes in a public place, his mother hits him on the back and says, 'Remember! Don't touch ANYTHING in the bathroom! Don't flush! Don't even wash your hands!' This makes the SP even more afraid of using the public place. But his father hits him on the back and says, 'You have to go to the bathroom *now*. I don't want to have to stop the car.' This makes going an almost impossible task, since the SP's body reacts to both their commands by playing frozen, and then nothing can come out.

Solution 1

Try to make the bathroom a nice place to go, not a dirty, filthy place where germs lie in wait to make the SP sick. Be patient with him. He is trying the best he can, but his body doesn't always cooperate. Give him a packet of wipes to put in his coat, so he can wipe himself away from home and not have an itchy bottom.

Problem 2

[*By James*]: When an NP has to poop, it barrels out of him like a cannon. Then he feels fine and clean after he poops.

When an SP has to poop, he is filled with terror that he is about to lose something, so that he holds his poop in and gets constipated. Then he suffers the rest of the day from a poop stuck in his body. Then he goes to the toilet and pushes. This is what he does whenever he has to poop, push everything out, because it does not barrel out like it should. Then the mother hits him on the back and screams, 'Stop pushing your poop! You might get hurt!' Then the SP says, 'But then it won't come out.' Then the mother says, 'Well, maybe it is not ready to come out. It will come out later.'

But then the SP is worried because his mother told him a couple days ago that if your poop does not come out, you could get sick, so he is worried he will get sick since he did not get his poop out. So the SP keeps pushing because he is used to pushing and then the mother screams at him the same way she did, as shown above. Now the SP feels sad.

Solution 2

Do not yell at him. That will hurt his ears. Try to tell him that the poop is not ready to come out at that minute, and that it must sit for a couple of hours. Also tell him that he should not push, just wait until that minute comes, then get it out. And don't tell him that he will get sick, because then the poop will only get more stuck.

17

Breathing Problems*

Problem

When an NP goes to sleep or grows up, he somehow learns how to breathe, and gets used to that and it will become a habit in his own life.

When an SP goes to sleep or grows up, he does learn how to breathe normally at birth, but when the SP is seven or eight, he is so into doing things and is into thinking his own thoughts, he cannot catch his breath when he moves, which makes him forget about breathing, so he holds his breath. So he gets used to that, and is not fully aware when he needs some oxygen, or when to breathe in or out. So he does not breathe when he is doing something, because his mind has completely forgotten about breathing. So when he starts breathing, he only breathes for a couple of minutes. He is only a shallow breather. Finally, the mother of the SP will hit him on the back and scream, 'Breathe! You're gonna die if you don't!'

Also, when he is going to sleep, he does not know how fast to breathe or when to breathe in or out. So he breathes too loudly, or he tries to hold his breath. His mother hits him on the back and says, 'Breathe normally!' But he doesn't know what that is.

Solution

Even though there is no problem with his lungs, you can treat him like a person with asthma. Asthma people have to be put on something (but make sure it's not a medicine or antibiotic or steroid). Put him on a mechanism that is connected to the SP, which will get him to breathe, but make sure a source of air is being blown in the SP

* By James, age 8

when the mechanism is being used. Or you can buy a nebulizer. A nebulizer is the best thing to use, since it helps with breath control.

[*By Mom*]: Believe it or not, breathing is a major problem for James when he gets into bed at night. Perhaps the lack of something to do makes him anxious; perhaps the sound of his breathing is annoying. Whatever the reason, he somehow thinks it is suddenly his job to control his airflow, and he becomes incapable of breathing normally. He starts hyperventilating or holding his breath so that it's impossible for him to relax and fall asleep. Only when he gets drowsy and relinquishes conscious control can he breathe normally and fall asleep.

18

Teeth Problems*

Problem 1

When an NP goes to sleep, he says, 'Good night!' and goes to sleep. He doesn't grind his teeth at night; he just snoozes for the night and dreams a sweet dream.

When an SP goes to sleep, since he is afraid of saying good night, he does not say good night. Then he has trouble falling asleep because he is not sure how he should breathe – rapidly or slowly. (See Chapter 17: Breathing Problems.)

At night, he will grind his teeth because of all his troubles. Sometimes the mother will wake up because of his teeth grinding and say, 'Don't grind your teeth! That's bad!' But the SP will go back to sleep and keep grinding his teeth.

Solution 1

Do not force your SP to stop. He will not process your command just by hearing it once. Do not yell at him because that hurts his ears (see Chapter 2: Noise Sensitivity). Go to the dentist and get a plastic thing to put on his teeth so he can sleep with it.

Remember, you must get your SP used to the plastic thing because it is a change to him (see Chapter 9: Change), and he will not sleep with a change in his mouth.

* By James, age 8

Problem 2

When an NP gets a snack in a plastic bag such as potato chips, since his teeth are strong, he just opens the plastic bag with his teeth. He is not afraid to do this because he knows his teeth will not fall out.

When an SP gets a snack in a plastic bag, since his teeth are not strong, he is afraid his teeth will fall out if he uses them, and he knows he cannot open a plastic bag anyway. Often he asks his mother if she can open the plastic bag, but she does not open the plastic bag, she just says, 'Why can't you open a plastic bag with your teeth, like everybody ELSE!' Now the SP sits there confused and sad while everyone else is enjoying their snack. Finally the mother sighs and opens the bag for him. If she's in a bad mood, she might grumble, 'Your sister could open her own bag when she was a year old.'

Solution 2

Give your SP lots of bags of chips to open with his hands. Tell him exactly how to pull open the bag by putting his hands on either side of the back seam. He shouldn't be using his teeth anyway.

19

Space Problems

Problem 1

When one NP walks through a crowd of other NPs, he knows exactly how much room to leave around himself. He sees people coming and gets out of the way, or knows exactly when to say, 'Excuse me,' as he passes. If someone is coming at him, he knows how to step out of the way, and no one gets bumped.

When an SP walks through a crowd of NPs, many things happen: (1) he is bothered by the noise (see Chapter 2: Noise Sensitivity), (2) he is so overwhelmed by the sights and things to see around that he doesn't notice the people passing by, so he bumps into them, and (3) he is so stressed by the number of people around him that he tunes them all out, which means that he doesn't know when to step around them or say, 'Excuse me.' Every time he bumps into someone that he didn't notice, the NP says something mean like, 'Watch where you're going! You rude, clumsy child!' Then the mother hits him on the back and says angrily, 'What are you DOING?? Why did you bump into that lady?' The SP is now afraid to take a step, for fear of bumping into someone else he didn't see. In extreme cases, he might simply lie on the floor and refuse to move.

Solution 1

If the SP simply cannot figure out how to be in a crowd, don't take him to crowded places! If he lies on the floor in the mall, he is trying to tell you something. Don't take him back to the mall. If you take him to the Kid Zone and you find him lying under the slide, that means that he does not want to be in the Kid Zone and is 'cocooning' (see Chapter 50: Cocooning). If you have to take him into a crowded place, hold his hand or let him lean on you. Don't hit him on the back.

Problem 2 [Personal Space]

When an NK (normal kid) goes to school, he has a basic knowledge of what bothers another NK. NKs know how far to stand from each other (see Chapter 20: Knowing How Far Away to Stand from Other People) and how loud to talk to each other. This basic knowledge enables him to make friends and keep them.

When an SK goes to school, he is bothered by everyone and everything. (See Chapter 39: Going to School.) Therefore, he thinks that human interaction consists of one person bothering the other and the other putting up with it until he can get away. So the SK is constantly baffled when his behavior causes other people to say things like, 'Your noise is bothering me,' or 'You're standing too close,' or 'When you twitch, you distract me.' The SP doesn't understand what they are talking about (see Chapter 42: Understanding Other People), since he assumes that people are always bothered by each other, so why bring it up?

Solution 2

One of the best ways to help your SP develop a sense of placement in space is to blindfold him and walk him through the house. On the way, ask him where he thinks he is and encourage him to reach out and feel for a lamp or a wall. This may be hard at first, since an SP often uses his eyes and strictly visual input to orient himself. During your first tour of the house, perhaps give him a running commentary of where you are, so he can experience the route without using his eyes.

If blindfold games are not too stressful, try playing 'Pin the Tail on the Donkey' or 'Marco Polo' in the house. (Marco Polo consists of blindfolding one person, who shouts 'Marco' then listens as the other players shout 'Polo.' The object is for the 'Marco' player to capture the 'Polo' players by using auditory clues alone. Try not to make the game too frustrating at first. Don't elude the blindfolded player too well, or he'll see this as just another trap invented by NPs to fool him.)

Also, encourage the SP to crawl through the house playing 'Baby'. One of the things we realize over and over is that a current problem is the result of a number of milestones that were not properly reached, and hence to properly solve the problem, you need to go back and achieve those milestones. In retrospect, we realize that James crawled using the input from his eyes, not his body, so going back and teaching him to crawl 'correctly' helped his later space problems. Only when you've achieved those earlier milestones can you address a complex problem such as orienting yourself properly in relation to others.

Problem 3

When an SP walks into a new room, sometimes he purposely bounces off the walls, runs into the walls, hits the walls, climbs on the furniture or tables, or (if he's really weird) runs his tongue along the walls. The mother hits him on the back and shrieks, 'Get away from that wall! It's filthy! What are you DOING??' This confuses the SP, since all of the above activities were pleasurable.

Solution 3

As inappropriate as these behaviors are, they are the SP's way of trying to use his body to orient himself in space. He bumps against the wall to establish his location in the room. He licks the wall to get as close as he can to it. Give him the opportunity to do all these things at home, then tell him that he must stay away from the walls in public. If you know he'll forget, position yourself near the wall so you can catch him as he hurtles himself into the plaster. But remember, give him ample opportunity to do these things in a non-social setting. (If he insists on licking the walls, have him do it in the bathroom after you've scrubbed the tiles!) Practically ALL of your SP's weird behaviors are either responses to stress or *attempts to heal himself.* This is the third basic principle of understanding SPs. Try to see what the benefit of each behavior is then give your SP a safe environment in which to repeat it. When he's done acquiring whatever it is the behavior gives him, the behavior will probably stop on its own.

Problem 4

Sometimes when an SK feels connected to a NK, he may hug the NK. This will cause the NK to pull away or tell the teacher. This confuses the SK, since people are always coming too close to him and touching him when he doesn't want to be touched. When he complains to his mother that he didn't want Aunt Madeline to hug him, for example, he is often told that hugging is an expression of affection. His teacher, however, tells him not to hug other kids and that he needs to give the other kids some space, something that no one seems to give the SK. This is doubly confusing, since everyone is also telling him that he has to *reach out* to other kids, to express his feelings, to show other people that he likes them, but whenever he tries, he gets rejected or reprimanded. He tries to tell his mother that if grown-ups can hug children as an expression of affection, why is it inappropriate for kids to do the same? His mother may try to explain that there are different standards of behavior for adults and children.

Solution 4

The ideal solution to the social problems concerning peers is to keep your special kid away from his peers until he has a basic command of the personal skills of living and some rudimentary awareness of others. This might not occur until he is seven or eight. If you can homeschool your SK, keep him away from other kids until then. Don't worry that he is not learning any social lessons. Until he has a basic grasp of social rules, most, if not all, of his spontaneous social interactions will be negative anyway, and you will create a hostile, oppositional child who becomes impossible to control. You may also be dooming him to a life of depression, anxiety, and misanthropy. If you want him to experience positive social interactions, have playdates with selected kids (I actually paid kids to come and hang out with James, for about four years), and be in the room monitoring the situation at all times. This is very important! If you want your child to learn the foreign language of social interaction, you must be his interpreter. He will not learn or work things out on his own.

Try to script appropriate ways to express affection. Make up little plays featuring the SK and his chosen companion. Have the companion explain to him how she (or maybe he) feels when the SK touches her. Have the SK explain how it feels when someone touches him. But give him a blanket command not to touch anyone when Mom isn't present. Write the rule down in an official book, or post it on the wall in his room. Sometimes when you write something down, it is better understood by an SK.

20

Knowing How Far Away to Stand from Other People

Note: This is also a type of space problem, but since it is a crucial skill in social interaction, we gave this topic its own chapter.

Problem 1

When one NP walks up to another NP, both of them know how near to stand beside each other, in order to be heard and respected, but not too close so they can smell each other's body odors. They also stand the right amount of distance away so that they can nod to each other and even pat each other a few appropriate times during their conversation. All this makes NPs feel closer and warmer toward each other.

When an NP walks up to an SP, the SP feels as if he is about to be attacked and therefore he stands back. If the SP walks up to an NP, however, the SP does not get proper signals from his sensory systems, and thus often bumps into the NP or stands too close. As you know, the SP is constantly being assaulted by the NP world, so he does not learn how to behave in a non-assaulting way. He does not know how far away to stand so other people don't smell his breath, because he can sometimes smell someone else's odors across the room. And he can't figure out how far away to stand so his voice isn't too loud, because everyone's voice is too loud for him. But most of all, the SP does not want to stand next to anyone ever, at any time. He wants everyone to go away. Therefore, he does not practice appropriate distances when he is forced into a social encounter.

Solution 1

This is a tough one! There are some rules that the SP has to learn by rote, without understanding what's going on. Have him practice walking up to family members and stopping at a specific spot (close enough so that he can reach his arm straight out and touch the person, but not close enough so he can touch the person with a *bent* arm). Have him start observing other people's reactions to him, though this skill may be impossible for him to master until he is an adolescent. Keep encouraging him to at least try. If an NP starts shifting his body closer to the SP, then the SP is probably standing too far away. But SPs, if the NP does get close, don't suddenly feel as if you are about to be eaten in one gulp. He is merely practicing his NP manners, which say that it is polite to stand within easy hearing distance of another person. Remember that hearing is a very important sense for NPs. Don't expect NPs to understand all the terror that is rampaging through your body when he gets close to you. He won't understand, but you won't get eaten either.

Problem 2

[*By James, age 8*]: When an NP is at a gymnastics class, sometimes the NT (normal teacher) of the gymnastics class will tell the students to pick a place a certain distance apart. The NP knows that distance, and the NT will not yell at him because he knew the distance already.

When an SP is at a gymnastics class, and the NT tells the students to pick a place a certain distance apart, since he learns things slowly and he is delayed on many things, he does not know what distance he should pick. Sometimes the NT has to take 15 minutes trying to tell him where he must stand, at the proper distance, and the class gets delayed. The class is without parents, so the mother can't hit him on the back, but the NT may hit him on the back and say, 'You should know where to stand! Now the whole class is delayed because of you!'

The NT will then talk to the mother after the gymnastics class about what a pill the SP is.

Solution 2

Put pieces of tape on the floor at home, and practice standing the appropriate distance from people. Remember that you may have some tantrums if you change the distance, but do it anyway, so the SP will get used to a variety of appropriate distances.

21

The Inner Ear

Problem 1

When an NK develops, all his systems develop along with him. One of the most important systems is the inner ear system. The inner ear has many functions: to provide balance and stability for the body, to prevent motion sickness and headaches during motion, and it helps to hear properly.

When an SK develops, he is terrified of change (see Chapter 9: Change), and apparently, his bodily systems are afraid of change, too, because they don't evolve the way they should. They cling to their current stage of development and resist 'growing up.' Or a mechanism such as the inner ear can get stuck in one position. It may allow the SP to feel centered and balanced only if he is standing with one arm dragging and his head tilted to one position. His mother frequently hits him on the back and says, 'Stand up straight!' Then the SK dutifully tilts his body in the way that makes her say, 'That's right. Now you're straight!' (even though the SK feels as if he is crooked). As soon as she turns her back, the SK resumes his former posture, which makes her say yet again, 'Stand straight! I just told you that!' So the SK straightens his head again until his mother looks away because *straight* to him feels crooked.

Solution 1

To strengthen your SP's inner ear mechanism, have him crawl on the floor, swing, roll down hills, roll his head from side to side if he can stand it, bounce on a bouncy ball or trampoline, and walk on a balance beam. Don't prevent him from doing all those weird, 'autistic' things like spinning and walking across the top of the sofa. These are his attempts to stimulate his inner ear. As soon as the mechanism is working more normally, he will feel normal dizziness and stop spinning so much. (Now James can't stand any kind of swinging or spinning.) In his younger days, one of James's favorite activities was to be rolled tightly in a quilt then to unroll himself across the room. The pressure of the quilt on his body calmed his nervous system, and the rolling stimulated his inner ear. We'd often find him standing on the rocking chair and rocking furiously back and forth, which drove us crazy but helped him with balance and muscle control. He also enjoyed spinning amusement rides and fun houses with rocking floors, tilting doorways, and twisting slides. (Now he can't stand them.) Sports requiring balance, such as gymnastics and ice skating, are also valuable. Try to find classes for kids with special needs.

Auditory integration training is supposed to stimulate the inner ear as well. For a description of AIT, see Appendix I.

Problem 2

[*By James*]: When an NP swings, he likes to pump and swing beautifully, he does not get a headache because his inner ear has developed properly, and he loves the feel of the motion of the swing.

When an SP swings, he gets a headache (see Chapter 55: Headaches), suffers knee pain because of the pumping, and hates the up and down. Although he may have liked swinging when he was younger (because he didn't get dizzy, did not know what a headache was, and couldn't tell if he had one), he can now tell that he has gotten a headache from the motion of the swing, because he is older and knows what a headache is. Sometimes he tells his mother. Then the mother hits him on the back and screams, 'Stop complaining and keep swinging! Pump correctly! Your sister could pump when she was five!'

The SP, therefore, has to suffer swinging with a pounding headache, and with undeveloped legs which can't pump, so his mother has to push him.

Solution 2

What are you thinking about when you tell your SP that you do not care about his feelings? Who are you to ignore his pains? You must not say that because you must help him. So why are you teaching your child to suffer continuously in silence? Don't you know that he has important feelings too? Well, he does, and it's your job to take care of them, not ignore them. Your SP's not making it up!

To help with inner ear problems, start slowly. Roll the SP's head from side to side a little bit at a time, but stop if he says he wants to throw up. Swing him in a blanket, like a hammock. Encourage him to stop swinging in the swing if it is making him sick. He is so used to suffering that he doesn't know when he should stop doing what he is doing and when he should simply suffer.

22

Balance Problems*

Problem

When an NK develops, his neck is not tight on any of the sides, and both sides of his body are strong because of exercise. Now he will use both sides of his body whenever he does something.

When an SK develops, the systems of an SK resist growing up. Hence, all his systems don't develop properly. And because he sits down doing nothing all day, none of his muscles get exercised. So one side of the body gets strong, and the neck of an SK gets tight on that side to support the weak side. So one side works better than the other! So if the right side is the strong side, it will raise its shoulder up, and the left side will droop its shoulder down, because it is weak (or vice versa). Then the SK walks like this (one shoulder up, one shoulder down), and then his neck becomes crooked.

Because he is not balanced, one pupil is smaller than the other, one eye is smaller than the other, one nose nostril doesn't have as much circumference as the other nostril, and one hand works better than the other. And when he talks, he will develop a funny way of talking. Instead of talking with both sides of his mouth, he will only talk with one side of his mouth. The mother hits the SP on the back and screams, 'Use both sides of your mouth!'

Also, when he smiles, one side goes up shorter than the other side. The mother will hit him on the back then and scream, 'Smile correctly!'

* By James, age 8

72

Solution

Have the SP recite the vowels of the alphabet using both sides of his mouth.

[*By Mom*]: Have him say the vowel sounds with his mouth wide open, as loud and as exaggerated as possible. Do it in a mirror, so he can see his mouth. Chances are he can use both sides of his mouth evenly, open up the lazy eye, etc., but it doesn't happen naturally. But exercising in a mirror will allow him to see as well as feel what it's like to use both sides evenly.

23

Auditory Processing Delays

Problem

The NPs have set up the world for their own enjoyment. They turn up the volume to where they like it; they flash images across the TV screen at a speed they find exciting, and they prepare food that looks and smells the way they want it. And most important, they talk to each other at a speed that is easily processed by other NPs.

But SPs, since they rely so much on the right hemisphere for information processing, are slow *auditory* processors (though, as we've discussed, they are rapid *visual* processors). The right hemisphere is wired differently from the left, and spends a lot of time absorbing the texture and entirety of something without really analyzing it or breaking it up into components. That's why right-brained people are often good at memorizing but lousy at processing.

When James, as a toddler, received a new video, he didn't insist on watching the whole thing right away. Rather, he would watch tiny segments of it dozens of time, until he had digested each segment. Often it would take him a week of repeating the first minute or so before he went on to the next minute. This kind of repetition drives NPs crazy, but it is the way an SP really learns something that he hears.

Because the pace of NP conversation is too fast, however, the SP sometimes can catch only a word or two the first time someone says something. He might latch on to only the verb, for example. So that when you say, 'I just went to the store,' he hears only 'store.' He might say, 'What?' So the following might happen:

> You: I went to the store.

SP: Store? What about the store?

You: I said, I went to the store.

[*SP this time hears 'went store.'*]

SP: Who went to the store?

NP [*impatiently*]: I said, I WENT TO THE STORE! Are you deaf?

Now the SP has heard the first sentence, but he didn't catch the last part: He thinks 'Who's dead?' But he dare not ask, lest the NP yell at him again.

Sometimes the SP doesn't hear what the NP said until he hears three repetitions. Other times, he is too preoccupied with figuring out other things people said to him the day before to listen today. So here is what happens:

NP: Come here.

SP [*thinking*]: What did she mean when she said...

NP [*louder*]: I said, Come here.

SP [*still preoccupied*]: I wonder if it meant...

NP [*screaming*]: COME HERE! LISTEN TO ME WHEN I TALK TO YOU!

SP [*confused*]: Huh? [*thinking*] Why is she yelling at me?

Unfortunately, many of the things the SP actually hears are yelled statements, so he thinks the world is full of mean, cruel people who yell at him out of the blue.

Another aspect to processing delays involves the annoying habit SPs have of automatically repeating under their breath things they have just said aloud. Sometimes they even laugh at what they said, which makes them seem weird and stupid. However, they are simply reviewing what they said, to see if it made sense. You see, there is so much stress associated with talking that the SP speaks without being fully able to pay attention to what he's saying. If he has right-brain speech centers, which is a definite possibility, much of what he says comes from 'the unconscious' – it just bubbles out of his mouth. When he repeats it under his breath, he is confirming (a) that he actually said it, and (b) that it made sense. If it does make sense, he might chuckle or giggle out of joy that he was able to express a lucid thought. However, most NPs get annoyed by this whispering.

Sometimes an SP who has learned not to whisper under his breath may confirm what he has just said by writing with his finger in the air. James did that continuously until he was about ten and did not understand why it was inappropriate, since it wasn't noisy. Before he entered fourth grade (his first full-time schooling), we had to once more evoke the 'stupid NP' defense, warning him that the kids would tease him without mercy if he spent all day writing in the air. When I asked him to explain what was so important about this kind of writing, he said that (a) it helped him organize his thoughts in a visual format, (b) it was calming, since his attention was focused on something visual, but (c) conversely, if he needed to say something that was inappropriate, writing helped get it out of his mind (see Chapter 24: Having an Urge to Quote). To his way of thinking, he had devised a clever way of being socially appropriate. After all, he wasn't blurting the thing out, so he was once more crestfallen to learn that his new system wasn't socially appropriate either. However, our discussion made me realize once again the importance of those 'autistic' traits we try to extinguish. For James, it was a way of trying to relieve the tremendous inner stress of having something to say and not being able to say it. He also commented that sometimes if he was angry at me or someone in authority, he could write out the nasty thing he wanted to say to that person, and that would satisfy him without a direct confrontation.

Solution

There are several options: Teach the NPs in the environment to be tolerant of the SP's processing delays, and not to shout or be angry; or you can encourage the SP to do his left-brain exercises, to try and transfer his thinking and language centers to the left hemisphere. This is easiest before the age of seven or eight, when language tends to get fixed in one area, but you will help him tremendously if you don't interfere with his 'autistic' habits such as lining up blocks, memorizing phone numbers, counting his steps, or reciting the alphabet endlessly. He is doing left-brain calisthenics, which will pay off someday in better auditory processing.

As we discuss in other chapters, watching movies with the closed-captions on helps to reinforce the auditory information with visual input. Along those same lines, James came up with the idea of recording his favorite movies on audiotapes so we could play them in the car. (He simply puts a tape recorder up against the TV, turns on 'RECORD', then orders everyone out of the room.) When your SP knows a particular story and is familiar with the dialogue, he can listen and understand without struggling to comprehend each word. The visual distraction of the movie itself is gone, but the memory of those visual images helps with comprehension. James also records the sounds of his favorite computer games on audiotapes and plays them in the car. Until I stopped to analyze what was going on, I immediately condemned this practice as just another one of his weird ideas. But when I listened to *Mrs. Doubtfire* in the car and found that without the visual distraction of a movie, I was able to better concentrate on the words, I suddenly realized what a valuable exercise it was in auditory processing. Once more, the 'symptom' – the 'abnormal' behavior – was actually a powerful healing tool.

Auditory training, Earobics, and FastForword also help speed up auditory processing time. James did all of them, and benefitted from them.

For writing in the air, tell the SP that he can do it in private or in the company of other SPs, but not when NPs are present.

24

Having an Urge to Quote

Problem

As mentioned in the last chapter, when a normal person sees a movie, he says, 'What a nice movie,' then walks out of the theater and resumes his life. If someone asks him what the movie was about, he retells it briefly in his own words.

When an SP sees a movie, although he may not *process* very much of what he's heard, his mind might *memorize* it immediately like a tape recorder. This is the third major principle of understanding an SP: he may have a deficient ability to process auditory information but a superior ability to memorize it. We believe that an SP's mind is compelled to memorize something he hears so that he can process it later on and in little pieces. Not all SP minds do this; some SPs don't memorize or process anything until hearing it repeatedly.

When the memorizing type of SP leaves a theater, the movie he just heard keeps playing over and over in his head, and he cannot think about anything else. After a while, hearing some line ten thousand times gives the SP the urge to quote. Often, the line is something that his NP mother cannot stand. For example, 'That's a spicey meat-a-ball,' from *The Mask*. Eventually his mother will hit him on the back and say, 'Stop quoting!' or even 'Shut up! That's echolalia.' That will make the SP sad, because he cannot help it.

Solution

SPs, one way to get a quote out of your mind is to write it down in a special book, called the 'oubliette.' An 'oubliette' (from the French *oublier*, meaning 'to forget') is a place where you put something, in order to forget it. We use a special diary, and when my mom can no longer stand a certain line that my mind has fixated on, we write it down in the diary, then that helps me to get it out of my mind. Sometimes I tell her I'm not ready to give up a certain line yet. Then we don't put it in the diary.

Or take a drama class, particularly one where you read scripts and memorize lines. There your 'photographic memory' will be valued. You can think about becoming an actor, because they have to repeat their lines over and over and over again. The NP goes crazy with all the repetition, but the SP finds it comforting and safe, since it is not new.

25

The Music Playing in Your Head*

Problem

When an NP is busy working, he just works and only stops if he has to do something else or if someone has called him. He may not hear any music in his head, or does not care if there is any music in his head. He just keeps working. Frankly, we don't know any NPs that we can ask. The only people who will associate with us are SPs.

When an SP is busy working, though, music plays inside his head, and he does not know what to do about it. Sometimes the music prevents him from working or concentrating on something else he wants to do. Music will always haunt him inside, and he will not be able to stop it. So every day, when he wakes up, music will play in his head. It will always bother him, that is, unless he has control over the music and can choose what he wants to hear.

Solution

Now that you, mothers, know about this problem (it may not be a problem), you may possibly start asking your SP *what* he is playing inside his head. Then, you can understand him. You can also guess what is probably playing in your SP's head sometimes, because maybe he is humming (see Chapter 47: Mouth Control) the same thing that is playing in his head. If that is true, then your SP might be trying to get the music out, since it may be bothering him.

But still, don't bother him either. This may be a way for him to hear music instead of having to annoy you with playing CDs all day (see Chapter 30: Being Obsessed with Music).

* By James, age 11

Also, in my case, my mother hears music in *her* head, so we ask each other from time to time what is playing inside.

[*By Mom*]: We don't have a good answer for resolving this one. Since music emanates from the uncontrollable right hemisphere, perhaps encouraging your SP to become left-hemisphere-dominant (see Chapter 33: Left vs. Right-Hemisphere Processing) will give him some relief. Solving math problems or doing complicated workbook assignments may help turn off the music for a while, though the music may just keep on playing. If he is being driven crazy, let him turn on the TV or the radio to a talk show. There are even videos for autistic people that have no background music. If you can't find any, make some of your own.

As James discussed above, we deal with this problem simply by making it a normal aspect of everyone's life. (Many SPs experience this.) Since we *all* have music playing in our heads in our household, we frequently ask each other, 'What's playing in your head?' then we ask each other why, where it came from today, etc. We laugh and comment and validate each other's experience. Sometimes if one person sings what's in his head, his or her listeners may start hearing that song in their heads as well. This is a novel kind of social interaction, you might say. When we are all trapped in a car going to the latest therapist, we often sing for each other the songs that are playing in our heads. We try three-part harmony, rounds, and counterpoint.

26

Special Occasions

Problem 1

When an NP looks at the calendar and realizes that it is only a few weeks until, for example, Christmas, he says, 'Oh, boy! Christmas is coming! Presents! Good food! Lots of people over! Christmas carols! Noise! Mayhem! Celebration!' All the NP mothers spend time planning for Christmas, buying their kids lots of toys and goodies and telling them tales of Santa Claus. The night before Christmas, the mothers stay up really late wrapping presents and putting crumbs and soot on the hearth to make it look like Santa Claus came down the chimney, and secretly, some may be hating the whole process. By the time they fall into bed at 3 a.m., they are exhausted.

When an SP realizes that Christmas is coming, he is filled with terror. People will begin invading his home more and more, bothering the SP, particularly if they bring presents over (see also Chapter 9: Change). On Christmas Day itself, the SP would rather stay in his room the whole day. Every minute is a pain. The first thing that happens is that he has to wake up and listen to the squeals of his brothers and sisters opening their presents. This hurts his ears (see Chapter 2: Noise Sensitivity). Then he is expected to open HIS presents. But he cannot stand his presents, so he throws them over his shoulder, rather than have to deal with one terrifying new thing after another. His mother hits him on the back, really hard this time, bursts into tears, and says, 'I try *so-o-o-o* hard to make you happy, and nothing works!! *Boo-hoo-hoo!*' Now the SP feels guilty and worthless, but he starts laughing uncontrollably, since he thinks crying is funny (see Chapter 27: Being Polite when Someone is Crying). This makes the father of the SP extremely angry, and he starts shouting at the SP. So now the SP has to deal with more noise, which hurts his ears. All he wanted to do was stay in his room and miss the entire Christmas.

Besides, he had written only, for example, four things on his Christmas list, and his mother got him eight things, including four things he did NOT want! And then he was expected to open four presents he did not want, deal with the terror of their newness four times in a row, then get hit on the back, subjected to crying, and shouted at. All his brothers and sisters look at him angrily, because HE has spoiled their Christmas yet another year. Never mind that THEY have spoiled his December 25th year after year and not understood. They don't understand autism or being an SP.

The presents are just the beginning of the SP's terrible, horrible, no-good, very bad day. The rest of it is the food and the mayhem and the noise and the people in his house. Thank goodness Christmas comes only once a year.

Solution 1

Get the SP ONLY the presents he wants. If possible, tell him that he is getting, for example, four presents, and if he asks, tell him what they are. He does NOT want to be surprised! How many times does he have to tell you that he does not want to be surprised? He experiences surprise as a tornado in his heart. I actually take James with me when I shop for his presents now, and on Christmas Eve, he wraps them himself and writes out the 'To: James' cards. That way he knows what will be in every gift before he opens it, and he can experience the dual joys of familiarity and recognition. He even helps me wrap other gifts, so that way he can enjoy knowing what's in others' presents before they are opened.

Also, please be aware that SPs are often right-hemisphere processors (see Chapter 33: Left vs. Right Hemisphere Processing). Despite their seeming indifference, they often KNOW what you are thinking behind that phoney holiday smile. An SP KNOWS if you hate the whole Christmas thing, and he is having to process your hatred and resentment along with his own. He also resents the fact that you told him a bunch of whoppers about Santa Claus, and he has had to deal with the improbability of it for years. Let him take a nap, if he wants, and miss Christmas.

Problem 2

When one NP goes to a party given by another NP, or a wedding, the NPs think, 'Oh boy! Food! Music! Good stuff!' Social situations make the NP feel warm and happy.

When an SP goes to a party given by an NP, or a wedding, he is faced with the worst fear of his life. All of the horrible aspects of life happen at a social event. His parents do not know that he is experiencing this like a typhoon. Here is what happens:

1. First of all, the SP has to wear clothes that are weird and uncomfortable. His mother might make him wear a pair of pants with a zipper or a stupid shirt that scratches him. He has to wear the same kinds of clothes over and over to feel OK. (See Chapter 7: Touch Sensitivity.)

2. When the SP walks through the door, he is attacked by a thousand NPs who say hello to him. (See Chapter 1: Saying Hello).

3. The SP immediately goes into shock and forgets how to talk. His mother hits him on the back and says angrily over and over, 'Say hello...say hello...say HEL-LO!'

4. After the SP has said hello over and over, he is then expected to converse with strangers. This is even more terrifying than saying hello, since the noise around him hurts his ears and he immediately tunes everyone's questions out. (See Chapter 48: Tuning Out.) Plus his mother expects him to invent his own conversation, which is a lot more difficult than saying just 'hello' and immediately playing frozen.

5. The only thing an SP can do that is socially acceptable is eat. However, chances are the party food is unfamiliar and looks weird and smells weird and requires the SP to scoop things on to a plate, which might end up in a spill or accident, which will cause the SP's mother to yell and scream and hit him on the back, saying, 'Oh no! Not

again! You are such a jerk! WHY CAN'T YOU BE MORE CAREFUL???'

6.   By this time, the SP wants to fall into a hole and never come out. If he is lucky, there is a computer somewhere and the NPs who are having the party will let him hide in front of the computer screen until the party is over. Also, if he is lucky, there will be some other miserable SP at the party, who has also escaped into the computer room, and they can play a game of 'QUAKE', for example, and imagine that all the aliens that get blown up are the NPs at the party.

7.   When it is time to leave, the SP has to say 'goodbye' to all the people he didn't want to say hello to (see Chapter 84: Saying Goodbye). His mother, as usual, hits him on the back and says, 'Say goodbye...say goodbye...say GOODBYE!!!' If the SP can't say goodbye because he has shut down, the mother still hits him on the back and says to the NPs, 'He is such a pill. He's so hard to raise. I don't know what's wrong with him.' Other NPs will nod sympathetically and say, 'I don't know how you do it. Isn't there a special school you can send him to?' Then the mom says, 'I tried to send him to school, but he just hated it and played frozen and went into a coma state.' Then another NP might ask, 'Isn't there a boarding school you can send him to?' Then the mother feels terrible guilt for wanting to abandon her SP, so she goes into the car and apologizes to him for making him go to the party, then the father and the mother have a big fight, saying, 'I can't do anything with his kid! He's wrecking my life!' The father goes into a rage and yells at the SP, which hurts the SP's ears (see Chapter 2: Noise Sensitivity).

Solution 2

Don't let the SP suffer like this! Hire a babysitter. Let him stay home. You don't want him at the wedding, and he wants to be alone. Even a young SP will do better home alone than at a party. Have people come over to your house so the SP can be with them wearing his own clothes and having his own computer room to escape to. Don't make him eat weird food (see Chapter 11: Food Sensitivity) and please don't say horrible things about him when he's there. He may be tuning out all the questions, but he can hear you when you tell everyone what a pill he is.

Problem 3

Getting invited to a birthday party is one of the greatest pleasures of being an NK. Not only are the parties fun, but an invitation is a sign of social acceptance. NP mothers are fond of bragging to each other about how many parties their darling little NK got invited to.

But to an SK, a birthday party is perhaps the worst nightmare of life. Fortunately, SKs generally behave so badly at the first birthday party they are forced to go to, that nobody invites them to another. In fact, the mother often complains to her friends that her SP child hasn't been invited to a single party the entire year.

Most mothers of SPs don't realize how much their kids detest birthday parties, and so when the SP's own birthday rolls around, the mother plans an enormous celebration to compensate for all the parties her SP didn't get invited to. This sends the SP into paroxysms of fear and dread, but the mother thinks she is doing a kindly, benevolent, almost sacrificial thing overcoming all the major problems involved in planning the event.

For one thing, there is no one to invite. The SP has no friends. So the mother gets on the phone and begs all her own friends to bring their children to the party. In the background, she can hear comments from the kids such as 'No way. I don't want to go to party for that weirdo,' 'He's strange,' 'He never listens,' etc., so she decides that she will make it a super-sized, super-fun party to con the guests into having a good time. This compounds the SP's stress, and he announces he's not going to the party at all. The mother then hits him on the back and says, 'I try so hard to make you happy, and nothing works! Next year you're not having a party!' Which, of course, is what the SP wants, so he continues acting weirdly whenever the subject of his party comes up.

When the day of his party dawns, the SP wants to throw up or stay in bed. For one thing, his mother has bought new party clothes for him, which send him into a state of panic because they feel different. (See Chapter 7: Touch Sensitivity.) Plus he is now a different age, which is a change, another source of panic in itself (See Chapter 9: Change.) By the time the party begins and he sees all the screaming kids giving him presents that he does not want, the SP either has a tantrum or plays frozen (see Chapter 49: Playing Frozen). He may spend the entire party huddled in the corner of the room while the guests riot around him, or else behave in a rude, inappropriate fashion to get people to leave him alone. The mother maintains her composure during the party while the rage boils inside her like a pressure cooker. The SP realizes this and spends the entire party dreading the explosion that is sure to follow when the last guest leaves.

When it is time to sing 'Happy Birthday,' eat cake, and open presents, the SP is so discombobulated that he tunes everyone out. He is also angry that he can't eat the cake due to food allergies (see Chapter 12: Food Allergies). He may refuse to open the presents, since he doesn't know what's in the boxes and that compounds his fear, or he may rip them open with a stone-faced expression and throw them over his shoulder. Every time he opens a present, the mother will hit him on the back and command, 'Say thank you,' which he thinks is the height of stupidity, for why should he thank someone for causing him such distress?

Solution 3

Don't throw a party for your child unless he clearly wants one. If he is non-verbal and rejects other children, you can be sure that a birthday party will be torture for him. If he is verbal and says no, respect his wishes. Ask him what he wants to do on his birthday, and if he says he wants to play computer games, let that be your gift to him.

On the other hand, if your SP says he wants a party, let him have total control over the planning of it. Despite his desire, he will still have to confront his fears, so rehearse the party moment by moment, discussing all the possible things that could happen. About a week before, buy a birthday cake and every night at dinner, decorate it with candles, sing 'Happy Birthday,' and have him blow out the candles. Practice doing all the goofy, unpredictable things that kids do (such as adding 'Cha cha cha' after every line of the song, or trying to blow out the candles themselves, or smearing their faces with frosting) so that there will be as few surprises as possible. The week before James's seventh birthday, I gave him a wrapped package every morning at breakfast, and he practiced opening it, admiring the gift for a polite amount of time, then smiling and saying, 'Thank you!' This was a terrifying exercise to him, but during the actual party, he was poised and polite and the marvel of all the parents present. No one could tell that he was nervous inside, but having a successful birthday party was such a boost to his self-esteem that he remembered that party with fondness and nostalgia.

Problem 4 [Travelling]

As you all know, NPs like new things. So when an NP travels to a new place, he enjoys all the new sights, sounds, smells, tastes, and objects. Since the world is populated mostly by NPs, any city an NP travels to will be set up to please him.

But, as you also know, the world is NOT set up for SPs. Therefore, when an SP travels to a new place, the same problems that the SP faces at home will be in the new city, except that the new problems are NEW.

In a new city, the SP is hit with a thousand problems. For example:

1. Where does he go to the bathroom? What if the toilet is too high, too narrow, or stinks? What if his mother runs out of his favorite wipes, and he has to use foreign toilet paper, which doesn't work well?

2. What if the food is a different color, or the new vanilla ice cream has dark specks in it?

3. What if the sidewalks are harder than the ones at home, and cause the NPs feet to hurt? (See Chapter 53: Foot Problems.)

4. What if the SP's mother and father are yelling at each other? Then the SPs ears hurt (see Chapter 2: Noise Sensitivity), and he also is afraid they are mad at him (see Chapter 38: Anger). After a short period of time, the parents really do turn their anger at him, since they are always angry at him to some extent, but now they are less able to control themselves. At these times, they are most likely to call him 'jerk,' 'clumsy,' 'dumb,' and 'weird.' So not only does he feel bad, but he experiences their anger along with his own. So now he has three angers to deal with, and that gives him a huge headache. (See Chapter 55: Headaches.)

5. Often the brothers and sisters of the SP want to go to places that terrify the SP, such as Great America, and the NPs want to do sickening things like go on roller coasters or the Haystack. Great America is the worst collection of rides and overloads that the SP can imagine. By the end of the day, he wants to kill himself. His NP brothers and sisters have ridden on things like 'Tidal wave,' but the SP always rides on a tidal wave – he does not need a mechanical one.

6. If the SP has inner ear problems (see Chapter 21: The Inner Ear), a long car ride can be sickening to the SP. After hours and hours of being sick, he can't take it anymore. But his mother hits him on the back and says, 'Stop complaining.' The SP is not telling a whopper, though, and he says, 'But I have fierce car sickness.' The mother is tired of hearing him complain, so she says, 'Just be sick then. I don't care.' This makes the SP feel even worse than before.

7. If the SP's parents make him go out to dinner, all of the previously explained problems with new food apply (see

Chapter 11: Food Sensitivity), and he ends up starving, which gives him a worse headache and makes his car sickness worse.

8.   Also, sometimes the restaurant is crowded, and the SK has to wait in a line. (See Chapter 60: Waiting Problems.) This puts him under more terror, and makes him afraid of going to a restaurant because pain awaits him in many ways.

Solution 4

Try to let the SP stay home as much as possible. A negative social experience is worse than none at all. Try to have people come to his house to interact with him, so he only has to deal with the terror of new people, not new people and new places. Get him a babysitter if you are going to Great America, and don't lie to him if you are going to force him to go after all. Don't say, 'We'll hire a babysitter for you,' then at the last minute make him go along.

If you have to take him with you, let him sit in the front seat of the car, since that may help his car sickness. Sometimes a drink with salt may help the headache.

Remember that the SP does not WANT to go with you, but you expect him to act pleasant and happy when you go somewhere (which he does not do). You have also been telling him that he should express his feelings, but every time he TRIES to express his feelings, you hit him on the back and complain and call him 'weird' and 'impossible.'

He does not have to do a thousand new things to have a good life. If you have to take him somewhere, bring as many familiar things for him as possible. Let him bring along his own food. Tell your hostess, or the waiter, that your son has severe diabetes and has to be on a special diet. Most people will respect the requirements of a real disease, particularly if they have heard of it, and won't give the SP dirty looks.

Above all, try to keep remembering what your SP is feeling. It is a pain and a drag, but you wouldn't do any better than he's doing if you lived in a world that continually caused you pain.

27

Being Polite When Someone is Crying

Problem 1

When a normal person feels sad, he cries and other normal people give him comfort and sympathy. When a normal baby cries, his mother picks him up and soothes him and makes him feel better. This is how it has always been with NPs.

When an SP feels sad, he sometimes grieves for things that an NP doesn't understand, for example, the SP orders his favorite French vanilla ice cream and the color is a tiny bit different (see Chapter 11: Food Sensitivity) from its usual color. This means that something has changed (see Chapter 9: Change) and this causes the SP to feel intense fear and grief. He cries and longs to be comforted. His mother, however, hits him on the back, and says, 'You're being silly again! The ice cream tastes the same.' Now the SP feels even sadder than before because he has been yelled at and been hit and misunderstood. He cries harder. Suddenly the mother bursts into tears, too, and says, 'Nothing makes you happy! I try *so-o-o-o* hard to make you happy, and nothing works. *Boo-hoo-hoo!'*

The mother is crying so loud that it hurts the SP's ears (see Chapter 2: Noise Sensitivity). This makes the SP angry at his mother and at the world for misunderstanding him and for not comforting him when he is sad. Therefore, when an SP sees another child crying, he immediately wants to laugh. For once, someone else is getting hurt and misunderstood! The SP may try to be polite (see Chapter 66: Being Polite), but he can't help himself. After all, nobody responds appropriately to HIS feelings, so how is he supposed to know how to respond appropriately to theirs? Nobody seems to give the SP sympathy, which is what the SP needs to experience in order to learn how to give other people sympathy.

Solution 1

[*By Mom*]: Listen to the SP when he is in distress. If you don't understand what the big deal is about a dish that got moved, ask him to explain in words why he is so upset. If he can't use words, pretend that you are him with all his autistic tendencies and ask yourself why you think he is so distressed. Show him how to respond appropriately to the distress of others by responding appropriately to his grief.

Solution 2

[*By James*]: Remember that the SP cannot control a lot of what comes out of him. It just rushes out like a tidal wave or like the contracting muscle that causes you to throw up. The laughing flies out of him, it is a strong force that cannot be controlled. Ask the SP to leave the room if he cannot stop laughing or chanting or jumping around. He wants to be alone anyway.

28

Being Obsessed with the Alphabet

Problem

When an NK develops, he learns how to talk at two, then around the age of five or six, he learns how to read in school. Generally, the talking comes spontaneously, then the reading has to be learned. Parents praise their NKs when they learn to read and they buy them readers and spellers and say, 'How smart you are!'

When the SK develops, all the noises of the world hurt his ears (see Chapter 2: Noise Sensitivity) so he never listens to what anyone is saying. Hence, he often fails to learn how to talk. On the other hand, he may focus on a form of communication that doesn't hurt him – printed words. Because the SK processes visual images so quickly, all the print in the world rushes into his brain, and pretty soon he figures out how to read, spontaneously, at the age of three or earlier. However, instead of praising the SK, the parents take their SK to the therapist, who says he is reading 'too soon' and that he has a condition called 'hyperlexia'. If his parents read a book by an expert, say Jane Healey, they will be warned that reading at an early age is a sign of mental retardation and they should discourage their SK from looking at books. If the parents are stupid enough to listen to this advice, the SK may search desperately for any printed letters he can get his hands on. He may insist that the closed captions be turned on when he watches TV, or he may fixate on the logos, on buildings or on people's clothing. Pretty soon he becomes obsessed with finding the alphabet in the environment.

When the SK goes into a store, furthermore, all the visual images flood him like a tidal wave. Therefore, he tries to find little images that don't flood him. Generally, those are little things, like letters. Letters are comforting and soothing, because the SK can recognize and process them, and they never change. An A is always an A.

Unfortunately, the therapist tells the mother that this is an obsession, and that the SK cannot spend his life staring at the alphabet letters in the store. So the mother hits him on the back and says, 'Stop being weird! Look at this toy instead.' But the SK does not want to look at a toy that he doesn't understand and which hurts his eyes. He wants to look at something he can understand.

Solution

The alphabet is the key to learning how to communicate if it is impossible to listen to other people's voices. The SK knows this somehow, and knows that those 26 letters are the key to being understood, and so he worships them, like 26 gods. They become the one true source of security the SK has, and so he focuses on them whenever he can.

[By James]: Mom realized firsthand why SKs focus on the alphabet. Reading this story tells you how she realized it. One gray afternoon, about a week before Christmas one year, Mom rushed over to an unfamiliar shopping center to buy a last-minute gift that was only available at that place. When she got out of the mall, she had only 20 minutes before she had to get to her part-time job. She'll tell you the rest:

In a rush, I [Mom] used the wrong exit out of the mall, leading into the western lots rather than the eastern ones. I had driven there in a new gray car that I hadn't yet learned to recognize immediately. The lots were full and seemingly endless. The day was gray, and suddenly every car in the lot, and everything in the world, seemed gray. I was scared and disoriented in this entirely gray world. The only thing that helped me make sense of the world was that my license plate was WRT 855. I became fixated with locating WRT 855. Only one gray car in the world would have that on it! I started reading license plates to the exclusion of everything else. My eyes focused on one set of digits after another. Finally it occurred to me that I was on the wrong side of the mall altogether, and I rushed to the eastern lots. When I finally found WRT 855, I was thrilled! It was a joyful, soothing sight.

And I realized a little better WHY James focused on the alphabet for so many years. They were his anchors in an incomprehensible world. The alphabet, reading, and finally typing, ultimately became James's native language. Speaking will always be a second language to him, but at least he has one form of communication that is spontaneous and natural, and in the academic, literary, and computer worlds, they give him a tremendous advantage over other children.

Therefore, let your child be obsessed with the alphabet. Buy him every alphabet video, computer game, board game, and book you can get your hands on. Drill him on flashcards, which he may love, since a single word is on every card. Keep the TV's closed captions on at all times, which will provide a visual reinforcement of the words he hears. (Don't YOU understand the French in a movie better when you read the subtitles as well we listen to the dialogue?)

Let him recite the alphabet for hours. First of all, the order will calm him down and stimulate the left hemisphere of his brain, which needs stimulation for social and language learning. But more important, recognize that, in the absence of an ability to generate sounds spontaneously, this is your children's attempt to babble (i.e., experiment with generating sounds).

The alphabet is also a good socializing tool. If you invite a child over and your own kid is tuning him out or playing frozen, start playing the alphabet game. Each child has to find something in the room that begins with A, then B, then C, etc. This game requires only parallel play, but both NKs and SKs seem to like it. Since the alphabet is a normal part of a five-year-old's education, the NK won't think your SK is weird by being interested in it.

Encourage your child to learn how to type and to do language-based computer games. (He may enjoy the visually-based games, but the left brain's language centers aren't stimulated by them.) Don't pull him away from the computer because it isn't social. If he can't communicate, socializing is fruitless anyway. The computer will give him the tools for future communication.

We actually used alphabet letters for rewards. James's favorite playthings were those wrought-iron or sticky letters that people attach to their houses and mailboxes. Whenever he achieved a given behavior goal, he was allowed to pick out one or two letters from the hardware store. If he was especially good for a series of days, we'd buy him a large brass house number, which he'd carry around lovingly like a teddy bear. He acquired quite a collection of letters and numbers, which he stored in a metal box and which always fascinated other kids. And of course, our house was full of plastic magnetic letters, peel-off letters sets, store-bought cardboard signs that said things like 'NO HUNTING – PRIVATE PROPERTY,' and stencil kits!

When the obsession with letters evolves into an obsession with words, start writing everything down. And I mean everything. Every request, every command, every bit of information you give your child. (You can also print your instructions out on the computer and collect them in a folder.) Have your child read everything you've written down, and have him point to each word. Buy a huge newsprint tablet for your writing. Then if you need to use the same request over and over, such as 'Wash your hands for dinner,' you can refer to a previous page. This may seem like a pain, but it's well worth it. Once your child can communicate with you, he is well on his way to becoming a fully functioning human being.

29

Being Obsessed with Time

Problem 1

When an NP wakes up in the morning or has to go to a class, he gets dressed, eats, gets ready, then leaves the house. He organizes his day to fit in all the things that he needs to accomplish. At least, some NPs do this.

When an SP wakes up in the morning or has to go to a class, he immediately panics. First of all, he is afraid that he will not have time to do all the things he has to do, then he feels confused about how to do them, then he feels afraid that he has forgotten something, then he feels overwhelmed that there are so many things to think about. The NPs have a saying, 'I can't think straight.' This is how the SP is all the time. (See Chapter 34: Thinking Styles.)

If the SP wakes up too late, this jolts his nervous system. He feels even more out of control than usual. Life is flying by and he is hanging on to its tail, as if it were a giant bird.

So, when the SP tries to deal with time, he finds a safe, concrete way to handle it – that is, with predictable measurements: seconds, minutes, and hours. If he is always aware of what time it is, or how long it takes for something to happen, he becomes more in control of it. That is why he becomes obsessed with knowing what time it is. Also, events rush by very quickly for the SP – often too quickly for him to process them – so by timing how long something takes, this helps him 'get a handle' on the event (another NP expression).

Solution 1

Let the SP be obsessed with time measurements. It is helping him bring order to his day. Let him time how long a song lasts, or how long a journey takes. Let him make elaborate schedules for himself.

These are good ways of processing time information, and besides, measuring is good left-brain stuff, which the SP needs.

Also, please remember that there are some times when you should not let your SP be obsessed, for example when he HAS to have a full hour of doing something somewhere. To help with 'full-time' fixations, be late to everything (this comes naturally in our house) so your SP will get used to being late and not being anywhere the entire amount of time on the schedule. He will have a lot of tantrums and angry outbursts, but eventually he will fixate on the fact that you can't be everywhere on time, and this will seem normal and safe to him.

Problem 2

[*By James*]: When an NP wants to do something, he does it as long as he does not have a headache (see Chapter 55: Headaches) or a stomachache (see Chapter 54: Stomachaches). If he is suffering from anything, he stops doing what he is doing and eats if he is hungry, or takes medicine if he has a headache.

When an SP does something, even if he is suffering, he is afraid that if he stops, he will not have enough time to do the thing he was doing. Also, it is a change to him (see Chapter 9: Change) because this interruption has not happened before in his life. So the SP continuously suffers when he is doing something. Yet on some level, he enjoys suffering, since he has suffered before and therefore it is not a change (see Chapter 9: Change) to him. But his mother hits him on the back and says, 'If you are suffering when you're doing something, stop doing it! Don't be obsessed with time!'

So the mother will command the SP to stop doing it, but the SP will just try to keep doing it and suffer and complain about how much his head hurts. Finally, the mother will give up and say, 'Just suffer then. I don't care. Just don't complain anymore.' So the SP suffers and does not complain anymore, but on some level, he is happy since he got what HE wanted!

Solution 2

Make a STOP sign out of red paper, and make it look like the STOP signs on the street, so it will not look NEW, and therefore, it will not look scary. [*From Mom*: Note the visual cue.] Train your SP to stop whenever he sees the STOP sign raised. Never force him, though, if he cannot stop what he is doing, or you will put him under worse stress.

Problem 3

[*By James*]: When an NK grows up, his brothers and sisters will go to many classes and learn a lot of things. NKs learn that they need extra time to get to their classes. They learn that you can't leave at the last minute or you will miss your class.

When an SK grows up, he is so obsessed and confused about time that he can't figure out when the appropriate time is to leave for something. (Also, if his mother has gotten him used to being late everywhere, he has an even harder time.) Although it is very possible to teach an SP to leave early for everything, he has a terrible time waiting (see Chapter 60: Waiting Problems), and his mother knows that if they arrive early, the SP will be jumping around and nervous. Sometimes the SP might even 'reach his limit' before the event begins. Therefore, the mother tries to arrive at everything at the exact moment it is to begin, which puts everyone under a lot of stress.

Solution 3

[*By Mom*]: Note that this contradicts Solution 1, but NPs aren't consistent: If being on time remains a major, ongoing obsession, try to arrive a little early when you go somewhere, but come armed with puzzles and storybooks that will keep your SP occupied until the event begins. Don't expect your SP to wait patiently for something if he is already terrified about participating in it (see Chapter 60: Waiting Problems) and is jumping out of his skin from anxiety. Bring something that he is currently fixated on, or better yet, allow him to do a *certain puzzle* or read a *certain book only* when he is waiting for something to begin. Then he will start to associate waiting with the pleasure of getting something that he wants.

30

Being Obsessed with Music*

Problem

As we have discussed in six chapters: (1) Chapter 2: Noise Sensitivity, (2) Chapter 25: The Music Playing in Your Head, (3) Chapter 50: Cocooning, (4) Chapter 48: Tuning Out, (5) Chapter 47: Mouth Control, and (6) Chapter 49: Playing Frozen; noise hurts the SP's ears. But in this chapter, we will tell you that your SP has another defense system against it.

Noise is the SP's natural enemy, and he tries to get rid of it every day. Since he cannot get rid of noise because NPs make it all the time, he may become more and more obsessed with music to block out the noise. I became obsessed with music, and because I was so obsessed, I had to have some kind of music playing from dawn to dusk. We had to take the tape recorder everywhere. I would listen with no expression on my face, no eye contact. Nobody knew that my obsession with music came from my sensitivity to noise. Also, my uncle has noise sensitivity (see Chapter 2: Noise Sensitivity), and his noise defense system is also listening to music. Like me, he has to listen to music wherever he is to protect himself from the noise.

When I was two and three, my mom used to take me to a mechanical duck which cost a quarter a ride. My mother kept feeding quarters into the machine and sometimes let me have three dollars' worth of rides. I liked it because it played music during a ride. I would ride with no expression on my face. People would come by and say hello and I would make no answer. We had to do this every day.

* By James, age 8

When the SP has to hear the same tape or music every day, finally his mother will go crazy from all the repetition, so she will hit the poor SP's back again and scream, 'You shouldn't have to listen to music all day! Why are you listening to music all day?' Then the mother turns off his music. That happened one day when we were in Boston visiting our relatives when I was a year and a half old. We were having Thanksgiving dinner, and I had to listen to the University of Michigan Fight Song all day long. Our hostess could not take the music anymore, so she turned it off. I turned it back on. She turned it back off. She didn't understand me.

I had to listen to the Rolling Stones every night to help me go to sleep when I was three. I did not understand the signals my body was trying to tell me every night. Usually my mom could nurse me down, but if that failed, my dad would have to take long walks with me riding in his backpack. Pretty soon, my dad was very angry, because I would often stay awake and drive my dad and mom crazy. So listening to the Rolling Stones helped me go to sleep.

Solution

Do not turn off the music deliberately; your SP may be using it as a soother or as something to help him. Let your SP listen to it in a soft volume, so it won't bother you. Also, if he is humming, ask him what noise is bothering him. Then try to remove the noise rather than screaming at him to stop humming.

31

Being Obsessed with Numbers*

Problem 1

When an NP goes on a trip in the car, he may want to find out how many miles it takes, but since he likes new things (see Chapter 9: Change), he does not care if his NP mother or father wants to take a new route that takes fewer miles than the previous route, to a certain place.

When an SP goes on a trip in the car, if he wants to find out how many miles it takes, he is afraid that his NP mother or father will take a route that takes fewer miles than the route they used the last time. We take a trip to my uncle's house twice a year. On August 16, 1997, we went to our uncle's house again to celebrate my ninth birthday on August 20. Well, we were driving to Indianapolis, and I wanted to find out how many miles it takes, but my dad decided to take a route that takes fewer miles, so I couldn't get a complete calculation of the number of miles in the normal route. I burst into tears. My dad told me that we would take that route going home, but it was still a change.

Solution 1

Take routes that take fewer miles on every trip if you have a new route you want to try with your SP or if you have a new route you want to take that day. Then change will become the regular thing and not scary.

* By James, age 9

Problem 2

When an NK grows up, he learns to talk spontaneously, then he must learn reading. The NP will learn reading at school during kindergarten. As we have discussed in Chapter 28, when the NP learns to read, the parents of the NK praise the NK. Then, in second grade, he learns to read big numbers like 20,000. The parents of the NK praise the NK again for learning how to read big numbers by saying the same thing they said about reading: 'How smart you are!'

When an SK grows up, however, as we have discussed in Chapter 28, he learns to read spontaneously, then he must be taught to talk. By the time the SK is eight, he may have already learned to read big numbers. However, instead of praising the SK, the mother may go to the therapist and say he has a condition called 'hyperlexia,' as discussed in Chapter 28, or that he 'perseverates,' or that he is weird. Then the mother may hit the SP on the back and scream, 'Stop reciting numbers! It's weird!'

Solution 2

Numbers are like letters, so let your SK be obsessed. He is acquiring an important tool and exercising the left hemisphere of his brain. [*By Mom*]: We used to walk around the house marching and counting our steps. James loved this seemingly 'autistic' behavior, but as he just mentioned, it activates the left hemisphere of the brain. Since that's where those dormant speech centers are, keep counting!

32

Being Obsessed with Perfection*

Problem

When an NP makes a mistake or bends a little corner on his work, he more often than not will not care. He just accepts it and does not do anything to fix it; he simply keeps it as part of his work. He may care if there is a spelling mistake, but he will probably just look it up in the dictionary and fix it.

When an SP makes a mistake or bends a little corner on his work, he gets a severe jolt to his nervous system. He is filled with stress. He tells his parents he must begin his work again because he made a mistake. The mother hits him on the back and says, 'Nobody cares! Why are you crying about something so stupid? That's weird!'

The SP starts over anyway, and the mother gets mad at him. The mother calls her friends (if she has any left, since her SP has alienated most of her friends), and tells them what a pill the SP is.

For example, when I was three, I had a fit because I was spelling names of cars and I made a mistake on one of the letters. My mom videotaped this story because she was already filming us, and it is on one of our family tapes. Here is the story:

> Mom and I were having a wonderful time writing 'OLDSMOBILE.' We wrote it together, since I did not know how to write some of the letters, such as S. When I was in the middle of drawing the I, Mom told me to draw the L next, and I mistakenly turned the I into an L. Then I begged her to turn the page and start over again, since it was not perfect and not my way. I had a big tantrum because it was her fault. 'No finish Olds-mobile,' I shrieked repeatedly, but Mom did not let me

* By James, age 8

start over again, because she remembered that my grand-mother had said not to give in to my obsession with perfection.

Also, my mom had to cut my cheese into letters, since I was obsessed with the alphabet, and they had to be perfect letters. Any mistake and I would get mad at my mom or refuse to eat the letter.

Solution

Tell him it is not something to have a big fuss about. Encourage him. He does not understand you. Start making everything not perfect, and he will get used to and need to have things imperfect. For example, my mother is a real slob, and the house is always a mess. It drives my father nuts, but mess is the only thing I have ever known. Therefore, I get upset when the house is in order and go nuts when I am forced to clean up.

Tell your SP that if you spend too much time obsessing about the little things, you forget about the big things. For example, we know an SP who was so busy choosing the cover color and the typeface for his book that he didn't even write it!

33

Left vs. Right Hemisphere Processing*

Problem

When an NB is born, he is a right-hemisphere processor, but he becomes a left-hemisphere processor at 18 months. By the time the NB grows into an NK, he will have become a left-hemisphere processor, so he has normal and good judgment, and is now a logical thinker. By the time the NK grows up into an NP, he will become a businessman and earn a lot of money. This is how it has always been with NPs. They always think logically, or you can say, they think sequentially. They are fast processors, because there is not too much processing going in the left side of the mind. Sometimes thinking sequentially is bad (see Solution 1 in Chapter 34: Thinking Styles), but if everybody was a right-hemisphere processor, no houses or buildings would be built, but a lot of books would be written.

When an SP is born, he is a right-hemisphere processor but something different happens at 18 months. The SP stays a right-hemisphere processor forever unless his mother trains him to become a left-hemisphere processor.

Right-hemisphere processors are slow processors because there is too much processing going on in this hemisphere of the brain, and it takes a long time to process all that stuff. So the right-hemisphere processing unit is jammed up inside there, and is so confused (see Chapter 41: Verbal Confusion) because the right-hemisphere does not know which information to process first.

* By James, age 8

106

So, if it takes about a year longer to process everything in the right-hemisphere, it is not ready to learn new skills at the appropriate time, because it is too busy learning another new skill. In fact, all right-hemisphere processors are delayed in everything, which means they learn differently. For example, I learned to talk three years late, which means that I learned at five instead of two.

But remember, as long as there are SPs, they are going to be right-hemisphere processors.

Solution

This is also a tough one! Have your SP do his left-hemisphere sequencing cards, but not too much. Make your SP half-global and half-sequential. Half and half is better than thinking in one hemisphere completely.

Also, as we've discussed at the end of the solution in Chapter 43: The Rules of Language, let him have his way and do his left-hemisphere activities until your SP can completely handle your way of thinking, and also remember that global thinking is not always bad. There are times when it is necessary. For example, helping our global community survive will require having people who don't always think in a straight line.

34

Thinking Styles

Problem 1 [Global Thinking]

NPs love to think logically: *A* leads to *B* leads to *C*, and so forth. They try to instill this way of thinking into NKs from the beginning of school. Schools teach NKs to make outlines and go from Step 1 to Step 2 to Step 3.

But SPs don't think that way. Because they process information in the right hemisphere of their brain, they think *globally* rather than *sequentially*. What is a globe? It's a circle.

SPs think like this: Someone says, 'Look at that beautiful sunset.' The SP hears all the words but, like the Internet, he clicks on whatever word happens to stand out. In this case, for example, the stand-out word is 'sunset'. That is also the name of a food store near us. So the SP thinks: *'Sunset Foods – they carry my favorite roasted chicken'*. Then he remembers the time he and his mom had a wonderful dinner together eating chicken at 'Brown's Chicken.' Then he thinks about their French fries, and then his mind clicks on the word 'French' and he remembers that his mother wants him to learn French, but he wants to learn Spanish. So he gets angry at his mother and his mind clicks on the time when she made him eat something that he didn't like, then she hit him on the back and said, 'Don't be so picky. You're going to drive your wife crazy.' Then the original speaker says, 'Didn't you hear me? Do you think the sunset is beautiful.' Then the SP barks, 'NO!' because he is very angry at his mother for having hit him on the back.

Solution 1

This is also a tough one. Allow the SP to do his 'left brain' activities such as marching and counting, to help him with sequencing. On the other hand, the world is evolving into a global community, and that means right-brain thinking is going to be more acceptable than before. The Internet is a right-brain tool; that's why it drives many NPs crazy. But Bill Gates and the other computer nerds are not NPs, and it was they who fashioned computer software to think the way they do. So your SP is well suited to dealing with the chaos of the future, which mimics his own mind.

The bad part of about being a left-brain, sequential thinker is that those types only go in one direction – they want more, and they want faster, and they want better. Because of their non-global way of thinking, they have ruined the earth, because all they care about is cutting down more trees and amassing more money and buying more land. If the earth is to survive, we need more global thinkers, who think of a tree in terms of its life cycle (which is a circle), not in terms of cutting it down and that's it. So make your SP do his sequencing cards, but not too much so that he loses his sense of totality, which will be needed if the global community is to survive.

Problem 2 [Negative Thinking]

When an NP grows up, he has a variety of experiences with other people – some good, some bad. So when he meets a new person, his mind reserves judgment about whether the experience will be good or bad.

When an SP grows up, however, virtually all of his interpersonal experiences are negative. And because he lacks social judgment, he is always saying or doing the wrong thing. In fact, every time he tries to do the right thing, it turns out to be the wrong thing. Therefore, HIS mind says, 'If everything I decide to do is wrong, then I better do the opposite of what I think is right.' This establishes negative thinking in the person's mind. After a while, his mind starts translating everything into the opposite. So when he feels happy, he frowns, and when he likes something, he says it's ugly, the way Oscar the Grouch on *Sesame Street* does.

Solution 2

Negative thinking is something that evolves slowly, and you can nip it in the bud if you're observant. If you find yourself criticizing your

SP for everything he does, limit his activities to things that he is truly capable of (it is easier to do this if you are homeschooling). If he is going into a new situation, go over in detail what may or may not happen. Allow him to make decisions on matters that he can handle, so he experiences some success and mastery for a change. Praise him lavishly whenever he does the right thing spontaneously.

When he makes a mistake in judgment or does something socially inappropriate, sit down with him and analyze exactly what led him to do it. If you can explain (even though you can't approve of) his behavior, you can both learn from the experience, and he won't feel like such a dolt and have such a negative opinion of himself.

Note: This problem is in code to show you an example of mixed-up thinking.

Problem 3 [Thinking mixed-up]

[*By James*]: One when talks NP another to they NP, each understand and other a have time good.

An when talks NP an to the SP, words become mixed up. Example, for you if 'What said, is time he it?' hear, might is 'Time or what?', weird something that. Like Establishes this thinking mixed-up requires and the that translate SP that everything hears, he takes which The time. hits mother on him back the says, and you 'Didn't what hear said? I me! Answer' The on side, bright SP the very is at good puzzles solving 'Word like since Jumble,' for EVERYTHING is jumble at him.

Solution 3

Him give of lots puzzles word solve to. Will this his perfect skills. translating He soon become may 'simultaneous instantly translator', what translating heard he into back you what said.

Problem 4 [Literal Thinking]

When an NK grows up, he learns the proper steps for doing everything (do this first, then this second, and so on), and whenever his mother says something like, 'Put on your shoes and socks,' the NK already knows that the steps for putting on your shoes and socks are putting your socks on first, then your shoes, so he does not follow exactly what she said but re-interprets it correctly.

When an SK grows up, since the speech centers in his left brain are not ready to process language and its context, when his mother says, 'Put on your shoes and socks,' the SK thinks that, if his mother told him in that order, he must have to do it in that order. So the SK ends up putting his socks over his shoes, and the mother hits him on the back and says, 'Why don't you use your HEAD?'

Solution 4

At first, you have to be very careful with what you say. Be very explicit, and don't use idioms. If you say, 'Hold your tongue,' your SP may try to grasp his tongue and pull it out of his mouth. As your SP gets older, try using a few idioms, but always explain them fully, including how the idiom got started and why it is used to mean what it does. James and his speech teacher have been collecting idioms for over a year now, and he reminds me of 'My Favorite Martian' as he learns all those illogical expressions that NPs use. His fifth grade class now is treated to the 'idiom of the week,' thanks to James.

Problem 5 [Different Rules]

[*By James*]: When there is something new in an NP's life, since he is not terrorized by change (see Chapter 9: Change), he does not care. If there is a change in the rules (for example, you don't have to do something one day, and then the next you do), he does not care because he does not fixate on the rule being the same all the time.

When there is something new in an SP's life, however, since the SP is afraid of change (see Chapter 9: Change), he cares whenever a change happens. So when the mother tells the SP to do something, he gets fixated on that as a rule and wants it to stay the same. Then the next day, the mother will tell the SP not to do the thing he did that other day (or vice versa), but since he has fixated on that rule and what was right to do yesterday, this will confuse him terribly. In order to feel safe, he feels compelled to do the thing that was right yesterday. When the mother finds out the SP disobeyed her, she will hit the SP on the back and scream, 'Why did you do that? I told you NOT to!'

Solution 5

The only solution we have to tell you is to keep explaining contexts to an SP. Keep telling him why this day was different from that one, and how this event differs from that one. Keep trying. Even invent some circumstances in which details change, to help the SP learn how to reason rather than memorize rules.

Problem 6 [Reasoning]

[*By James*]: When an NP has to do his work and there is something in the way of where he wants to go, he stops walking and moves the thing away to give himself some room. Then he walks by and does his work. He does the same thing if it happens again.

When an SP has to do his work, though, since he does not see that there is extra room to move things aside, and it doesn't occur to him that he can move something, he does not move it. Also, sometimes he does not see the thing, so he bumps into the thing that is blocking his way. Often he complains, 'Mom! What can I do? This thing is in my way, and I cannot go anywhere.' So the SP just lies down on the floor paralyzed and unable to move. The mother goes to the SP, gets him up from lying down, hits him on the back, and screams, 'If something is in your way, MOVE IT! It's not bolted to the floor. Why don't you use your head?'

Solution 6

Buy a critical thinking book to teach him to reason. Give him lots of sample problems in which people have to use their head to do something. Try to give the SP an example of every possible Problem that he could face. Hopefully, the SP will someday learn to apply these possible outcomes to his daily life.

Problem 7 [Absentmindedness]

When an NP puts his book or something else down on the table, his mind makes an automatic note of where he left it. Then when he wants to go back and get his book, the NP immediately goes back to the table and picks it up. All day long, the NP is doing things and remembering that he did them, and his life goes along smoothly.

When an SP puts his book or something down on the table, sometimes he remembers where he put the book, but often he does not. When he puts his book down, his mind might be in a whirl, thinking about a dozen other things so that his hands are working on their own, putting the book down out of habit rather than conscious decision. Then his mind, which is processing other things, does not process the fact that the book got put on the table; it keeps wondering when Daddy is going to buy 'Clue,' so they can play it to improve the SP's reasoning skills.

When his mother asks him where his book is, he might not remember it at all, or he might remember where he put it last week but not this time. When he sees her angry face, he goes into a panic, and then he can hardly remember his name. He cries, 'I don't remember!' expecting her to start yelling. The mother hits him on the back and says, 'Think harder! How could you not remember where you put the book?'

Then she roams through the house, complaining and getting angry, trying to find the book. Along the way she finds all the other things that were lost in the previous two weeks, and that makes her a little happier, but not much (since she already had to replace most of the stuff, which cost her a lot of money). Finally, after a half-hour of looking, the mother hits the SP on the back and says, 'How could it disappear? Did you HIDE it?'

Solution 7

Have scavenger hunts at home. Ask your SP to hide a bunch of things around the house then have him go and find them. The purpose of the game is not to conceal things but to encourage the SP to remember where he put them. Also, ask him to pay more attention to what his hands are doing (although this will be very hard for him). Even an SP's brain needs only a little bit of attending to where something is put down in order for it to store the memory of where it was placed. However, the SP is often totally absorbed in his own thoughts and does things without being aware that he did them.

Problem 8 [Picky Thinking]

[*By James, age 11*]: SPs do not know why, but NPs, when it comes to clothes, are picky thinkers. They want your clothes to be in top shape, no holes or anything. And SPs can't understand WHY. After all, they think, 'What's the point about stupid clothes? You should just wear them and not worry about what's WRONG with them.'

So SPs can't understand why their mothers are always forcing them to change clothes because they have holes in their favorite clothes. This always makes the SP angry, since he is always uncomfortable wearing new clothes. They scratch his body. (See Chapter 7: Touch Sensitivity.) Because he does not want his body scratched, he refuses. This may cause the mother to hit him on the back and scream, 'I DON'T CARE IF YOU'RE NOT WEARING YOUR FAVORITE CLOTHES! YOU WEAR THESE BECAUSE THEY LOOK GOOD!' Then she forces her SP to suffer in silence, wearing itchy clothes. She thinks it's more important to look good than to feel good, which is confusing to the SP since she always tells him she wants him to feel like an NP. Also, she tells him that the tiny hole in his clothes is important even though the tiny spot on his paper, she said yesterday, was NOT important. But the SP doesn't understand why the picky things that she points out are important, but the picky things that he points out are NOT important. This makes him decide that the NP world is too weird to figure out.

Solution 8

Mothers, it's best to just let your SP wear whatever he wants. Just be thankful that you are not the one who is going to be teased, he is. This may seem a little mean, but it's best for him not to be uncomfortable. However, if the SP complains about being teased, you will have to tell him it is better for him to wear clothes without holes.

35

Stress*

Note: This is a chapter about how an SP suffers many different kinds of stress all the time.

Problem 1

Because an SP is a right-hemisphere processor, he cannot keep secrets at all. If he must keep a secret, he is put under a huge amount of stress keeping one. For example, the mother is getting old and has to take a pill to keep her healthy, which the SP cannot tell anyone else about. This puts the SP under a huge and terrible amount of stress. So he may not be able to keep the secret, and the SP must go do a lot of things to tell somebody (when the mother is talking to somebody):

1. If the mother is talking to another mother or another adult, the SP must get the adult's attention, so he does this by interrupting (see Chapter 65: Interrupting Other People), and the mother hits the SP on the back and screams at him, 'Why did you interrupt us?'

2. The SP will tell the adult who talked to the mother, if he can talk, 'There is something I must tell you in private, so my mom won't know.'

3. The SP and adult go to a private place and the secret (which is the pill the mother is taking) will burst out of the SP's mouth like a bull from a cattle chute or like a burst out of a cannon.

* By James, age 8

4. Then the adult goes back to the mother and tells what the SP did.

5. The mother hits the SP on the back and screams, 'Why did you tell that adult? Didn't you know it was a secret?'

But the mother doesn't understand that the SP was trying to keep the secret, but since the SP is put under a huge amount of stress keeping secrets, and the mother doesn't even know that he is thrown under a huge amount of stress keeping secrets, the mother thinks that the SP was TRYING to be inappropriate and rude. But the SP was NOT trying to be rude. The mother doesn't understand, as if the SP were a broken machine and the mother didn't even understand why the machine was broken.

Solution 1

Get the SP used to keeping secrets by asking him to keep an easy secret every day. Have him keep it from just one other person, who is specifically stated. This way the rules are clear to the SP.

Problem 2

As discussed in Chapter 39: Going to School, the SP is bombarded by kids at school and a teacher who doesn't understand anything about an SP. When the SP knows that the class is taught by an NT (normal teacher) that does not know about an SP, the SP will get afraid of going to school every day. So when his NP mother forces the SP to go to school, the NT or the kids at the class will tease him, which will put him into a horrible, terrible, and 'humongous' amount of stress. All stress is like an evil spell somebody has put on you, for example, how in Power Rangers, the villains put the Power Rangers under their own spell. Also, the newness of the class and the school puts the SP in even more stress. So the mother, after she has heard tons of stories about hating school, will hit the SP on the back and scream at the SP, 'Why can't you like school and not be afraid of it, like everybody ELSE!'

Solution 2

Try enrolling your SP into the Calvert School (see Appendix I), an organization where they send the workbooks home for homeschooling. Then your SP can work in peace and in quietness.

Problem 3

Because an SP resists growing up, his NP mother will force him to do everything and grow up. Then the NP mother becomes very pushy, which bothers the SP, so he will scream at the mother. So the mother will keep torturing the SP, until the mother gets tired of listening to the screaming SP, and be so embarrassed because of the screaming SP that she will hit the SP on the back and say, 'Stop screaming! That hurts my ears!'

Then the SP must suffer inside a huge and terrible amount of stress because somebody is trying to force the SP to do something he resists every day.

Solution 3

Forcing your SP is not going to do any good, because stress may affect the SP's brain, and the SP may become brain-injured. So don't force him, but help him by doing things he likes to do in a way that he can learn some new skills.

Problem 4

Because an SP gets fixated and used to many things that an NP doesn't get fixated on or used to, he wants things to stay the same all the time. So since the SP hates change (see Chapter 9: Change), the SP is put under a terrible amount of stress because the SP hates change, and a change has happened. Finally the mother hits the SP on the back and screams at the SP, 'Why can't you like change and new things? You should like change and new things! Why are you under stress? Don't be under stress! Don't be in fear! Don't be in terror! Why are you in fear and terror? You look silly!'

Solution 4

Don't shove a change into the SP's face. Why are you changing things without even telling him? To help, tell your SP what change will be happening before you do it so it will not be new for the SP anymore.

Problem 5

Because an SP often hates social situations (see Chapter 26: Special Occasions), he always wants to get away from them. Playdates, parties, weddings and funerals always put the SP under a lot of terror. So when the SP's mother tells the SP about a social situation that is coming up, the SP gets the worst fear he has ever had. Also, the SP is put under a horrible amount of stress, because the SP knows that he hates social situations. So the SP may play frozen at the social situation when it is happening, and the SP is under a huge amount of stress too. Every minute is a pain. The SP just wishes the social situation to be over. When the mother finds the SP suffering in silence, playing frozen, in stress, and not paying attention to anybody, the mother will hit the SP on the back and scream at him, 'Stop playing frozen! You're supposed to like social situations!'

Solution 5

Don't let the SP suffer like this! Hire a babysitter whenever you must have a social situation, like to your cousin's wedding or a birthday party.

[*Note from Mom*]: Half of your SP's problems stem from neurological delays, sensory problems, and physical problems. The other half of his problems are the result of stress. Many of your child's behaviors are attempts to lower his stress level. They are symptoms of stress overload. So rather than trying to extinguish the symptoms (such as hand flapping), why not extinguish the stress first, and see what symptoms drop away?

Stress is your child's No. 1 enemy, worse in some ways than the autism itself. Stress makes your child sick and kills off his badly needed brain cells (see Chapter 48: Tuning Out). Every time you force him to 'get used' to something, you are destroying a little bit more of his nervous system and making him less able to cope with life in the future. You are also making him more resistant to new situations yet to come (see Chapter 38: Anger). Oh, you may be teaching him some new skills by rote, but you are not helping him become a fully functioning human being.

Go and observe your child in school. You may be appalled at the amount of stress he is under all day long. Hours and hours of stress will break down anyone quickly. Don't add to his problems.

36

Behavior Problems*

Problem 1

When an NK develops, he develops good judgment. When an SK develops, though, since he does not have that fully developed judgment NKs have, all of his social situations are negative. Also, you know how you are leaving him alone inside the house because you are afraid he will embarrass you? Well, though staying alone helps with some sort of suffering the SK has to face, it is making your SK more and more used to house behavior, which, as you all know, is chanting and making funny noises (see Chapter 47: Mouth Control), quoting (see Chapter 24: Having an Urge to Quote), jumping around, kissing the walls, and sticking your tongue out. So all of his social situations are negative because he is used to house behavior, and lacks public behavior. As you all know, house behavior inside a public place is embarrassing to the SK's mother, so if she realizes the SK is not behaving properly, she will walk up to the SK, hit the SK on the back, and say, 'Why are you acting like this? You are acting crazy! Who taught you to act like this?'

Solution 1

Remember that the SK cannot control a lot of what he is doing. It just rushes out of him like a tidal wave, a strong force, so strong it never can be controlled. Go to a public place every day and help him by telling him how to behave in that public place. You will have to tell him everything; he will not learn it on his own.

* By James, age 8

Problem 2

[*By Mom*]: When an NK goes to the doctor or a therapist, the child is generally the focal point of the appointment. The doctor asks the NK pleasant questions to pass the time and tries to make the experience as painless as possible. If something is going to feel weird or uncomfortable during a physical exam, the nurse may smile and apologize to the NK, perhaps even giving him a lollipop or a sticker for being so brave. This makes the NK try his best to remain polite and well-behaved during the entire exam. Everyone feels good about the experience, especially the doctor, who prides himself at being able to handle kids… Normal kids, that is.

When an SP goes to a doctor or a therapist, the doctor generally tries to establish his control of the situation from the very first. All of his training may have been geared toward controlling SKs rather than empathizing with them. He expects the child to misbehave and act up, so the moment the child opens his mouth to speak, he is immediately commanded to keep silent. If the child tries to touch or examine something interesting, the doctor grabs it from him and tells him he must keep absolutely still while the doctor and the mother talk. When the SK realizes that all the talking is about him, he may try to put in his own two cents, which causes the doctor to command him to be silent once again.

When it is time for a physical exam, the doctor again tries to maintain control over the child, whom he secretly regards as a defective alien and a nuisance who needs to be subdued by drugs or harsh punishments. Sensing this, the child tries to elude the doctor, or behave in such a horrendous way that the mother is too embarrassed to come back for the next appointment. If the mother goes home with a plan for curbing the child's behavior, this may prompt the child to start misbehaving every time he sees that doctor. After all, nobody respected him during the exam, so why should he respect the examiner?

Solution 2

If your SK's behavior is unusually bad during doctors' appointments, try to analyze what is going on. Apart from the considerable stress of being poked and tortured by a stranger, is the doctor an arrogant control freak who thinks of special-needs children as unruly humanoids that need to be subdued? Can he empathize with special children, or are they 'other' to him? Does he talk to you about your SK as if the child weren't in the room? Does he dismiss or squelch the child's attempts to present his own opinion? Does he see every trait your child has (particularly self-assertion and curiosity) as a symptom of his 'disorder'? Chances are your SK's behavior problems are the result of resentment, anger, or stress resulting from the therapist's callousness. Stay away from control freaks when selecting a therapist, or better yet, forget about expensive therapy, save your money, and start a home program. For information about home programs, see Appendix I.

As mentioned elsewhere, the worst thing you can do is turn your child into a reactionary, someone who defies authority as a reflex. This will indeed occur, however, if you consistently try to curb and control him rather than understand him. SKs do not misbehave (in the beginning, at least) because they are 'bad'. Either they do not understand what is expected of them, or they are overly stressed. To figure out what is going on, *empathize, empathize, empathize*. Become your child. Get into his mind. Only then will you be able to understand the logic of his 'bad' behavior. This does not mean that you automatically allow the bad behavior to continue. Empathy is not the same as unconditional acceptance. It is necessary to change the situation, but you have to figure out which aspect of the situation needs changing. If the environment is placing an intolerable stress on your child, change the environment, not the child. You may find the behavior problem resolves on its own.

37

Discipline

Problem 1

When an NK develops, he learns the rules of behavior then instinctively tests them out. Sometimes he feels it is necessary to test the limits of a given rule or even to break it in order to see what happens. This is a normal part of the NP learning process. Sometimes he gets punished by breaking a rule: his mother may catch him and force him to do some sort of penance, or he may get hurt in the process of breaking the rule. In either event, the bad consequences teach him to follow the rule for his own good. In fact, as an NK grows older, he learns that good things happen to people who follow rules. On the other hand, occasionally breaking the rules becomes a way of asserting oneself in the face of authority. This is something that an NK's nature compels him to do as he grows into an NP. It is also a way of having some fun at the authority figure's expense. Since the United States was founded by rebels, free thinkers, and hopeless criminals, our gene pool has a lot of naughtiness and defiance of authority in it. So disobedience is a genetic trait among American NPs. American mothers know this, and they take classes on effective parenting and 'Discipline in the New Millennium' and go home and try to assert their authority in the home. The goal of this, however, is to teach their children *self*-control and *self*-discipline, so that they learn how to do the right thing because it is right, not because there is a rule about it.

When an SK develops, however, a lot of the rules he is forced to follow cause him pain or add to his stress. This is the result of having NP rules imposed upon him when he belongs in an SP world. Therefore, he learns to break NP rules whenever he can to *avoid* pain. Avoidance of pain, after all, is a human trait. Furthermore, because he is so overwhelmed by the NP world, he lives a defensive, reactive kind of life. He is in no position to 'test the limits' of anything, since he is like an exhausted swimmer hanging on to the side of a raft. Survival, not growth and development, is his only thought.

When the SK's mother realizes that he is disobeying all of her rules and requests and is fighting her over everything, at first she tries the logical tactics: she yells, she punishes, she uses time-outs, she takes away privileges. When she finds that this isn't working, she may buy a book on discipline or see a therapist. If she goes to a behaviorist, a type of therapist who believes that human beings (especially SPs) are no different from rats and monkeys, he may give her several stimulus-response, positive-reinforcement-type schemes for controlling her SK. These may include star charts, reward schedules, and the like. If what she is asking the SK to do is hurtful or scary, however, he may keep disobeying her and say, 'I don't want a star.' She may go back to the therapist, who may then recommend one of the negative-reinforcement-type schemes such '1–2–3, you're out' or a similar way of trying to turn a child into a 'Stepford' android.

Here is an example of the '1–2–3' method of discipline:

> SP: Mommy, these socks don't feel right. [*Actually he is experiencing the seams as razor blades across his toes*]
>
> Mom: That's one.
>
> SP [*whining*]: My toes hurt!
>
> Mom: You're not supposed to whine. That's two.
>
> SP [*agitated*]: But Mom, my ——
>
> Mom: That's three. I warned you. Now you have a ten-minute time out.
>
> SP [*screaming*]: But my ——
>
> Mom: Get upstairs! And if I hear anything more, I'll add ten minutes!

After months of this, an SK might either just give up and do whatever his mother wants, despite the pain, or what's more common, he may learn to fight her tooth-and-nail on everything as a way of maintaining his human dignity. By employing a stimulus-response type of learning, the mother has taught her SK a stimulus-response mode of behavior: *She commands; I disobey.* This becomes automatic, and you may end up with an SP who now has oppositional-defiant disorder as well. Or you may teach your SK that he gets to disobey twice before he is punished, so by golly, he'll disobey you twice every time you ask him to do something.

Solution 1

[*By Mom*]: Unless you have a totally non-verbal child who can only be taught with a behavior modification plan, such as that of Dr Lovaas, avoid these humiliating techniques altogether. The behaviorists put children in the same category as lab animals, and if you keep treating your child like an animal, he'll become as stubborn as an animal – a mule, that is. Whenever he resists you, ask him why. If he can't speak, look around and theorize as to *why*. Chances are he is attempting to avoid pain or minimize stress. Remember, you are not dealing with a normal child, and to cater to his needs in this understanding fashion is *not* the same as spoiling, as it could be for a normal child. Understanding his needs is not going to 'spoil' him. It is the constant and continuous lack of respect for his needs that spoils him.

Also, please avoid the temptation to subdue your child with drugs unless you've created such a hopeless situation with an older child that drugs are his only hope. Your goal, if it's still possible, is to raise a fully functioning human being, not a medicated or well-trained chimp. A smart, verbal child will particularly resist the '1–2–3' type of enforcement plans, since they insult his intelligence. We know of families in which these plans have turned the SKs into little 'Rambos', fighting their parents on everything. The parents go back to the therapists, who come up with even stronger forms of this humiliation, and the children react even more negatively. Ultimately, everyone ends up on some kind of medication – including the parents.

Problem 2

[*By James, age 11*]: Because an SP doesn't know what is happening in the NP world, when he disobeys something, he often maybe didn't understand (see Chapter 42: Understanding Other People) what he was meant to do. This normally gets the SP's mother mad because she thinks the SP doesn't want to do what she wants. This often results in a punishment for something the SP didn't know was wrong.

Here is a story about how disciplining was handled in bad ways:

I go to an SP art class at the high school with my friend, Katie. It has been a mystery to me why she is always misbehaving and not paying attention during group time, until now. This story tells you why.

My mother goes to ballet with my sister, Lauren, the same time I go to art. Her lesson ends at 5:00 pm, the same time my group ends. But since it takes time for Lauren to change her clothes, etc., Mom doesn't pick me up from art until 5:15. So I stay after with my art teacher. But one day Katie stayed after too, until she heard her bratty sister Christina say, 'It's time to go! We're late!'

However, Katie wasn't ready at that time, so her mother Linda came into the art room and said, 'If you're not ready in ten seconds, I'm leaving without you. Mr. Kilner, if she's not ready and I'm gone, take her to the intersection of Charles + Jones Road (a long way from her house) and drop her off there, OK?'

Mr. Kilner said yes, and Katie wasn't ready, so Linda left with Christina.

'Too bad you can't get a ride,' the sister teased.

I followed Katie out the door as Linda's car just left. 'Wait! Wait!' Katie screamed, but Linda showed no sympathy as she drove faster out of the parking lot. I saw her turn the corner.

Two minutes later, my mother came into the parking lot and picked me up. I told her all about what had just happened. On Charles Road, we saw Katie running on the sidewalk on the left of the street, while Linda had her car parked in the distance on the right side. It seemed as if Linda was waiting for Katie. Mom thought Linda was going to pick her up, so she pulled up to Linda's car and asked, and Linda said yes. Then we left them and went home.

One week later, when we went to art, Katie didn't pay attention a lot more today than she had done before. In the middle of the lesson Katie said that her mother was busy and might not pick her up at all. She told me that last week her mother was only fooling us by stopping her car, and that after we left, the mother drove off without Katie, who had to walk miles in the dark. Then I said, 'We'll take you to your house if you don't get picked up this time.'

After the lesson, we had a snowball fight outside. We saw Linda's car outside too, except empty. Then we saw Linda through a window. Soon, I was getting cold, so I went inside the high school. Wondering what Linda was doing, I went into the hallway and saw that Linda was talking to Jackie, another mother whose kid was in the art group. I overheard their conversation. Here is what they said:

> Linda: You shouldn't give in to waiting for your kid to get ready. It's useless, and besides, your child isn't learning anything being allowed to dawdle like that. For example, my daughter Katie wasn't ready last week, so I left without her and she ran all way to Main Street before I picked her up.

> Jackie: That was a good thing to do. Your kids should now be learning that there are consequences when you do bad things.

At that moment I felt so angry at them that I talked to Linda. I asked her, 'Why did you make Katie run all way to Main Street?'

Linda said, 'I wanted to teach my child a lesson. My rule is if my kids aren't ready, I make them suffer the consequences, which are, they have to walk home themselves. So, at Main, I picked up Katie and she didn't go to Girl Scouts because she had done that and I made her stay home and had her do something I hate to do myself – the LAUNDRY!!!'

At this, Jackie nodded and said, 'That was the right thing to do.'

Then I said, 'We were about to pick Katie up before we thought you would do it.'

'You were doing a bad thing. If you had picked her up, you wouldn't have let her learn her lesson about getting ready. You would just let her get away with it, and not make her suffer the consequences,' said Linda in a cruel manner.

When I left her, she was laughing as if she were a witch.

A few minutes later, Christina and Linda were leaving. They were about to leave Katie behind when she came with them.

Then, my mother came to pick me up.

After that, I told my mother. She was shocked and she felt bad that parents could act that way. Then, I knew that what Linda had said last week was a trick. I never felt as angry as at this time, when I saw this terrible thing happen...

Certainly what you just heard was totally barbaric. It also shows you that Linda, Katie's mother doesn't understand SPs. But, this story is true, and it shows you how some mothers discipline their children in ways that don't work.

Solution 2

[*By Mom*]: When the relationship between a mother and her SP breaks down to this level, it is necessary to start over. If I were Katie's mom, I would pull Katie out of all her activities and let her stay home for a while, engaging in activities that are limited enough for Katie [who has some form of ADD] to handle and be successful at. The cruel punishment of leaving a child behind in the dark teaches her nothing but resentment and prompts more disobedience and defiance.

In the case of the art class, Katie is probably confused as to why her mother is so angry at her. After all, Katie is staying behind to comfort and interact with James, while he waits for me to pick him up. For years, she has been encouraged to interact socially with her peers and to try to make friends. Now that she is interacting with her friend and entertaining him rather than abandoning him while he waits for a ride, she is expecting to be praised. Instead, she gets punished. This must be terribly confusing to her, and it actually encourages her to abandon her friend the next time, the way her mother abandoned her. So what is the message in this encounter? That keeping to a tight schedule and being obsessed with time are more important than interacting with a friend and giving him your company and comfort? (See Chapter 29: Being Obsessed With

Time.) Is it any wonder why SPs find the NP world so baffling and inconsistent?

38

Anger

Problem 1

[*By Mom*]: When an NP hears shouting and screaming, he stops what he is doing and sees whether the shouting and screaming is being directed at him. If it is intended for someone else, the NP goes back to his work and tunes the screaming out. If the screaming is directed at him, he straightens up, gets his denial mechanism activated, and prepares to argue with whoever is attacking him.

When an SP hears shouting and screaming, he goes into a panic. He assumes that if some mistake was made, HE is to blame, since he is usually to blame for every bad thing that happens in the entire world. He then immediately tunes out and plays frozen, so that he won't have to deal with the yelling. For example, the parents could be yelling at each other about...

1. A stupid thing the SP did and how much he embarrassed one or the other of them. However, because each parent has different things that drive him or her crazy, the parents might be disagreeing as to *how* stupid the thing was.

2. The condition of the house. The father is yelling at what a mess it's in while the mother is trying to tell him that between the SK's multitude of therapies and lessons and the NK's endless playdates, which trash the house each time, there is no time to fix it up.

3. How they never have enough time together, because the SP has taken over their lives.

After a while, the SP's frozen mechanism doesn't work so well, and he starts listening. No matter what the subject is, he assumes that the real reason they are yelling is that they are stuck raising him. This makes him very sad.

Solution 1

[*By Mom*]: Parents, try to yell at each other behind closed doors. Your SK may appear not to notice about what is going on around him, but he cares more than your NKs. Since everything in the environment hits him like a typhoon, he has to build walls to protect him from the onslaught. But that doesn't mean that he is not getting drenched by the emotions pouring out around him. He wishes you could spend one day in his body, then you'd know. Also, long after your fighting is over, the words you shouted are playing and replaying in the SP's mind and he can't get them out. Pretty soon he might have the urge to quote you (see Chapter 24: Having an Urge to Quote). Don't yell at him if he does so! He is just trying to get your words out of his mind.

Problem 2

[*By James, age 11*]: When an NP gets angry, he yells a little bit, but it doesn't take long for him to cool down and often he is over it and he talks with the NP who made him angry.

When an SP gets angry, it's a different story. Since he can't control his anger, he yells and screams at the NP who made him angry, and doesn't let him talk. Normally his mother hits him on the back and screams, 'CALM DOWN AND LET HIM TALK! HE KNOWS WHAT HE DID WRONG, SO STOP YELLING AT HIM! BECAUSE YOU DIDN'T STOP, YOU ARE GETTING A TIME-OUT! UP TO YOUR ROOM FOR TEN MINUTES!'

But this makes him confused. After all, NPs do not get time-outs when they are angry, so why should an SP get a time-out then! It just isn't fair. But that is the way it is with an SP – it's unfair for them. This is what your SP possibly is thinking when you send him up to his room.

Solution 2

First, you can teach your SP basic ways of cooling down anger, like counting to 10, the way NPs normally do it.

If the SP fights you when you try to teach him, though, talk to your SP about it before giving him a time-out. If the SP will talk to you, you can discuss the anger and calm him down at the same time, so the anger will stop.

However, if your SP is so angry that you can't talk to him, then give him a time-out anyway. This will cut down on all the images attacking him, and that will calm him down.

Problem 3

[*By Mom*]: When an NP grows up, he and the environment engage in a basic dance of give-and-take. Sometimes he asserts himself, and the environment adjusts; other times, the environment demands that he adjust, and he learns to do so. There is a pretty good fit between the NP and his NP world, and this gives him a basic sense of trust and comfort in that world (see Chapter 67: Trust Other People). When things go wrong, therefore, he gets angry, but then cools down and resumes his life.

When an SP grows up, he is constantly and continually locking horns with an environment that does not understand him. He is seen as rigid and illogical, but to him, the *environment* is rigid and illogical. He is constantly accused of having to do things his way, but to him, the environment is always demanding that he do things *its* way. After a while, the SP feels like a victim of outside forces, and this makes him angry. When he tries to assert himself, he is put in time-out, subjected to humiliating behavior modification schemes such as '1–2–3 you're out' (see Chapter 37: Discipline), put on medications that rob him of his will, and is essentially told that he has no say in his own decision making. This makes the SP even angrier, so that eventually, every little upset becomes an opportunity for his mounting rage to come blasting out. Add to this the fact that the SP, in general, doesn't have a lot of control over what comes out of him, and you have created a person who blows up at every little thing.

Solution 3

[*By Mom*]: Limit your SP's environment so that he isn't always in conflict with it. Homeschool him, and don't force him to have playdates or go to social situations. If he is blowing up over every little thing, ask him what bigger thing that little thing reminded him of. Give him the opportunity to make decisions on small matters such as his own clothing, the route you take to therapy, etc. Give him a sense of control over his life.

Parents have to be very careful not to create an antagonistic situation between themselves and their SPs. We have seen over and over the tragic results of behavior modification schemes such as '1–2–3 you're out,' or '1–2–3 Magic.' When you treat a human being like a rat in a Skinner Box, he starts behaving like a rat: a creature who acts on impulse. Furthermore, he'll start seeing you as the enemy, and he will try to get away with as much as he can. If you start a countdown every time he tries to talk to you, he will assume that you're not listening to him, and he will stop listening to you. Once you've created an oppositional situation, you've given your child yet another burden to deal with by himself – oppositional defiance – and he will start defying everything and everyone. If you keep counting down as a reflex, your child will start defying you as a reflex.

If this happens, stop *everything,* and start from scratch with quiet holding, rocking, etc. (See Chapter 71: Loving Other People and Chapter 79: Needing Other People.) Don't let an oppositional situation get established. Your child wasn't born full of rage; the NP world made him that way. It's your job to undo the damage, not make it worse.

39

Going to School

Problem 1

When a normal kid begins kindergarten or any other kind of normal school experience, he is excited because he will spend the day with his peers. Peers are 'his own kind,' i.e. beings who are like him.

When a special kid enters a normal school, he is abruptly removed from the only safe people he knows – his family – and thrown into a room full of aliens. However, they do not perceive themselves as aliens, they perceive HIM as the alien. Since it is not in human nature to accept aliens, the NKs immediately reject the SK. This usually begins on the first day of kindergarten and lasts through high school, college, graduate school, or any other school the SP attends.

Solution 1

The ideal solution is not to send the SK to school. He doesn't want to go; the kids don't want him around; and for once, the NPs and the SPs agree on something. However, most SPs cannot stay at home during their entire childhood, because their mothers want to get rid of them. That way the moms can pretend they live a normal life and are not stuck dealing with a kid who is NEVER happy. Therefore, the next-to-ideal situation is to send the SK to a special school that is filled with other SKs, so he can be educated with his peers, that is, people who are *really* like him. The SP may not like the special school, but none of his classmates will like it either. So they will all have something in common.

However, thanks to a terrible thing (invented by NPs) called 'mainstreaming,' most SPs cannot be educated among their own kind. They have to be distributed around all the NP classrooms, so that each classroom can have its alien-in-residence.

There is no good solution to mainstreaming except to fill the SK's life with positive experiences outside of school. To give the SK lessons in how to interact with other kids, hire some nice neighborhood NKs to come over and play with the SK. These nice children are often termed 'rent-a-friends.' If possible, hire four or even five NKs to come over every week, so the SK will have lots of positive play experience with nice people. The NKs will discover what a nice and loyal friend the SK can be when he is not being bombarded by too many sensory typhoons. Then word will spread around the neighborhood that not only is the SK OK and should not be teased, but that playing computer games with him after school is the easiest paying job in town.

Problem 2

When an NK enters first grade, he has acquired working skills from his previous experiences in the NK world. He knows how to talk and interact with other kids, and he is ready to learn how to read.

When the SK enters first grade, he may already know how to read but not to communicate (see Chapter 43: The Rules of Language) or interact with other kids. He also has a hard time understanding things that he hears (see Chapter 42: Understanding Other People). Therefore, his alien status in the classroom is made worse by the fact that the work is impossible for him. He can't process what the teacher is saying, so he tunes her out. The other kids bother and/or reject the SK, so he tunes them out as well. On the other hand, the reading, writing, and math are so easy, since the SK did the same work at home a number of years earlier, that he gets bored and tunes out the work, too. Therefore, he fails in school.

Solution 2

See Solution 1 for ideal and next-to-ideal solutions. If these are not possible, then the SK can perhaps qualify for a class for the learning disabled. These classes are generally populated by nice kids who are themselves the victims of social rejection. Or the mother of the SK can do some sneaky stuff (see Chapter 45: Telling Lies and Keeping Secrets) and order the school books, so the SK can review his work at home. In the case of work that is boring, give the SK problems to work on in his head while he is bored. Perhaps the teacher can give the SK some 'enrichment' material, if she is a nice NT.

Problem 3

When normal teachers hear about SKs, they immediately think, 'There's nothing wrong with that kid. His mother is the problem. She is the nut case who hates males and therefore is inventing lies about her son to destroy him. She's the one who needs help.' Then the NT (normal teacher) begins her two-step process of getting the mother out of her way and planning out all kinds of schemes for forcing the SK to become normal. This generally has disastrous consequences. For example, James's second-grade teacher made him have his photograph taken eight different times for her Open House slide show, even though photographs are like blasts from a machine gun, in James's experience. Even though James's mom asked that he not be photographed, the teacher did so over and over. When school picture re-take day came, James threw up all over his desk in terror, and had to be taken home. The teacher still doesn't understand what she did wrong. To this day, kids bring up the time that James 'threw up all over the place.'

Solution 3

See Solution 1 and 2 for ideal and next-to-ideal solutions. If these are not possible, then the SK is stuck. There is no NP on earth who understands an SK, especially an NP who is a teacher! The SK and the SK's parents should keep complaining whenever something horrible happens. The normal teacher will not change, but maybe the SK will receive a label of 'behavior-disordered,' and if his behavior gets bad enough, maybe he will qualify for a special school.

Problem 4

When the SK becomes the resident alien in a classroom, all the kids will tease him to some extent, but the worst teasers will be THE BULLIES. They will flock to the SK like flies to honey. The bullies are dependent on SKs for their very identity. Bullies generally have deficiencies in many areas except negativity. Therefore, they enjoy hurting other people because they do not feel so great about themselves.

One day, for example, James was teased by the high school kids who sell popcorn in the movie theater. They wanted to punish him for not taking a long-enough time eating his popcorn before he asked for his free refill, and they said he had to clean the counter, or they would call his mother. James did not clean the counter, but he accurately surmised that those kids did not feel good about themselves and thus had to tease a second-grader. After all, they were only minimum-wage flunkies who were bored and frustrated and thus had to take their frustrations out on a child who was having a good time with dad, and who was free to come and go as he pleased, not stuck behind a counter, selling popcorn!

Solution 4

There is no good solution for bullies except to raise their self-esteem, so they don't have to hurt other people to feel good. However, since there will always be bullies in the world, the best thing for the SP to do is avoid them, and if he can't, to ignore them, and if he can't, to play frozen. Or try to echo all the stupid things the bullies say back to them. Echoing comes naturally to SPs, but it drives NPs crazy.

> Bully: Hey, you're gay.
>
> SP: Hey, you're gay.
>
> Bully: I'm not gay, you are.
>
> SP: I'm not gay, you are.
>
> Bully: Shut up.
>
> SP: Shut up.

In the field of echolalia, the SP is unsurpassed, and so he should put his talent to work to defeat the bullies!!

Problem 5

[By James]: When an NK goes to school, since he has acquired modern learning skills, he knows how to do schoolwork the way any other NK does schoolwork. As we have discussed above, most NTs (normal teachers) do not like it if someone in the NT's class does schoolwork the way they want to do it! Since the NK does not want to be punished, he works the way his other classmates work.

But weird things such as breves and macrons you put on letters for telling what sound a letter is making during phonics; making a K-W-L chart before you read a non-fiction story; using a stupid writing process by drafting, editing, responding and revising, and publishing; asking predicting, observing, judging, and connecting questions before, during, after reading a story are very hard for the SK to deal with. These are the goofy learning processes of the new world he is living in, rather than the way you learned when you were just a kid. You didn't even do this stuff! That's why you don't understand your kid's homework. Well, the SK doesn't understand any of this either.

The SP, although he is forced to use these hard and goofy ways, will think of his own way. So when the SK goes to school, he does the work he is supposed to do his own way. But since the NT does not like the SK's way, he will fail in school because he did it the wrong way, not because he did the problems right. My friend Will from Saskatoon used to get only partial credit for his math problems because he wouldn't show his work on his paper. It didn't matter that he got the right answer. Will is an SP, and he used to get so mad at not getting full credit that he'd kick the garbage cans in the hall at school.

The SP's mother will have many meetings with the teacher (like my mom had with my teacher), but it won't go any good. NPs only understand their own ways of doing things.

Solution 5

Enrole your SP in a homeschooling program so he can have the books at home and work his own way. Or you can order the books that he has at school, and let him read them at home.

Problem 6

[*By James, age 11*]: NPs are not scared of school at all, as we have discussed in the previous problems. They are also not scared of the noises you hear at school, such as the bell, the teacher talking, and the fire alarm (when there is a fire drill), the sound of the PA, etc.

But as we have discussed in the previous problems, SPs *are* scared of school in every single way. They are also scared of the noises because they have noise sensitivity (see Chapter 2: Noise Sensitivity). So the SP feels like he has heard a balloon pop three times as loud as normal whenever the bell rings, the teacher talks, the fire alarm rings when there is a fire drill, or the sound of the PA.

The school bell always used to hurt my ears. So your SP will always be afraid that the bell will ring any second of the day. Or if he knows the time the bell rings, he can be afraid during those time periods. For example, these are the times the bells ring in our school:

8:40 a.m. Arrival Bell

8:45 a.m. Tardy Bell

11:30 a.m. 1–2 Grades Lunch Bell

12:15 p.m. 1–2 Grades Recess End Bell; 3–4 Grades Lunch Bell

1:00 p.m. 3–4 Grades Recess End Bell

3:05 p.m. Bus Dismissal Bell

3:10 p.m. Walk Dismissal Bell

So, in my school, an SP would be scared at these times.

The teacher talking also hurt my ears in school, so I tried to tune my teacher out (see Chapter 48: Tuning Out), but I failed. So I invented something called 'EAR PRIVACY.' I patted my ears rapidly with my hands, so I only heard bits of what was being said, but not too much. Finally, the teacher caught me and she thought I was weird. I didn't know what to tell her, so I made up the name 'EAR PRIVACY.' At this the class laughed and laughed, but that was how I was able to ignore my teacher.

But now, the one and only thing that scares me in school and might also scare your SP is the fire alarm, which goes off during a fire drill. Since fire drills are unexpected and the bell is so loud when it happens that I used to be scared every day in school that there would be a fire drill. Your SP may think of it as 'a red thing on the wall that goes off whenever it feels like it.' But I am now calming down because my mom talked to the principal and she told my mom that there is a drill once a month, so I am now only scared at the beginning of each month until the drill, which is much better for me, because at least I'm not scared every day!

Also, the PA system in the school may also be scaring your child. In my case, the PA system always goes on in the morning, and then the PA being used again is unexpected, for example, if someone has to go home early from school, or if someone has to stay in the office (see Problem 7). So your SP may be scared the whole day because you never can tell when something will be said over the PA system, or the intercom, etc.

But your SP may still be scared of many sounds in school. So you have a choice, NMs (normal mothers). You can make your SP keep suffering in mainstream school, or you can pull him out of school. (You will learn more about what happens if you pull your SP out of school in the solution.)

Solution 6

There is no way you can escape a fire drill or the school bell or a PA system. But the best thing to do is something that may change your entire life style, but it's the best for your SP. And that is to pull your child out of school and homeschool him. I benefited a lot when I was homeschooled, because Mom and I were an unbreakable team. Your SP will benefit, too. From then on, he will no longer have to worry about hearing the school bell, no longer worry about hearing a fire alarm (because you certainly don't have fire drills in the house), and although he will have to listen to a person talk, it will be his mother, which is much better than a stranger.

Problem 7

When the mother of an NP goes into a public school, the office staff greet her with a smile, ask her some pleasant questions, then let her into the building. After she's been buzzed through the main door, the secretaries might comment about what a nice person she is and how great her kids are.

When the mother of an SP walks into the office of a public school, she is greeted either with scowls or perhaps with silence. If she has come to drop something off for her child (because he walked out of the house without his backpack again, or perhaps without his shoes), the office manager rolls her eyes, murmurs something under her breath, then informs the mother curtly that she is not allowed to enter the classroom area. Another mother may be let into the classroom area immediately, but that's because she has three cute kids in the school, none of which are in special programs.

If the SP's mother insists that she needs to see her SP, the office manager may announce over the PA system that Johnny [or whoever] must report to the office immediately. This blast from the ceiling hurts the SP's ears (see Chapter 2: Noise Sensitivity), forces him to disrupt his work, which is a terrifying change to him (see Chapter 9: Change), and alerts the entire school that he once more forgot something or did something horrible. When Johnny finally comes into the office, he is greeted by the same scowls that his mother received, except that he doesn't notice them since he refuses to make eye contact (see Chapter 3: Eye Contact) and automatically tunes the office staff out (see Chapter 48: Tuning Out).

After both of them have left, the office staff may spend the next half hour talking about what a pill the SP is, how unfriendly and rude his mother is, and indeed how weird the entire family is. The mother may get into her car vowing never to walk into that office again or deciding to pull her child out of that school forever and homeschool him.

Solution 7

If you can afford to homeschool your SP, do it! Subjecting him to the scowls and rejection of school employees only intensifies his hatred of other people. But if you are stuck sending him to school because you need to work to earn his therapy money, then use the unpleasant experience of the school office as a valuable lesson in what your SP feels. When you walk into that office, does your skin start to crawl? Does your head start to pound, does the room start to spin, and does fear start filling up your chest? Do you want to look down and just wish those scowling faces would disappear in a puff of smoke? Do you feel tongue-tied and filled with terror and guilt, as if you've just done something horrible? If so, remind yourself that this is how your SP feels *all* the time. Every social encounter for him is like your interaction with the school office staff. It's as if you have been tried and sentenced to death by their stares for the bare fact of being who you are. Is it any wonder that your child acts 'autistic' in the presence of others?

Problem 8

[*By James, age 11*]: When a NP student goes into a school as he normally does, he is threatened by the Safety Patrol to WALK, TAKE YOUR HAT OFF, etc. Although the NP thinks they are bossy, he knows the Safety Patrols are only trying to help him or her.

When an SP student goes into school, the Safety Patrols do the same things. But not only are they bossy creeps, they decide to pick on one person, one person that they can control so that person can not be able to do something because they are the Safety Patrol. Say the SP is chosen. For example, before school, say the SP is swinging on the playground minding his own business when a safety patrol kid comes and steals it. Then he brags about how he is more important than the SP, and how he deserves the swing more than the SP does. Also, this may not just happen to an SP, this may happen to an NP, but there is a greater chance that it happens to an SP.

Then, in the middle of the day, the SP is going to the bathroom when a safety patrol kid arrives and says, 'You can't go into this bathroom until I am done. I am in the Safety Patrol, meaning I am more important than you, so you must wait until I am done.' Then, probably, the safety patrol kid may take as long as he can to keep the SP waiting, which makes him angry. (See Chapter 60: Waiting Problems.) This also makes the SP sad, and when he is done, the teacher may yell at him for taking so long in the bathroom.

Safety Patrols, however, will not change. They will always be there to get you, and to think they are the kings and queens of the school. For example, I pass the Safety Patrols in the hallways, and I see them doing bad things to kids. I also see them stealing swings outside. In my perception, the Safety Patrols haunt the two main sections of the school: the hallways and the playground. I have two stories about safety patrol – fake or real – stealing things from students who wanted to have a good time. The students may not be SPs, but they show how the Safety Patrol really is, unlike the way adults say they are. And, just to tell you, I am NOT in the Safety Patrol, and never will be. I fear I will turn into a bossy creepy kid like the other patrol members, which is not the way I want to turn out to be. I want to be nice, not mean.

Now, on to the stories:

1. Everyone wants to be in the Safety Patrol so they can overpower kids. This is a story about a kid who wanted to be in the Safety Patrol so much she faked it to steal a child's swing. Although this story may be about a person faking being a real patrol kid, she acts as if she *was* a person who belonged to the Safety Patrol.

    I am swinging on the swing when I hear a small kid crying. (Swing-stealing happens all the time.) I look and see a big kid swinging, and a little kid talking to her. Here is what they said:

    Little Kid: Give me back my swing.

    Big Kid: I am in the Safety Patrol, and I deserve the swing.

    Little Kid: But it was my swing.

    Big Kid: No, now it's my swing.

    Little Kid: You give it back, Miss Safety Poop-troll! I want it back!

    Big Kid: You insulted me. For that, you're getting Respect Time, miss.

    Now, I stepped in. Something was off...

    James: Hold it! If you say you're in the Safety Patrol, where is your vest and badge?

    (All safety patrol people have special badges and vests saying 'SAFETY PATROL' on them.)

Big Kid: I forgot it today, OK!

Little Kid: Give me back my swing!

The Little Kid decides to give up, so she leaves and plays with her friends. The story is over.

2.   I am walking down the hall when I see two safety patrol people telling a child he cannot use the bathroom until they are done. Here is what they are saying:

Safety Patrol: You cannot go into this bathroom until we are done.

Child: Why?

Safety Patrol: Because we are the Safety Patrol and we get first dibbs at everything.

Child: Well, I have to go. Bad.

Safety Patrol: Well, you must wait for us.

Child: You let me go in there. Let me in!

I just walked by, so this was all I heard. But this still tells you how horrible and dishonest those two safety patrol people are.

The Safety Patrol will always be there to haunt the hallways and the playground before and after school. Although there are punishments for safety patrol kids, they often get away with it, so they normally can't be stopped. They will be out to get you. You must ignore them, SPs.

Solution 8

As said in earlier solutions of this chapter, the best way to resolve this is to homeschool your child. If you do not do this, you will make him suffer having to deal with the Safety Patrol, and your SP can't ignore them finally after millions of sad days with them.

Problem 9 [Self-Defense]

By the time an NP goes to school, he has learned the basic rules of self-preservation and when to employ them. Because he has established a sense of basic trust in this world, the NP world, he knows when he is safe and when he is in danger. He is encouraged by adults to be assertive but not aggressive, to defend himself but never to attack anyone else. Because he is basically comfortable in his world, he can also recognize when something hurts and can take measures to avoid pain or to ward off a physical attack.

When an SP develops, however, everything and everyone causes him discomfort, so he develops a self-defensive personality. He builds walls to protect himself from the assaults of the world and other people, and his parents, teachers, and therapists spend much time and energy tearing down those walls and stripping the SP of his defenses. Therefore, he learns that he is not entitled to defend himself against discomfort but to endure the pain and become a Stoic. So when a school bully attacks or causes the SP pain, he may simply stand there and let it happen. If he reports the incident to his mother, she may exclaim, 'Why didn't you STOP him? Why didn't you defend yourself?' This is confusing to the SP since she doesn't allow him to defend himself against her attacks with combs, toothbrushes, and dental floss, so why should he be allowed to fight a bully's fists?

Furthermore, his teacher and the social worker have drummed it into his head that he needs to be flexible with other people and to allow them to have their way. So when a bully twists the SP's arm behind his back, the SP may let him do it to be sociable and accommodating to the other person. He may also be afraid that if he complains to the teacher, she may tell him the pain is just his 'misperception.'

Solution 9

Encourage your SP to tell you everything that happened in school. He will probably be good at providing every detail. If he describes an abusive event, tell him that the other person acted inappropriately, then re-enact the scene over and over but with your child responding with reasonable self-defense techniques. Also have him act out telling the teacher. Write out a list of rules about when it is appropriate to call out, scream, etc. to get an adult's attention. This may be very confusing to your SP at first, since the message you've been giving him so far is to break down his defenses. You may want to enroll him in a martial arts class to help him gain an automatic ability to defend himself in a physically threatening situation.

40

Teasing

Problem

Whenever an SP ventures out into the NP world (which is essentially the world), he becomes the subject of teasing. School is the worst place, because bullies hang out there (see Chapter 39: Going to School), but as long as there are NPs and SPs, there is going to be teasing.

The NPs don't realize they are doing it; they just expect everybody to be like them, and so when one person ISN'T like them, that person has to be behaving weirdly on purpose, and hence deserves to be teased. The SP doesn't know he is behaving inappropriately (or if he does, he can't help himself because he is unsure of the right way to act), but generally he is made aware of his transgressions when the teasing starts. This makes him feel both sad and insecure. After all, how can he correct his behavior if he doesn't know in advance what to correct?

Solution

The ideal solution is to keep the SP away from school, away from kids his own age, and in fact, away from kids in general until he displays social interest and some rudimentary social learning ability. Until those two things emerge, your SP will continue to behave weirdly and get teased. If you surround him by grown-ups, however, he will not get teased much, if at all. And besides, when he shows some initial social interest, grown-ups will help him learn the rules of responsible, reciprocal behavior, not the laws of the jungle. After all, if you were going to hire a tutor for your child, would you hire one who was 5 or one who was 40?

Teasing, unfortunately, will not stop as long as children are allowed to play unsupervised in groups. The worst thing you can do to your SP is plonk him down on a playground or in a play group to let him 'get used to it' or 'work it out for himself.' Neither of these things will happen. It has been said that the behavior of children mirrors the behavior of adults in previous eras, and that personal behavior evolves along the same path as human culture (just like the body follows the same evolutionary path that the animal kingdom followed, from a single-celled animal through the classifications of animals, and finally up to man). We believe that teasing and ostracism served an important cultural purpose in previous eras, dating back to when people lived in small family or tribal groupings. In those times, it was absolutely essential that everyone pull his weight and participate in the community. A weird kid was a liability. Perhaps SPs were killed outright in simpler times, or perhaps they were sufficiently ostracized that they were never able to secure a mate and pass along their weird, antisocial genes to their own children. If an SP's genetic material died with him, then the tribe would no longer be plagued with his dysfunctional personality. (Can you imagine the problem a rigid kid would be for a nomadic tribe? 'I don't want to leave this forest!' he'd scream, and cling to the tree he absolutely had to hold in order to fall asleep.)

Ostracism helped rid a group of undesirable genes, and perhaps the kids of today are re-enacting behavior from those earlier times. Indeed, when an SP is let loose amid a group of young NPs, they become like a pack of Neolithic hunters, with the SP serving as their marked prey. Although we live in an era where every person (even SPs) allegedly has the right to live and be himself, children in groups don't know that. If you're a weird kid, you're as good as dead in kid culture. For that reason, it is necessary to remove your SP from that culture, and teach him to behave like a grown-up. In one area, then, he'll be way ahead of his peers.

41

Verbal Confusion

Problem 1

When one NP talks to another NP, the first NP listens, understands, then responds. All this is normal and pleasant to the NPs.

When an NP talks to an SP, as we discussed above, the SP feels fear and sickness and ear pain as soon as the first word is spoken. And he also feels confusion, since NPs talk too fast. The SP is still struggling to understand the first word after the NP has spoken ten words or so. Sometimes he is thinking about something else, and does not hear the NP. Or sometimes something the NP says reminds him about something else, and the SP's mind immediately goes to that something else, the way the Internet accesses a new topic immediately by simply clicking on a word. The SP's mind works like the Internet, which means that it is hard for the SP to stay on the topic that you're on.

Also, sometimes the SP mishears one word and misunderstands what the NP is saying. Since the SP is afraid and stressed all the time and does not want the NP to know that he does not understand, and he doesn't want his mother to hit him on the back and yell at him, the SP fakes it. For example, the mother says, 'Put on your pajamas', but the SP hears 'bananas.' The SP dutifully goes into the kitchen and peels a banana. The mother starts screaming that he just brushed his teeth and it's time to go to bed and how could he want MORE food? The SP, then, is so confused that he forgets how to talk and cannot tell her that he is only obeying orders. Then the mother hits him on the back and says angrily, 'Just spit out the words, would you?' Now the SP is so totally confused that he starts to cry, which causes the mother to call up her friend and complain about what a pill he is and how he is so hard to raise. This makes the SP so sad that he cries harder, since he thought he was being a good kid and obeying his mom's orders.

Solution 1

When the SP is doing something weird, ask him why he is doing it. Chances are there is a logical reason for it: he heard you wrong, he is doing something that was the right thing to do yesterday, he is obeying what he thought was a rule. As a right-brain processor, his thought patterns aren't always the same as an NP's, but they have their own logic.

Also, please accept when the SP says, 'I don't understand.' What may have been obvious and simple to you is not obvious to him. After all, you can't understand his world – why should he understand yours?

Problem 2

[*By James, age 8*]: When an NP mother gives a command to an NK, he immediately gets up and does what she says. This is because he does not want his mother to get mad at him.

When an NP mother gives a command to an SP, he is filled with terror and does not hear her properly. Often, he hears the opposite of what she said, for example, she said, 'Don't hit the wall!' and the SP hears 'Do hit the wall.' And the SP starts doing the opposite of what she said. The mother hits him on the back and screams, 'I told you not to hit the wall. Listen to me when I talk to you!'

Solution 2

Tell your SP many times what you want him to do. He hears messages incorrectly and slowly, but after ten times, he may be able to obey you.

42

Understanding Other People

Problem 1

NPs communicate on two levels: with words and without words. NKs become bilingual naturally, and by the time they can use words, they can also communicate effectively without words.

When SKs are very young, they have a horrible time learning how to use words. Because they are so young, we don't know why, but we suspect it is because they do not hear words properly. James heard the word 'vitamin' and pronounced it 'bivin.' 'Vitamin C,' which he took every day, was 'bah C.' When you say, 'Do you want some milk?' to an SK, he might hear it as 'Byouwansummil?' He might memorize the entire phrase and attach a meaning to it, but there is no way he can divide all the sounds into words and use them to formulate other unique sentences. Therefore, he may simply give up on understanding other people.

When James taught himself to read, one of the first things he did was take a pencil and draw thick black lines between the words, as if he was emphasizing that these combinations of sounds were separate units, not a continuous string. However, by learning words through written language, what he learned was their meanings on paper, devoid of context or emotional impact. He did not learn the different ways each word could be used in normal speaking. So even though he became fluent in the English language, his knowledge came from silent symbols on a page, not from the fluid, ever-changing ways other people spoke. And the nonverbal messages — tone of voice, volume, intonation, emphasis, etc. — that accompany spoken language were missing altogether.

Solution 1

Watch movies and analyze what the NP characters are thinking and feeling through their dialogue. Remember that an SP can learn, but not at the pace of normal life. A movie can be rewound and re-viewed repeatedly, typed up into a script and read, watched with the closed captions on, and played in slow motion, to give an SP multiple opportunities to learn something at a slower pace.

Have the SP analyze the tone of voice, whether the person is being ironic or sarcastic (very difficult for SPs to figure out, since to them words are what they are, not the opposite of what they are), etc. Speak freely about your own feelings, and inform the SP if you yourself say something sarcastically or in a mean way. Encourage him to state, 'She didn't mean that,' or 'She said that in a mean way,' or any other valid emotional observation. With his analytical mind, the SP will often become obsessed with finding the right feeling for a given comment. In fact, you may eventually have to teach him when it is NOT appropriate to be frank about another person's intent.

Problem 2

Because an SP often lacks normal body awareness and spends a lot of time tuning out the environment, he doesn't have years of observing other people's body and non-verbal facial language. In fact, he is probably so scared of other people and so distracted by details in the environment that his eyes cannot focus on body language. So he misinterprets hand gestures (or fails to notice them), makes inappropriate gestures of his own, and does not pick up on the fact that he is boring you and you wish he would be quiet. Sometimes he'll alter his voice and become very dramatic when he tells you a tale, but he does not realize that you don't have a half-hour to listen to him tell you every detail of the movie he just saw. He doesn't understand the cues you give him that you don't want to listen to him anymore. Sometimes the first inkling he has that he's boring you is when you scream, 'Enough!' Sometimes his mother hits him on the back and says, 'Stop talking! I'm sick of your talking!' Then the SP, in shock, feels depressed and worthless and unloved, because he was only trying to make conversation, and got hit on the back.

Solution 2

This is one of the hardest problems an SP faces, and there are no easy solutions. Continuous outside feedback seems to be the best strategy, telling the SP throughout the day how he misinterpreted something or behaved inappropriately. If he's giving you an epic history of highway construction in America, let him know early on that he's boring you – before you explode. The best thing the SP can do is to listen and accept what the NP is saying, without arguing and trying to assert that he, the SP, is right. SPs are almost never right when it comes to social interaction, and once the SP learns this and doesn't protest, he can improve much faster.

One game we use is called, 'What is Mommy feeling?' We invent scenarios, then we analyze what each person in the scene is feeling. James is always a character. In real life, when something goes wrong, we play the game too, analyzing what everybody is feeling under the circumstances. An NP sibling or a rent-a-friend will have a better grasp of the game at first, but eventually the SP will be better able to participate. I'll never forget the time my four-year-old Lauren fell off her two-wheel bike and screamed for my assistance. When I rushed over to her and cried, 'Are you all right?' she corrected me, 'You're supposed to ask, 'What is Lauren FEELING?'

The games that help with facial recognition (see Chapter 4: Recognizing Faces) will also help with the non-verbal messages those faces convey. Always remember that messages that appear on paper, computer screens, and other visual formats are better assimilated than messages presented by flesh and blood. Information conveyed by people rushes by too quickly at first and will not be processed or understood by the SP's brain. Don't rely on other people to teach your child anything at first.

43

The Rules of Language

Problem

When an NK learns to talk at age two or less, he somehow processes language correctly, so that he picks up all the illogical aspects of language with hardly a problem. At first, he might say 'gooder' and 'bringed' and 'foots,' but these are a good sign – the NK has processed the RULES for language: 'Add ed for the past tense,' or 'Add s for a plural'. This is a sign that his LEFT hemisphere is acquiring language, since the left side is the rule side.

When an SK learns to talk, chances are his left-hemisphere speech centers are not ready to receive language yet. Therefore, he rightly ignores all the things that people tell him, since he is not able to process language properly. However, as he is floating around in his prelingual world while all the other NKs are saying, 'Bye-bye, Mama' or 'Hi, Dada,' the mother of the SK gets scared. After all, she doesn't want a late-language processor as a kid, does she? So whenever someone says to the SK, 'Hi!' the mother hits him on the back and commands, 'Say Hi!' The SK doesn't know what is going on here, but after a number of punches on the back, he figures he better do something, so he says, 'Say Hi!' just like his mother does. This generally satisfies her, although not for long.

By the time the SK is three, everyone is disturbed by the fact that he can't talk to them. Outsiders will say, 'He's spoiled. He's lazy. He's antisocial. You've ruined that kid.' The mother gets even more nervous, and starts insisting that the SK say something when a person talks to him. The SK still doesn't have the faintest idea what to say, but he still figures if that person said, 'What a nice day,' and nobody hit HIM on the back, it must OK to say that, so the SK says, 'What a nice day.' The mother is still worried because he's supposed to say, 'Yes,' or something that indicated he processed the NK's question. Or she might still hit him on the back and say, 'Don't copy! That's rude!'

The SK, in desperation, starts trying to pick up language with the only resources he has: his ears, which simply hear, and his right hemisphere, which copies but does not process. And here is what happens:

NP: Hi, James, how are you today?

SK [*ears hear, RH memorizes*]: Hi, James, how are you today?

NP: No, I asked you.

SK: No, I asked you.

NP: Don't echo me.

SK [*trying as hard as he can to think up the right answer*]: You are fine.

NP: No, you call yourself 'I'.

SK [*thinking a bit*]: But James must be a 'you' since people call James 'you'.

Later on...

SK: You want milk.

Mother: No, say 'I want milk.'

SK [*thinking*]: Mommy wants milk? Mommy says 'I' to mean Mommy.

Mother: Do you want milk?

SK: You want milk.

Mother: No, you are an 'I,' not a 'you.' I am an I.

SK [*totally confused, thinking*]: Mommy is 'I.' But Mommy is not James, so James cannot be 'I,' too.

Mother: Answer me!

SK [*getting a brilliant idea*]: *James* wants milk.

Mother [*hits him on the back and cries*]: Why can't you understand? You are an I. I am a you. When you talk about yourself, you say I. When you tell me something, you say you, and I say I back. When I ask you a question, *you* are supposed to say I! It's an easy system. Why can't you get it?

SK [*thinking*]: It's a dumb system.

Mother: Now let's try again. Say, 'I want milk.'

SK: *Mommy* want milk?

Mother: No, say, 'I want milk.' That means YOU!!

SK: You want milk.

[*Mother bursts into tears and gives up.*]

SK [*feeling sad*]: Why I am crying, Mommy?

Mother: Because you'll never learn. It's hopeless.

SK [*thinking*]: It's a dumb system.

Solution

Don't force your SK to learn how to talk before he is clearly ready. If he is echoing and mixing up his pronouns, he has only his ears and perhaps his right hemisphere to work with, and they can't process language. If you keep insisting, he will do the best he can – by listening as hard as he can and repeating as much as possible. As a result, you child will end up with hyperacute hearing (which you'll later have to fix) and a dominant right hemisphere language center, which will doom your child to slow, weird speech.

Jane Healey, a brain researcher, warns parents that if you force a child to learn a major skill before the appropriate brain center is ready to receive the information, then some other brain center will store the learning. But generally the only brain centers that are ready are intended for earlier, less specialized learning. So the learning is imperfect or often inappropriate. We all know what happens when a resistant child has toilet training forced on him. Somehow the reptilian portion of the brain (which is the least specialized) takes over the task of toileting, and you have a child who behaves like a stubborn dinosaur over the issue of where and when he is willing to go.

The right-hemisphere speech center is not as well supplied with neurons as the left side, so a right-hemisphere speech center will always remain deficient. On the other hand, because of the strong associative powers of the right brain, you may end up with a son or a daughter who tells puns endlessly, laughs uproariously over strange, language-based jokes, and drives everyone nuts with riddles and word games. You don't want to raise a crashing bore either.

Instead of forcing *him* to speak, just keep exposing him to speech. If he isn't overly sensitive to your voice, keep talking. Make audiotapes of your voice, and play them in the car. Play talk radio rather than music. Also, let your child engage in those mindless, repetitive things that therapists call autistic, in order to stimulate his left brain. Let him march around the house and count endlessly. Smile when he recites the alphabet or reads off house numbers while you're in the car. He is trying to heal himself, and when he is ready (perhaps by the age of five), he can learn language properly, just a little bit later.

Sometimes your SK will start processing a few sentences and use them over and over. Don't try to change that. If he says, 'Yeah milk,' or 'No milk,' instead of trying to use pronouns, reward him for communicating, and let him use his system until he can clearly handle your systems.

James has developed a technique for understanding people which involves typing out what they say on a computer screen in his head and reading what he has typed. His mental computer is always booted up to a word processor. When he hears words, the computer picks that information up and types it out for him, thereby converting it to a visual format. (Remember, SPs are rapid visual processors.) He can do this without any conscious effort.

44

Literal Language

Problem

When an NP learns how to talk, he uses the left hemisphere, which processes language. As he gets older, he learns not only the meanings of words but their hidden meanings. Then he picks up expressions such as 'That's the way the cookie crumbles,' though he knows that there is not a real cookie crumbling on the carpet.

When an SP learns language, because he uses his auditory centers and the speech center on the right side of the brain, his understanding of language is different. He learns the literal meanings of words but has a hard time understanding the inner meanings. This makes the NPs think he is stupid, whereas the SPs have a hard time understanding NPs.

Solution

Get a dictionary of idioms and slang out of the library, and study it. Teach the SP expressions one at a time. Eventually he will understand them. He may even start collecting them, making lists of them, and using them compulsively. That's OK, since non-literal language will help him understand the subjectiveness and illogic of the NP world in general.

45

Telling Lies and Keeping Secrets

Problem

When an NK turns three or so, he or she starts engaging in pretend play and make-believe. When he pretends to be someone else, he is grasping an important, distinctly human, concept: the idea that some things are not true. Only human beings, it has been said, can imagine things that aren't there.

By the time the NK is four, he suddenly realizes that if there is such a thing as an untruth, then he has the power to SAY something that is not true. Tentatively he begins to make up stories, particularly ones that get him out of a jam. 'My sister spilled the milk,' that sort of thing.

At first the lies are transparent, and even cute. But after a while, the parents of NKs start reprimanding them and even punishing them for telling lies. The parents want their NKs to know the difference between truth and untruth, and to CHOOSE the truth. However, in order to choose the truth, you have to experiment with it; hence, the NK may simply withhold the truth, particularly if the truth may lead to punishment. That's how the NK learns how to keep a secret.

All this is normal and natural, and although society frowns on both lies and secrets, a child cannot develop a conscience or a moral side without experimenting with going against the rules.

When an SK turns three or so, however, he is so overwhelmed by his sensory, motor, and perceptual problems that he is barely treading water on the tidal wave of his life. He cannot even say his name, let alone tell a lie. He can't keep a secret if he has no language. He can't tell a lie if he can't communicate. And he certainly can't understand the difference between truth and untruth if he doesn't know the difference between yes and no.

Hence, the SK does not engage in any imaginative play or make-believe at the appropriate time.

When the SK goes to school unable to engage in any imaginative play, this causes another problem for him. If he is still processing on the right side of the brain, he will take everything literally and refuse to do anything that isn't true. So, for example, if the kids are doing a play and he has to read the part of the rabbit in *Alice in Wonderland*, for example, he may refuse to do so because he is not a rabbit. He may announce to the whole audience, 'I am not a rabbit.' His mother may walk up to him, hit him on the back, and say, 'So what if you're not a rabbit. READ YOUR LINES!!' But this makes the SK confused, and he may lie on the floor and refuse to do anything more, which will make his mother furious and embarrassed. When they get home, she may scream, 'Don't ever embarrass me again! Just do what you're told. Why are you so WEIRD??'

Eventually, if the SK learns how to talk, he will get the same fascination with pretend play that NKs get. He'll start experimenting with lies probably around the age of eight (if he sorted out the I/you problem at around age 5). However, when an eight-year-old starts telling lies, it is not as cute as when a four-year-old does it. Eight-year-olds are supposed to know better. So when the eight-year-old SK walks into his mother's bedroom and says, 'Mom, I blew up the vacuum cleaner,' she might hit him on the back and scream, 'HOW COULD YOU BE SO STUPID!! WHAT'S WRONG WITH YOU???' This response makes the SK very sad, because he thought she would laugh and understand his joke.

Her reaction will probably encourage the SP to start keeping secrets. If he DID really blow up the vacuum cleaner, he may not tell anyone. Or if he accidentally peed on the floor (see Chapter 59: Aiming Problems), he may try desperately to clean it up so his mother won't hit him on the back. And if he can't clean it up, she starts screaming, 'WHO PEED ON THE FLOOR??' This will prompt him to keep a secret about who peed on the floor, yet instead of being happy that her kid can withhold the truth (whereas a truly autistic person cannot), she might scream even louder, hurting the poor SK's ears (see Chapter 2: Noise Sensitivity).

On the other hand, keeping a secret is very, very difficult for an SK. He feels intense stress when he has to keep a secret, and so he often cannot hold it in. You see, the SK has a hard time figuring out what is appropriate and what is not. NKs are always telling him to express his feelings, which is a stressful situation to begin with, but then when he does express his feelings, people are always hitting him on the back and telling him that what he just said was inappropriate. So he is never quite sure when he is going to get hit and screamed at. Often he gets hit and screamed at for NOT saying something; other times he gets hit and screamed for SAYING something. This makes it almost impossible for him to do anything. An added stress, too, comes from the fact that the right hemisphere is not known for its duplicity. Lies and secrets are more appropriate to the left hemisphere. (Note: the Roman word for 'left' was 'sinister.') So if the SK learns something and stores it in the right hemisphere, it is always ready to burst out like a bull from a cattle chute. Keeping it in requires superhuman effort, especially when everyone is hitting the SP on the back and commanding, 'Talk!'

Solution

Don't assume your SK should behave like an eight-year-old just because he is eight. Treat him like a five-year-old if he's emotionally only five. And be very, very happy if he starts lying and keeping secrets. That means that he is not hopelessly autistic, but can evolve to someone who lies and cheats like you do! Lying is the first step toward normal moral development. And keeping secrets means that the left hemisphere is working to some extent. Be thrilled! And don't hit him on the back!!

46

Using Your Voice Politely*

Problem

When one NP talks to another NP, nobody is bothered by the noise. When an NP talks to an SP, however, since the talking of the NP hurts the SP's ears and puts him under intense stress, the SP tries to block out the NP, and here is what happens:

> NP: It's really cold today, isn't it?
>
> [*The SP's ears are hurting, so he tries to block out the NP.*]
>
> SP [*loudly*]: Did you see **Aladdin**?
>
> [*The NP is annoyed because the SP talked too loud.*]
>
> NP [*louder, so the SP will learn a lesson*]: Don't switch the topic. And you're talking too loud.
>
> [*The SP's ears are hurting worse.*]
>
> SP [*again, loudly, to block out the noise*]: Did you see **Beauty and the Beast?**
>
> NP [*angrily*]: You're talking too loud.
>
> SP [*even louder, since the NP is ignoring his questions*]: Did you see **The Return of Jafar?**
>
> NP [*screaming*]: How many times have I tried to tell you. You're talking too loud!

* By James, age 8

And this happens over and over again, until finally, the NP gives up and goes away. Then the mother hits the SP on the back and screams, 'Why did you talk too loud to that person? Lower your voice!'

But the SP doesn't know this, because EVERYBODY talks too loud to him, and nobody tells them to be quiet. In fact, his loud voice is his friendly voice, because when he is speaking, no one else is hurting his ears (see Chapter 2: Noise Sensitivity).

Solution

Instead of teaching your SP how to talk at the right volume, get him Auditory Integration Training, which will help with other things, but will also help the SP hear the same way an NP hears, so he'll know if he is talking too loud or not. The first thing that happens before AIT is that the SP is given an audiogram, to see how he is hearing. This may help you learn about his sound sensitivities.

47

Mouth Control*

Problem 1 [Funny Noises]

When one NP talks to another NP, the noise does not hurt the NP's ears, so he does not have to make funny and inappropriate noises to block out the sound of the NP's voice.

When an NP talks to an SP, since the noise hurts his ears, as we've discussed above, the SP plays frozen (see Chapter 49: Playing Frozen), and makes funny noises which he uses as a defense system for noise. The mother of the SP will hit him on the back and say, 'Stop making funny noises. That's rude and inappropriate.'

Solution 1

All funny noises probably come from noise sensitivity (see Chapter 2: Noise Sensitivity) because the SP is using them to block out noise that hurts his ears.

The best solution is AIT (Auditory Integration Training). See Appendix I for information.

Problem 2 [Chanting]

When an NP grows up, he does not chant. Because he does not chant, he does not develop any funny voices to use for chanting. He also tries to deal with the situation when he is frustrated instead of going crazy and using a funny voice. Sometimes an NP wants to chant and use a funny voice, but he does not.

When an SP grows up, he does not know which behavior is right or which is wrong, so he decides to do what feels good. So he chants

* By James, age 8

164

and finally he will decide to do it in a particular way. He decides to make up a funny voice (or a funny accent) to use when chanting. So he gets used to using that special accent when chanting. He uses tactics like this when he is frustrated, because when he is frustrated, he is mad because using his own way did not work the way he expected it. Since he does not know how to deal with his anger, he makes funny noises and chants in his own funny accent, and cannot control himself during frustration. His mother will finally get bothered by the new accent the SP invented, and by the fact that he is frustrated and cannot be controlled, so she sits the SP down, hits him on the back, and screams, 'Why do you chant??? You should not chant!! If you are frustrated, don't get out of control!! You should be able to control yourself when you're frustrated!!' This puts the SP under intense stress. Not only did he do the wrong thing, he got hit on the back and yelled at just because he tried to do the right thing, but didn't as usual. Sometimes when somebody talks to an SP, he thinks that the only defense is to bother the NP. So here is what happens:

> NP: Do you want to play with me?
>
> SP [*chanting*]: Oh yeah, you cut the carrot in half.
>
> NP: Don't chant.
>
> SP [*chanting again*]: And then you grate the carrot with a cheese grater.
>
> NP [*more sharply*] Don't chant.
>
> SP [*again, chanting*]: And then you put it in hot water.
>
> NP: [*even more sharply*]: Don't chant.

And this happens over and over again, until the NP walks away. Then the mother hits the SP on the back and screams, 'Why can't you talk normally, like everybody ELSE!' However, the SP is happy because the annoying NP went away.

Solution 2

[*By Mom*]: Every time your SP talks too loud, chants, hums, or makes annoying noises, ask him what's bothering him. At first, he may not know how to answer you, but eventually he will become more aware of his own motivation. All of his annoying noises are a form of non-verbal communication, and finding out the message therein will help both of you understand the behavior.

If your child can't talk, try to figure out for yourself what is bothering him. Listen to the environment. See who's around. Try to determine if there is anything overstimulating. Also try to detect a pattern. Does he always go nuts in a particular place? (James had a fierce tantrum every time we took him to a playground or a museum.) If so, what is so upsetting about that environment? By locating and removing the source of the annoyance, sometimes your SP's annoying reaction to it will cease.

Problem 3 [Humming]

[*By Mom*]: When an NP goes to school or to a lecture, he learns to listen to the teacher or lecturer. He sits quietly so he can hear him or her better.

When an SP goes to school or a lecture, the noise bothers him, but he tries his best to sit still so his mother won't yell at him. However, since the noise will drive him crazy if he doesn't do anything about it, he may start to hum softly. Pretty soon he learns to focus only on his humming and to block out the outside world. If the person sitting next to him in school or his mother hears him humming during the lecture, they may tell him to stop bothering other people. The mother may hit him on the back and whisper, '*Shh!* That noise is rude. Be quiet.' This is confusing to the SP, since every noise to him is rude but nobody else is getting hit on the back.

Solution 3

If your child starts humming, immediately ask him what's bothering him. If he can't tell you, listen to the environment for a fan or other annoying noise. If he continues to hum in school, pull him out. He's not learning anything anyway. If you don't pull him out, insist that he be allowed to sit by himself at the back of the room. Chances are he'll then be far enough away from the other students so no one else can hear him. He won't hear anything the teacher says, but if you've decided to keep him in school, at least he won't be bothering you or the other students for six hours a day, and he will be learning a discreet method of blocking out the rest of the world and calming down his nervous system.

48

Tuning Out

Problem

As you know, the SP is surrounded by noise, outside and inside. Noise is his primary enemy, and he cannot control it in any way. Even when the world is utterly silent, the noise persists in his head. Quotes repeat themselves endlessly, driving him nuts, just the way his mother is driven nuts when he chants aloud (see Chapter 47: Mouth Control). So sometimes, just to escape all the noise, the SP tunes out, or shuts down his nervous system, the way *C3P0* shut down his computer systems in the first *Star Wars*. It is like pulling a plug.

Solution

To help the SP tune out the inner noise, give him a hard math problem to solve, or give him a large pack of cards to count, or give him some words to copy by hand on paper.

The problem with the uncontrollable noise is that it originates from the right hemisphere of the brain, which is more autonomous than the left. Since the SP's left hemisphere is where the delay and deficiency lie, encourage left-hemisphere activity and development. This is accomplished through boring, repetitive, sequential tasks, such as counting, reciting the alphabet or marching. (You know, all those things your therapist told you to prevent your SK from doing because they are weird?) Without knowing it, you have further delayed his left-hemisphere development, and made him more victim to the chaos of the right hemisphere. So when he is going crazy inside, give him a column of a dozen numbers and have him add them up. If he insists on a purpose for any activity, make them dollar amounts, and tell him you want to know how much you spent at the grocery store or give him a hard division problem. That will satisfy him, and keep his left hemisphere dominant for a while, which will be a relief for him as well as you.

An older SP might try meditation, which encourages repeating the same sounds over and over. By giving the SP a higher purpose for the repetition, he may feel soothed by the knowledge that, at last, he is not doing something weird, but worthwhile and even recommended by wise people from other countries.

49

Playing Frozen

Problem

[*By James, age 8*]: When one NP talks to another NP, the NP listens and is interested in what the other NP is saying.

As we've discussed in Chapters 1, 2, and 48, an SP often plays frozen when an NP talks to him. He is playing frozen because that is his defense system from noise, since talking hurts his ears (see Chapter 2: Noise Sensitivity), and noise is his enemy. The SP also has other defense systems – making funny noises – and humming and chanting. But if noises or chanting aren't sufficient, the SP plays frozen, paying no attention to the NP, making no eye contact with the NP, and not responding to the NP. This behavior usually drives the SP's mother nuts, since he does it in front of other people and embarrasses her. She often flies into a rage, not only hitting him on the back but shaking him and screaming in his face. Some SPs respond to this abuse by going 'comatose,' while others wake up out of sheer terror and start saying, 'Hello! Hi! How are you! I am fine! Nice to know you! Good-bye!' Anything to get his mother to stop screaming at him.

Solution

[*By Mom*]: NPs and almost all animals play frozen if they are under extreme stress. This means that they fear they are about to die. But because this is an extreme measure, many NPs live out their entire life and never have to use it. The fact that your SP is playing frozen over and over means that his nervous system is undergoing the kind of extreme stress that will eventually break him down and make him sick. Playing frozen is a form of communication – an SOS. Take it seriously. Don't push your SP, even if he is embarrassing you.

Explain to the NP that your child is having a panic attack and to leave him alone. If the NP starts asking embarrassing questions about your child, change the subject. Your SP can hear you when you talk about him.

Recently I read about a new twist to the good old 'fight-or-flight' response. We all know about that response; the one that was supposed to help Neolithic hunters escape a saber-tooth tiger once a year but is used repeatedly in modern life to deal with all the unnatural stresses of our lives. Well, children supposedly have a 'fight-flight-or-freeze' response, with the freeze mechanism being activated by a sense of profound helplessness (*I can neither fight nor flee so I'll shut down*). Neurologically, the 'freeze' mechanism is the most damaging of all, since it causes the nerves and immune system to go into a kind of suspended animation. Some body cells die off during *every* freeze, because the freeze lowers the energy level, and cells cannot function without proper fuel. Nerve cells die, too, and as you know, they never regenerate. Playing frozen, then, promotes nerve cell death, as well as sickness and allergies, since the immune system is compromised. Is it any wonder our children are prone to allergies and get sicker more frequently and for longer than NKs? This is the most compelling evidence I've ever heard for keeping an SP out of stressful schools, programs and social situations.

50

Cocooning

Problem

NPs do not cocoon. Therefore, we cannot comment on whether they like it or not. We suspect that they hate it or think it is strange.

But SPs cocoon to protect themselves. Cocooning is similar to tuning out or playing frozen except that it involves a small place.

[*By James, age 8*]: When an SP is bombarded on all sides, particularly in a playground, or in a room with a lot of screaming kids, sometimes playing frozen is not good enough. He has to find a small place to hole up in. He might lie down under a slide, or hide in a tube, or play behind a park bench. That way, he is better able to block out all the sensory darts. Often the SP's mother drags him out from under the slide, hits him on the back, and says, 'Get up, you lazy jerk! Don't you know there are germs under there? Why can't you play like every other kid? You are so weird, I can't stand it anymore. Nothing makes you happy!' However, the SP WAS happy under the slide. Mom didn't hear him complaining. Now that he is exposed, he is dreadfully unhappy, and he has had to be yelled at to boot. This makes the SP even sadder and more determined not to play in the playground the next time.

Solution

Let the SP cocoon. If you are going somewhere where there is no appropriate place to do cocooning, let him stay in the car, or let him lie down in a quiet room and roll him in a blanket. Maybe take along his mummy sleeping bag, so he can cocoon in it. Again, why force him to be social and in the middle of things when all you are doing is teaching him to seethe and hate people and suffer in silence?

51

Exercise

Problem

When an NP exercises, he grumbles a lot and longs for it to be over, but he feels really good afterward so he forces himself to do his routine.

When an SP exercises, he not only hates it during the exercise but hates it afterwards. He hates moving his body because of all the trouble he has with balance (see Chapter 22: Balance Problems) and proprioception, and all the other systems that don't work right. When it is time to exercise and the SP attempts to play frozen, his mother hits him on the back and warns, 'Do you want to die of a heart attack when you're forty? You can't sit in front of a computer your whole life! How will you ever get married and find someone to take care of you if you look like MUSH??' Exercise is generally a sore subject between the mother and the SP, and it is during exercise that the SP hates his mother the most and wishes he could belong to another family.

Solution

Start modestly. Have the SP exercise his fingers if that's all he can do at first. (After all, he can type, can't he? That's finger exercise.) Find something that an SP generally likes to do, like bounce on a bouncy-ball, jump on a trampoline, swing, or bounce off the walls. If he hates standing up, teach him to ride a bike and let him bike everywhere. Encourage him to crawl, which does not require the same degree of balance as walking.

Often giving the exercise some higher purpose will do the trick. Take the SP's pulse, and record it each time on a chart. He might see how high he can make it, or how it diminishes over time with conditioning. That's good left-brain stuff, and will help with neural organization.

Keep trying! The SP's depression will lift with a bit of movement. And so will yours.

52

Pain Problems*

Problem 1

When an NP gets hurt, he says, 'Ow!' and tells his mom, 'I got hurt!' Then the mother of the NP will come to him, look at his injury, and if it is bad, the mother may put some special medicine on it to help it feel better. Then the mother may give the NP sympathy, so he does not feel so bad anymore. He always feels some pain when he gets hurt. That is because his nervous system works normally.

When an SP gets hurt, he still says, 'Ow!' but sometimes he does not tell his mother because he remembers that his mother has hit him on the back when he has a headache (see Chapter 55: Headaches), saying, 'Why do you have a headache again! You shouldn't have a headache! How can anybody have a headache for TWO YEARS?', and did not care about the SP's pain. Hence, the SP gets afraid to tell his mother: she did not care about his headache, so why would she care if he got hurt?

The SP now suffers in silence. Finally when the mother discovers that her SP got hurt, she may hit him on the back and say, 'Why didn't you tell me? Didn't you feel it?' Of course he felt it, but since she didn't care about his headaches, why would she care about his other kinds of pains? (For example, we lived in New York, and on July 30, 1992, we moved from New York to Illinois, where we live now. During the trip, I accidentally put my finger in a hot cigarette lighter. That made a big burn on my finger, but I didn't tell anyone. Later my dad discovered that I had a burn on my finger, and he was sad that I hadn't told him.)

* By James, age 8

Solution 1

Believe your SK when he says he has a headache, and don't ignore his pains like you're doing. Because you have ignored his pains, you have made him more and more afraid of telling you about them. So care about his pains, and your SP will not be so afraid to tell you about them anymore.

[*By Mom*]: Several years ago, I had James crawl around the house for a half-hour every day to help with brain development. Although we tried to make a game out of it by 'petting the dog' every time he came by, one day he complained that his knees were killing him, so I bought him some knee pads. The first time he wore them, he said his knees felt worse and he wouldn't crawl. I told him to be quiet, that he was just reacting to a new thing, and I forced him to crawl his allotted half-hour. He trudged through the house in tears while I hardened my heart against his SP sensitivities.

After the crawling was over, James insisted that the pain was horrendous and he wasn't crawling anymore. Angrily, I put the knee pads on and began to crawl, to show him that he was overreacting. The pain was unbelievable, like barbed wires boring their way into my knees. I stopped immediately and said, 'These are horrible. Why didn't you tell me?' James looked at me blankly, because he *had* told me. I simply didn't listen. Quickly I put myself in James's position and thought how I would have felt if I had been forced to endure a half-hour of that agony. Believe me, I would have been pretty angry, and in fact, I would have been indignant and simply refused to crawl, as James had.

It made me realize once more how we assume that something doesn't hurt our kids if *we* decide that it shouldn't hurt them. And somehow *we* are the authorities on what they are supposed to feel. Is it any wonder that our kids are constantly angry at us? (See Chapter 38: Anger.)

Problem 2

[*By James*]: Often, the father of an SP is not an NP; he is an SP himself. An SP father behaves just like your SP child. Like your SP, he sometimes makes very bad judgments about things.

For example, he makes bad judgments on movies, and lets his SP see brutal movies and movies about kids controlling adults and kids punishing adults. Since the SP cannot make the right choices and does not know which is right and which is wrong, he may think the violence is OK and not care about the pain in a brutal movie which the SP father has let him see. Or the SP may learn to be against his mother, since the father has let him see movies about kids having power over adults.

After a while, the SP learns terrible behavior from the movies the SP father has let him see. The mother will hit the SP on the back and scream, 'Why are you acting like this? Why are you hitting and kicking other people? Why are you trying to be the boss of me? Why are you against me like that?'

Now the SP, if he can talk, will tell his mother in shock and in tears, 'The reason why I am acting like this is because my father let me see those brutal movies, which taught me how to hit and kick other people, and my father let me see movies about kids being against adults, which taught me how to be the boss and be against you. I am sorry. I cannot make the right choices.'

Now the mother of the SP will get mad at the father, and destroy all the tapes with brutality and kids against adults in them. Then the mother will yell at the father, or the father may yell at the mother for destroying all the tapes that he paid lots of money for. The father doesn't know that the movies are bad and have a ton of violence.

Solution 2

Before letting the SP see a movie, watch it first to see if it has anything bad in it that the SP might learn, or anything bad that the SP might quote (see Chapter 24: Having an Urge to Quote). That will prevent the SP from seeing a lot of bad things which he can't process properly. Avoid movies, like *Liar, Liar*, which show a lot of inappropriate behavior. The SP won't be able to judge that it's inappropriate and will imitate it.

Also, make sure you tell the SP father what movies are OK for the SP kids to watch. If he insists on bringing a bad tape into the house anyway, record a good TV program over it when the father is at work!

53

Foot Problems

Problem

When an NB (normal baby) is born, he has what is known as a Babinski reflex in his feet. That means that when you stroke the outside of his foot, the big toe curls backward. This reflex helps with crawling, since it positions the toes to dig into the floor. By the time the NB is one year old (past the crawling stage), the Babinski reflex evolves so that when you stroke the foot, the toes curl forward. This helps in walking, since the toes then dig into the floor in a different direction, helping plant the upright foot on the floor properly. This also encourages the foot to develop an arch.

When an SB (special baby) is born, he may or may not have a Babinski reflex. He probably has one, but if he is born with touch sensitivity, his feet will share that sensitivity, and he will avoid sensations on his feet. If you stroke his foot, he may scream. Or after a while, he may play frozen. As the SB learns to crawl, he may dislike the feeling of the floor against his feet. So he figures out some way to move that doesn't require much pressure on his feet. Therefore, his feet don't develop properly.

This can cause problems with walking later on. If the bones of the feet and the arch don't develop, and the SK doesn't like the impact of his foot being placed on the floor, he may develop a funny way of walking. He may plop each foot on the floor, or to minimize the contact between his foot and floor, he may walk on his toes. As a result, his legs and knees get tired, and he hates to walk. Pretty soon, he spends a lot of time lying on the floor. His mother hits him on the back and says angrily, 'Get up, you lazy brute! You can't sleep your life away. Get up and move.'

She gets particularly angry when she tries to buy him shoes, and none of them feel right. She hits him on the back again, after they have gone to 20 stores and tried on 20 pairs of shoes, and says, 'Why are you acting like this? You are weird! What is wrong with you? The MAN says those shoes fit! Why are you saying they don't?' Finally she has to order a special pair, like the ones he used to wear, which don't have laces since the SP can't figure out how to tie them, and she is angry because of all the time and energy spent to get this pain-in-the-neck kid a pair of shoes.

Solution

Believe your SK when he says his shoes don't fit! Test his Babinski reflexes, and if he doesn't have one, take him to a foot doctor and get orthotics. If he is still growing, the orthotics will help his feet grow properly.

At home, practice developing a Babinski reflex. Put your index finger under his toes and encourage him to curl them around your finger. Remember when you used to put your finger in your baby's hand and he or she would grasp it? Your SK's toes need the same stimulation.

If the soles of his feet are still overly sensitive, try rubbing them firmly or brushing them. Once his feet are less sensitive, they can start catching up with other NFs (normal feet) in the neighborhood. This will also help the SP enjoy exercise (see Chapter 51: Exercise).

54

Stomachaches*

Problem

When an NP gets a stomachache, he either eats some food (if the stomachache means he's hungry) or stops eating (if the stomachache means he's full).

When an SP gets a stomachache, he is not sure whether he is hungry or full, since he can't remember whether he ate and he is usually unclear about his body's signals. So he continuously suffers from indecision. If he eats too much, his mother will hit him on the back and say, 'You're eating too much,' or she will say, 'You don't exercise enough,' (see Chapter 51: Exercise); 'you shouldn't eat like a football player.'

Sometimes the SP is afraid of eating. Often, though, he will get hit on the back because he is not eating the food that his mother gave him. His mother will scream, 'Why can't you eat normal food, like everybody else? You're driving me crazy!'

Solution

Give the SP something to eat every two hours. That will help a lot. Eventually he will learn the difference between being full and being empty.

But make sure he likes the food, or he will not eat it! If he says the food makes him want to throw up, believe him and give him something else.

[By Mom]: Don't expect your SP to regulate his eating. If he is like James and spent most of his early years starving until we could figure out what he liked, then he may eat compulsively now. When he stuffs

* By James, age 8

180

himself now, James says that he is 'catching up' on all the eating he missed. He reminds me of a dieter on a binge. When we go to an all-you-can-eat place, I have to regulate how much food goes in, since James generally won't stop until he is so stuffed that he can no longer sit upright. Be vigilant; you have to monitor your SP's food intake like everything else. He can't do it for himself.

55

Headaches

Problem 1

When an NP gets a headache, he takes an aspirin (if he's a grown-up) or a Tylenol (if he's a kid), and pretty soon his headache goes away. He doesn't ponder over where his headache came from, since it didn't last long.

When an SP wakes up, chances are he will have a headache, just from the tension of being alive in an NP world. He might never be without a headache. He might have a headache every moment of his life. He is always under a terrific amount of tension and stress, which would drive any NP crazy, but the SP is supposed to take the pain and shut up. Otherwise, his mother may hit him on the back and say angrily, 'You're just telling me a lie! You don't really have a headache. How can anyone have a headache for TWO YEARS??'

However, the SP is not telling a lie. He really has been in pain, and all the mother's attempts to cure him have failed. This makes him sad once again, and he stops telling his mother about any pain, even if he accidentally puts his finger in a hot cigarette lighter in the car. His mother, upon finding the blister, may hit him on the back and say, 'Why didn't you tell me? Didn't you feel it?' Of course he felt it, but she didn't listen to him about his headache, so why should she care that his finger is all puffed up and sore? The mother calls up her friends and sadly tells them that she thinks her SK is autistic after all. Otherwise, why would he have such a weird reaction to pain? The SP, meanwhile, sits in front of the computer, playing his favorite violent game using only nine fingers, and he wishes he could be one of the powerful characters in that game.

Solution 1

There are many, many treatments for a headache. Don't give up until you find the right one. In James's case, cutting out wheat and eating frequently did the trick. Three days after he went wheat-free, the headache and much of his car sickness disappeared. We figured that a wheat-free diet was a much safer thing than most of the drugs other SKs are on for behavior problems. Whenever James eats wheat now, the headache returns in full force. He still 'mourns' the loss of spaghetti, ravioli, pizza, and tortellini, but he doesn't miss the pain.

Also, try to remove the stress in your child's life. In our case, removing James from school eliminated most of the stress. After all, stress is one likely cause of developmental delay. To put a delayed child in a state of stress for six hours a day is certainly going to break down his brain even further.

Problem 2

When an NP rides in a car, he thinks, 'Oh boy! A ride! Places to go! People to see!' He loves the freedom of the car and enjoys the images whizzing by.

Driving in a car for an SP, however, can make his headache worse. He feels a pounding in his forehead, and he wants to jump out of his skin. When he tries to complain, his mother tells him to shut up (she can't hit him on the back because her hands are on the steering wheel), and the SP learns to be quiet; otherwise, his mother would get so angry that it affects her driving. Hence, he just closes his eyes and plays frozen as best he can, waiting for the ride to be over.

Solution 2

Put your SP in the front seat of the car as often as you can. It is said that worse carsickness comes in the back seat of any car. But if you have an NP brother or an NP sister who wants to go in the front, mothers, tell them about how your SP gets carsick and must be in the front to help it. Try also cutting out wheat, as explained above.

56

Neck Problems*

Problem

When an NP exercises, as we discussed in Chapter 51, he grumbles and longs for it to be over, but he feels good at the end of his exercise program. He does not feel pain during exercise, because his neck is not tight.

When an SP exercises, even though he grumbles and longs for it to be over, he does not feel good at the end of his exercise program. This is because his neck is tight and he experiences exercise as if it was pain. Also, when he is at the chiropractor (see Chapter 58: The Chiropractor), or if his mom is rubbing his back or massaging his neck, he feels continuous pain, as if she is torturing him. So the SP barks 'OW!' when the mother touches him. After a while, the mother will get tired of hearing the SP bark 'OW!' The mother will then hit the SP on the back and bark back at him, the same way the SP barked at his mother in saying 'OW!' She may say, 'I'm making you feel better! It's not supposed to hurt!'

This puts the SP under a lot of stress, which may make his neck even tighter because he is trying to feel good but he just can't.

Solution

Keep massaging his neck and keep rubbing his back, but gently. His pain will go away slowly. Chances are his stiff neck worsens his headaches (see Chapter 55: Headaches), and this treatment will help him. Please believe him when he says a light touch hurts. Be patient. Try all the different types of touches until you find one that doesn't hurt.

* By James, age 8

184

Try to find a good physical therapist who can work on the sore muscles in the neck. In my case, a physical therapist realized that the left neck muscles were much more developed than the right ones, which was putting an abnormal stress on my vertebrae. She is working on correcting the problem.

[*By Mom*]: I recently took James to an osteopath for some cranial-sacral work. She found some compression on the right side of his skull, which was consistent with the molding he suffered at birth. It also explained the tendency of his head to hang to the right and to use his left ear and eye to experience the world more than his right ones. The tightened left neck muscles are a kind of head-righting response, with the left side trying valiantly to re-center the neck. He has had this droopy head since he began walking, and as James described in earlier chapters, no amount of prompting could get him to straighten up permanently, since 'straight' feels crooked. This droop, however, has led to all sorts of skeletal and muscular problems.

57

Back Problems*

Problem

When an NK grows up, he cuts his life into three sections (partly exercise, partly work, and partly play). The partly exercise part helps stretch his back, so he does not get backaches and does not sit incorrectly.

When an SK grows up, he does not like exercise (see Chapter 51: Exercise). As we have discussed in another chapter, the SP does not feel good after exercising, because his neck is tight (see Chapter 56: Neck Problems). But also because of his touch sensitivity (see Chapter 7: Touch Sensitivity), his back shares that sensitivity, so lying down on a bed and sitting on a chair is not possible for an SK to do correctly. Lying on a bed is horrible sometimes because the SK has to deal with the contact between the back and bed. When he is sitting up, because his back hurts while being held up, he will start lying down on chairs (so he doesn't have to control his back, and keep it up). After a while of lying down, the mother will yell at the SK (she can't hit him on the back, because she can't reach it when the SK is lying down), 'Sit up!'

Solution

Take him to the chiropractor, but don't force him if he's in pain.

[*By Mom*]: To reduce tactile sensitivity, let him sleep in a tight cocoon-type sleeping bag (See Chapter 50: Cocooning). Let him drag it around the house like a security blanket, wrap it around his shoulders, and hop around the house in it (one of James's favorite games). If he wants to be in it when he sits down, let him. It's

* By James, age 8

probably making him feel safe and protected. Give the bag a special name, and make it a revered object in the house.

58

The Chiropractor

Problem

When some NPs get a backache, they go to a chiropractor. The chiropractor adjusts their neck, which hurts for an instant, then the NPs feel better and go home. It is scary, but the NP gets used to the fear because he knows that the pain will not last long. Besides, he only gets a backache once in a while.

When an SP gets a backache and goes to the chiropractor, the pain of the adjustment is like having one's head ripped off. After the adjustment, his head is pounding and he isn't feeling good, as he should. His mother hits him on the back, which makes his back feel worse, and says angrily, 'You're supposed to feel better.' 'But my head is pounding,' the SP says. 'It's not supposed to pound,' the chiropractor says. 'You're supposed to feel better.' The SP doesn't respond, because nobody understands.

Solution

Keep going to the chiropractor, but also keep insisting that the adults around you take your feelings seriously. Every time someone hurts you, *SPs*, say, 'That hurts! Don't do it!' Keep telling everyone your feelings until they understand. If you cannot talk, keep expressing your feelings by crying so hard that the grown-ups have to listen. If you can talk, keep repeating, 'That is how I feel. That is how I experience the world. It hurts me, even though it doesn't hurt you.' Eventually, the adults around you *may* understand.

59

Aiming Problems

Problem

There are many aspects to aiming problems. They are all related to vision problems (see Chapter 5: Eye Sensitivity and Chapter 6: Eye Teaming). In an NP, the vision systems (front and side) work in harmony, so that the NP is able to see clearly and accurately what is out there. So when an NK learns how to aim, he is able to do so with only a little practice.

When an SP boy is asked to aim, for example, during urination, his eyes give him all kinds of distorted messages. For one thing, if you are standing next to him, his nervous system goes on alert (he hasn't learned on a neurological level that you are a parent and not a predator), so he focuses on you with his overly developed peripheral vision. In fact, his head-on vision is probably lacking, and he is not used to focusing straight ahead of him. (After all, he cannot make eye contact [see Chapter 3: Eye Contact]; is afraid of looking at things because they are too powerful; and spends most of his time, like an animal on the plain, trying to detect other animals who are about to eat him.)

So when it is time to aim into the toilet, he often misses. His mother hits him on the back and says angrily, 'You didn't try! You have to try harder! I'm not going to clean up this mess every day!'

So the SP boy tries harder, but now he is terrified that Mom will hit him on the back again, and not only do his eyes not work but his hands don't work either. Sometimes the mother will not tell him that he has to hold his private part and actually aim it. She assumes that he will figure this out for himself. However, an SK does not figure out anything for himself, and while he may grasp the concept that the private part has to be lined up properly, he may try to do so by arching his back or digging his thighs into the toilet, or some other way of getting the private part lined up properly without the assistance of his hands. But this doesn't work well, since his legs are weak from lack of exercise (see Chapter 51: Exercise).

Solution

Go to a developmental optometrist and get your SP some vision therapy. You can also try getting him aiming games such as darts or bean bag toss, but if they are excessively frustrating, don't make your child play with them. Start with something easier such as pouring water or sand into cups.

When you teach your SK a skill such as standing to urinate, don't assume anything. He doesn't live in your NP world, and hence cannot learn by merely observing other NPs. You have to tell him every single step of a new skill, preferably by writing down the steps and numbering them. Tell him what to do with his hands, his feet, his eyes, his head, everything. Then be patient. He will learn, but slowly.

60

Waiting Problems

Problem 1

When an NK has to wait in a line, he grumbles and mumbles, but his mother says, 'Shh,' and eventually, as he grows up, the NK learns how to be patient.

When an SK has to wait for something, he has to deal with an internal typhoon. First of all, when it is time to do something, the SK does not want to do it, because it is a new thing and a change (see Chapter 9: Change). So he declares, 'No, I don't want to go.' His mother usually hits him on the back and says, 'You're going! I don't care what you want! Why can't you be like other kids?'

So the SK processes this command as best he can. But he processes on the right side of the brain, which suddenly tells him that he HAS to go. Remember, the tremendous force on that side of the brain grabs on to an idea and takes over his conscious thinking so that now he has to do this dreaded thing *Immediately*. He can't think about anything but doing the thing that he doesn't want to do. He gets on his shoes and gets in the car, because there is nothing at all in his mind now except following the orders of his right hemisphere.

His mother tries to get him to be patient and to stay in the house while she is getting ready, but the SK is already out the door, waiting in the car, even though it is -20 degrees Fahrenheit in the dead of winter or 105 degrees in the car during the summer because the SK doesn't think to put the windows down. When his mother finds him, he is either shivering, or sweat is rolling down his cheeks and his shirt is soaked, but he hasn't even noticed the temperature in the car.

Later, when they are in line for whatever it is the SK doesn't want to do, the NKs are waiting patiently more or less. But by now the SK is ready to explode out of frustration and he is jumping around and chanting and trying to get to the head of the line. 'Stand still!' the mother commands. 'I don't want to wait!' the SK cries. So the mother, of course, hits him on the back and screams, 'Why can't you act like those other kids? Why are you always such a jerk and an embarrassment?'

Then the mother secretly wishes that the SK would start playing frozen again (see Chapter 49: Playing Frozen), at least then he didn't embarrass her. Finally, she screams at him so much that her yelling replaces the previous command that he had to do the thing he didn't want to do. The yelling reverberates in his mind, and again he wants to go home. 'I don't want to do this,' the SK complains. Then the mother bursts into tears and imagines calling up her friend to wail about what a burden her weird kid is.

Solution 1

The best solution to this is understanding. Understand that your SK doesn't think the way you do, and that he is not in control of his thoughts. It is very difficult to live with your SK's 'typhoons'. However, he isn't misbehaving; he's doing the best he can. You wouldn't do any better coping with the forces he has to face daily, and you are an adult, whereas he is only a kid.

Problem 2

[By James]: During a thing an SK does not want to do, right after he had to deal with the terror and anxiety of waiting in line, more waiting often awaits him. This happens the worst in a restaurant.

Going out to dinner is very scary for an SK because the SK has to wait in line for the table (on a crowded night), which puts him under intense stress. He is also put under more stress because he is afraid the restaurant does not have the right food: he is very picky, so he only eats certain things. So in both parts of the thing he did not want to do (1) waiting in line for a table, and (2) eating (because he will not eat food that is new), his terror mounts.

The SP is terrified during the whole trip to the restaurant because pain awaits him. He may lie down on the floor as soon as he gets there, so he does not have to deal with the problem of standing up.

Then when the mother, father, and possibly a brother or a sister order, the SK does not order anything, owing to the terror and fear of new foods. Right after everyone has ordered, and when the mother discovers that the SK did not order anything, the mother will hit him on the back and scream, 'Why can't you eat normal food, like everybody ELSE!'

Now the SK has ruined the whole trip, and the mother has had to deal with another embarrassment, like she had to every other time they went somewhere.

Solution 2

Don't make the SP suffer like this! Hire a babysitter whenever you must go somewhere. Admit it – you don't want him around, and he is not learning anything in these terrifying situations.

61

Connecting with Other People

Problem

When an NB is born, he knows instinctively how to connect with people, and people know how to bond and connect with him. They take care of his needs, and he loves them for it.

When an SB is born, he may or may not know how to connect with other people. However, his needs are disregarded or taken care of inappropriately so many times that he starts withdrawing from other people. Other people are the enemy.

As the SB turns into an SK, his problems with the NP world intensify. He needs to do certain things like spin and jump and suck his clothes, while the world tries to get him to stop by punishing him and hitting him on the back and yelling at him. Soon he is sent to school, where he is abused and teased and tormented and called 'weird' by everyone he comes in contact with.

Hence, he never learns anything social, such as imaginative play and good manners. He tries his best to stay away from other people, by hiding in the computer room or by playing frozen. People continue to react negatively to everything he does, and hence he learns how to fear them but not how to connect with them.

By the time the SK is seven or eight, he has learned how *not* to connect with anybody. He learns all the bad lessons that his mother hits him on the back for, such as avoiding eye contact and refusing to say hello (see Chapter 1: Saying Hello, and Chapter 3: Eye Contact). By the time the SK grows up and becomes an SP, he wants to live on a different planet. Since he can't, he stays in his room most of the time, hating NPs and feeling bitter about his lot in life.

Solution

Most SPs never solve this problem. How can you connect with an abusive, oppressive OTHER? Normal people don't hang around people they hate, why should an autistic person hang around in a world he hates? However, connecting with another person can be absolutely wonderful, the best thing life has to offer (perhaps).

We recommend that the SP starts slowly, with a carefully engineered hug perhaps. Hugging babies is good because they can't figure out that you lack social skills. Also, they need a very simple kind of contact, without two-way verbal communication. They need only to be held and rocked. They don't expect you to say 'Hello' or 'I am fine.'

After the SP learns to hold and enjoy holding babies, he can attempt to interact with older children, perhaps two-year-olds. If he can learn to adapt his play behavior for beings who are not like him, then he is learning an important first lesson in connecting with others.

It is necessary first to normalize the tactile sensations (see Chapter 7: Touch Sensitivity), so that the hands are not overly sensitive. Practice with stuffed animals, soft cloths, anything that feels good. SPs, ask your family members if you can touch their skin, rub them, and experience them. Make sure they don't tease or ridicule you (see Chapter 40: Teasing) or accuse you of things you've never heard of.

When you start trying to initiate contacts, remember that taking the first step is hard for everybody. Don't try to pretend you are somebody different. A real friend will find out who the real you is in no time. Be honest about your fears, and remember that people are more likely to accept something once it is explained to them.

SPs, if you find that the snuggle centers in your brain are suddenly working overtime, so that 'all I want to do is snuggle' [James's words], see if your mother or sister can tolerate the increased snuggling. Your mom will probably have more patience for it; however, your sister may understand your sudden new need to be held (which hits you, as everything else, like a tidal wave). It is a good sign; don't be afraid to ask for a hug. You're on your way to full, normal connectedness and maybe even love (see Chapter 71: Loving Other People).

62

Saying the Opposite*

Problem

When an NP sees a decoration or a picture that a person has made, he says, 'What a nice picture.' He likes beautiful artworks, designs, and decorations.

When an SP sees a decoration or a picture that a person made, he is filled with terror because it is a change to him (see Chapter 9: Change), because he has not seen that picture before and he always tries to avoid change. Also, since he is a global thinker and a negative thinker (see Chapter 34: Thinking Styles), he cannot make good decisions or good judgment about anything. So instead of thinking, 'What a nice picture,' the way an NP thinks about a picture, he thinks, 'What a rotten, horrible, stinky picture.' So he spits out what he thinks (see Chapter 47: Mouth Control), and tells the person, 'What a rotten, horrible, stinky picture.' This is called, 'Saying the Opposite,' because the SP is saying the opposite thing to what he was supposed to say. Now the person who showed him the picture is embarrassed, his mother is embarrassed, and the mother will hit the SP on the back and say, 'You shouldn't say something is ugly; say it's beautiful!'

The SP then says that the picture is beautiful out of terror and fear.

Solution

Help him by drawing ugly pictures and drawing beautiful pictures. Explain to him the difference between beauty and ugliness in general terms (e.g., things that are life-giving are beautiful; things that represent death and evil are ugly). Eventually the SP will learn what

* By James, age 8

the NP world thinks is ugly and beautiful, and this will help him say
the right thing.

63

Things Mothers Do to Their SPs*

Problem

Sometimes an NP mother likes to play tricks on her SP. This often happens when a special occasion is coming, or they have to do something and the NP mother and father tell their SP, 'We'll hire a babysitter for you,' but then force the SP to go with them right out of the door, not hiring a babysitter at all. After a while, the SP will start knowing that the NP mother and father are telling a lie. I have three examples about tricks a mother might do:

1. Sometimes an NP mother and an NP father discover that there is a wedding coming up and do not tell the SP anything about it. When the day of the wedding comes, they force the SP to come with them, with many changes (see Chapter 9: Change) shoved in his face.

2. Sometimes an NP mother and an NP father have an SP that causes trouble and has terrible behavior at restaurants. But one day, there is a steak special at the restaurant, and the NP mother and the NP father really want to have steak. So the NP mother and the NP father tell their SP that he does not have to go, then drag the SP to the car when they are going!

3. Sometimes an NP mother and an NP father only have NP food in the house. You remember how an SP hates NP food from Chapter 11, don't you? Well, then the NP mother and the NP father say, 'There are tasty things to eat

* By James, age 8

198

tonight,' and the SP thinks that means they have tons of SP food, but that really means NP food. So the SP gets forced to eat a whole meal of new food that he is afraid of and that he is afraid he will not like, so the SP has to (a) suffer with stress, (b) feel horrible-tasting food in his mouth, and (c) feel pain from the thumbtacks scraping his mouth (how the SP reacts to bumpy things). So now the SP has suffered because he got forced to eat food that he didn't like, but got tricked because his mother said they would have something 'good' that night.

The SP is bombarded because of the nasty tricks and plans you have thought up to fool him. Because he has learned tons of lessons from you, he may think you are a horrible, insane person who hurts other people, because the SP reacts to you as a person who hurts him, so the SP thinks you hurt other people because you put him in pain and stress.

As discussed above, the SP will suffer the trip the NP mother and father are taking, so the mother, finally, or the father, will stop the car and scream, 'Stop complaining! Enjoy yourself! Be a normal person!'

But the SP was only responding to his own pains, which his mother didn't even know about.

Solution

If you keep hitting your SP on the back, think up evil plans for him, yell at him, force him, and play tricks on him, he will learn a ton of bad lessons by doing all that when he is a grown-up. How many times have you told your SP, 'You are going to drive your wife crazy.' Well, nobody wants their kids to drive their wives crazy when they grow up, and that is the one thing your SP will do because he has learned evil lessons from you. But you aren't noticing that you are helping the SP to drive his wife crazy, are you? So if you are not evil to your SP, the SP will not drive his wife crazy when he grows up.

Also, your evil tricks and plans put the SP under a lot of stress, like hitting him on the back and yelling at him do, because it hurts his ears (see Chapter 2: Noise Sensitivity). We have learned that stress kills people, if you have too much of it.

The best solution is understanding. Have the SPs read the next paragraph, because they are the only ones to help in this matter.

SPs, whenever your mother plays tricks on you, makes nasty plans for you, yells at you, if you can't talk, stop listening to your mother and scream loudly. This is the only way you can talk to your mother, because she will listen to you then. If your mother says, 'Stop screaming!' when you are screaming, ignore her and make her listen to you. Eventually, she may understand you. If you can talk, though, when your mother hits you on the back, say, 'That hurts! Don't do it!' Or if she plays tricks on you, say, 'I can figure out your tricks because I am used to them.' Or if she makes nasty plans for you, say, 'When I hear things like that, I already know you are thinking up a nasty plan. I can also hear you when you are talking to yourself about me. Please don't do that anymore, because I can find out your nasty plans easily.' Or if she yells at you, say, 'Yelling hurts my ears! Don't do it!' Eventually, she may understand you both ways (screaming and talking), and know that she should not play tricks on you, hit you on the back, yell at you, and make nasty plans for you.

Your SP will not learn the right things if you do those five things.

SPs, help your mothers understand and listen to you.

64

NPs and SPs Together: Part I*

Problem

When an NP invites another NP to come over to play, both NPs are excited because they like playdates and social situations (see Chapter 17: Social Situations). NPs like seeing other NPs.

But since no NPs invite any SPs to come over to play, the SP's mother invites NPs to come over to play. Since an SP is so afraid of his NP friends (if the SP has any friends) and other NPs, he just spends his whole life getting away from NPs. The reason why an SP gets away from an NP is because several things happen:

1. The NP will say 'Hello' (see Chapter 1: Saying Hello) to the SP, which will hurt the SP's ears (see Chapter 2: Noise Sensitivity).

2. The SP must say 'Hello' (see Chapter 1: Saying Hello) back to the NP that has come over to play, after the NP has said hello, which is very painful. The mother of the SP will hit him on the back and say, 'Say Hel-lo! Say Hel-LO! Say HEL-LO! Say HELLO! SAY HELLO!'

3. During the time when the NP said hello to the SP, and the SP said hello to the NP, the SP had to make eye contact (see Chapter 3: Eye Contact), and an NP's eyes are like two suns blinding him.

4. Then the SP has to play with the NP, which is very painful because the SP would rather stay alone. Also, since the SP

* By James, age 8

does not know how to play with anybody, often he cheats when they play a game, or starts a big fight with the NP.

5. During the time when the NP and SP tried to play with each other, most NPs like to talk to other people, which hurts the SP's ears. However, the NP does not know that the SP is an SP; he thinks the SP is simply a weird NP. So the NP does not know that the noise is hurting his ears.

6. When the NP is leaving, the NP says 'Goodbye' (see Chapter 84: Saying Goodbye), which hurts the SP's ears again (see Chapter 2: Noise Sensitivity).

7. Then the SP has to say 'Goodbye.' The mother of the SP will hit the SP on the back and say, 'Say Good-bye! Say Good-BYE! Say GOOD-BYE! Say GOODBYE! SAY GOODBYE!' The SP will say 'Goodbye' out of fear and terror.

When the NP leaves, the mother will have a big fight and will yell at the SP (see Chapter 38: Anger), because the SP ruined the whole playdate because he hates social situations (see Chapter 26: Special Occasions).

Solution

Hire a nice NP to come over every day and your SP will get used to playing with an NP. Pay the NPs like babysitters. Remember to limit the times he has to go over to another person's house, because then he has to face two changes. It is important to limit his changes, because if you don't he will be in more stress.

65

Interrupting Other People*

Problem 1

When an NP hears his two parents talking, he stops what he is doing and may want to listen to them talking. But if the NP wants to hear them talk, first he has to see if they are talking in private. If they are talking in private or not in private, the NP will not interrupt their conversation because the NP already knows he would be rude and impolite if he interrupted the two parents talking. So the NP just continues his work.

When an SP hears two parents talking, he does not know why they are talking but the SP gets an URGE to talk. If the SP does not know how to talk but really wants to express himself, probably the SP will scream at the two parents talking. If the SP knows how to talk, the SP will just say something that he's interested in, and that has nothing to do with what the parents are talking about. Let me give you an example of what would happen, first with the SP screaming, then with the SP talking about something he's interested in.

Example 1:

> [*One day, the NP mother and the NP father of the SP are talking about how weird and what a jerk the SP is.*]
>
> Mother: Our son is weird, right?
>
> Father: Yeah, he's a jerk.

* By James, age 8

203

Mother: We can't do anything with our kid – he's so rude.

Father: We can't go anywhere, just go to his favorite places every day, that we are tired of going to.

Mother: Yeah, our son is wrecking our life. We can't even go in the car because he has fierce carsickness. I think he is telling a lie and that he does not have carsickness. Do you think so?

Father: Yeah, I think he's lying.

[*The SP cannot talk. But the SP gets a strong urge to talk, so he goes to where the NP mother and father are talking and he feels sad because of what they are talking about and screams at the two parents.*]

SP: Wahh Wahh Wahh Wahh Wahh.

[*The mother stops talking to the father.*]

Mother [*hitting the SP on the back*]: Didn't you hear us having a conversation? Didn't you know we couldn't talk to you this minute?

Father [*hitting the SP on the back*]: Didn't you hear us having a conversation? Didn't you know we couldn't talk to you this minute?

SP [*still screaming*]: Wahh Wahh Wahh Wahh Wahh.

Mother: This kid is driving me nuts.

Father: He really is a jerk.

Example 2:

[*The NP mother and NP father will still be talking about the same thing as shown in Example 1.*]

Mother: He is such a picky eater.

Father: Why can't he eat normal food like everybody else?

Mother: Our son has told us that bumpy things scratch his mouth.

Father: That's stupid. What can we do?

Mother: Disguise things in his favorite food. Our son may not be able to notice them that way.

[*See Problem 2 in Chapter 11, about hiding new foods in old foods.*]

Father: But what if he notices the new food?

Mother: We'll just close his mouth so he won't be able to spit it out so he must swallow it.

[*The SP can talk. After a while of listening to the two parents, as we've discussed on Example 1, he feels so sad because they are talking about how weird he is. But the SP still gets an urge to talk, so he goes to where the two parents are talking and says...*]

SP: Haven't you seen Power Rangers? The rangers get shrunken by a evil monster.

[*The NP mother and father stop talking.*]

Mother [*hitting the SP on the back*]: Stop talking! Wait your turn to talk! You're changing the subject!

Father [*hitting the SP on the back*]: Stop talking! Wait your turn to talk! You're changing the subject.

SP: Then the rangers get sent to Divatox.

[*Mother and Father go away, rejecting the SP.*]

Now the SP is feeling sadder and rejected. He was only trying to make a conversation, but got hit on the back and yelled at.

Solution 1

Have your SP pretend he is 'zipping his mouth' so that he cannot talk and then he will not interrupt his parents when they are talking. Have him put his finger up to his lips and pantomime 'zipping' his lips shut.

[*By Mom*]: James once told me (around age seven) that when he heard someone else speak, he felt the urge to imitate. Someone else's speaking loosened something up in him and gave him 'permission' to talk. When the other person stopped speaking and it was James's turn, he had lost his urge to speak and, in fact, couldn't speak because there was no one to imitate. So what seemed like rude interrupting was actually a developmental problem, which James tried to cope with as best he could.

Problem 2

When an NP sees his mother or father working, he just goes away and does his work. He does not interrupt his mother or father working.

When an SP sees his mother or father, since SPs are slow social processors, chances are the SP has not processed the mother or father working yet. So this may happen:

> SP: Have you seen *Hercules*? This movie is about how a god named Zeus and his wife Hera have a newborn baby and the baby is given a horse named Pegasus and must stop Hades and other evil monsters. Have you seen it?
>
> Mother [*hitting the SP on the back*]: Stop talking! I'm sick of your talking! I'm working now and you can't have my attention!
>
> Now the SP feels sad and rejected.

Solution 2

Mothers, tell your SPs that you are working and that you cannot talk right now. Be patient, give your SP a chance to notice that you are working.

Problem 3

When an NP mother has to talk on the phone, she picks up the phone and dials a number (if she is calling somebody), or answers the phone (if the phone rings) and talks to that person. Since the NP is a fast processor, he processes the mother talking on the phone, so the NP does not interrupt his mother, because the NP wants to let his mother talk.

But when an NP mother who is raising an SP has to talk on the phone, as you all know, the mother does the same thing as discussed on the last paragraph. But since the SP is a slow social processor, he does not fully process that the mother is talking on the phone. So he interrupts. (Let me give you an example. Let's pretend the person the mother is talking to is named Jamie, and she is talking about what a burden her weird SP is):

> Mother: My son is a jerk and a big burden.
>
> Jamie: Why?
>
> Mother: He never acts the way normal people act.
>
> Jamie: Give me some examples.
>
> Mother: He won't eat the food we eat, he won't talk to other people, and he acts horrible during a social situation.
>
> Jamie: Tell him you are the boss.
>
> Mother: But my son doesn't trust me. He only depends on himself, by making his own decisions.
>
> [*The SP gets an urge to talk. But the SP does not realize the mother is talking on the phone, so the SP does this...*]
>
> SP: I want to show you something.
>
> Mother [*to SP*]: Be quiet!
>
> SP: I want to SHOW you something!
>
> Mother: Be QUIET!
>
> SP: I WANT TO SHOW YOU SOMETHING!

Mother: BE QUIET!

SP: I was just trying to show you something. [*He starts to cry.*]

Mother [*hitting the SP on the back*]: Why can't you be quiet, like everybody ELSE!

Solution 3

Make a STOP sign and hold it up to him when he is interrupting you on the phone. Make sure it is the familiar-looking one, so it isn't a change (see Chapter 9: Change).

66

Being Polite*

Problem

When an NP grows up, he practices the rules for being polite every day: 'Say please when you want somebody to do something; say thank you when that somebody has done the thing you wanted him or her to do or somebody has given something to you; say excuse me when you burp, hiccup, sneeze, cough, or bump into somebody or if you have to walk between them; don't call names when you are having a fight; don't chant or make funny noises in public, etc.' Since the NP must use these rules every day, he can learn them with only a little teaching and practicing. Because he knows how to be polite, whenever the NP ventures out into his own world (the NP world), everybody will like him because he has treated them with kindness and respect.

When an SP grows up, chances are he is not ready to learn the rules for being polite. And chances are he hates NPs because he thinks they will hit him on the back the way his mother hits him on the back. Hence, the SP ignores NPs and how they act with other people socially. Also, (1) NPs talk too loud, which hurts the SP's ears, and (2) NPs touch other people, which hurts the SP's body. This makes the SP afraid of NPs because they put them in pain. So the SP gets used to indoor, solitary behavior and does not practice being polite and good manners at all. Hence, he thinks that funny noises and chanting are OK and acceptable (see Chapter 47: Mouth Control).

So the SP floats around in his own world chanting and making funny noises whenever he feels like it, or being rude when he is with

* By James, age 8

an NP. After a while of being rude to everybody, the mother of the SP will hit him on the back and scream, 'Why are you so rude? You must say please when you want somebody to do something; you must say thank you when somebody does something for you or if somebody gives something to you! Do you understand?' [The SP plays frozen.] 'Hey, I know you're in there, so speak! Let me ask you this! What's your problem and what is wrong with you? Why are you so rude? All normal people are polite in their world while you are floating in this stupid old world that you should not float in! BE POLITE!'

Solution

This is a tough one! Act out plays in which the SP meets an NP. Have him practice being polite every day. Also, have your SP see how NPs behave by renting good movies for him to watch (See Problem 2 in Chapter 52: Pain Problems, concerning the renting of good and bad movies). Avoid movies in which the main character is acting in an inappropriate and antisocial manner. The SP will not be able to tell which is the good behavior and which is the bad behavior, and he will pick up the bad habits since SPs always choose the wrong thing. Only when your SP has learned the difference between right and wrong behavior you can rent a Jim Carrey movie. Otherwise, your SP may start speaking out of his butt, like Ace Ventura.

67

Trusting Other People*

Problem

When an NP grows up, he will learn to make proper judgments for himself. Since he knows other people have that same sense of judgment, he will know that he can trust everybody else. This is how it has always been with NPs.

But when an SP grows up, since he plays frozen with everybody, his own internal systems will also play frozen and resist 'growing up.' Also, because an SP often lacks normal judgment and often lacks social judgment, he may develop his own kind of judgment. As you all know, SPs like different things from an NP, so an SP has a different kind of judgment.

Also, as you all know, NP parents make decisions, and have commands for all the NPs to obey. So the SP often thinks, 'If parents make commands and tell people what to do, then I can make commands and tell people what to do.' So the SP may start making his own decisions, which, are of course, bad ones because of his lack of social judgment.

Also, because SPs make their own kinds of decisions, the SP may think that all NP decisions are bad, and all SP decisions are good. Because of that, the SP does not know how to trust other people, because how can he trust other people if he thinks that if he obeys an NP decision, something horrible and terrible is going to happen?

So if the SP's mother has a job for him to do, he might say, if he can talk, 'I am not doing your job. I do not want to do it.' Then the mother of the SP will hit him on the back and scream at the SP, 'You cannot make decisions! You are not the king! You will obey me!'

* By James, age 8

Also, since adults make decisions, if he wants to make a decision, he may think of himself as an adult. Finally the SP will get used to thinking of himself as an adult, without his mother even knowing, and will try to be the adult in every social situation he is in (see Chapter 26: Special Occasions), which will put the SP's mother into a worse fit because he can't behave properly.

Solution

[*By Mom*]: It is very important that the SP develops a 'sense of basic trust.' Without it, he can do no meaningful social interaction with others. However, it is extremely difficult for the SP to develop this sense, for reasons we have discussed elsewhere (for example, everyone is bothering the SP all the time; everyone talks too loudly; events rush by too fast for the SP to process; people are always accusing the SP of doing things that he didn't know were wrong, etc.). In addition, because the SP has developed a strong will in order to survive, he naturally resists obeying orders.

In order to help the SP develop a sense of basic trust, you have to give him the very early experiences that he missed. Play peek-a-boo with him; play patty-cake with him. Remove the stress from his life – starting with mainstream education – then give him the carefree childhood he never had. If he resists playing peek-a-boo, it could be that he hasn't yet established 'object permanence,' whereby a child realizes that something doesn't cease to exist if he no longer can see it. If he gets agitated, try something even more fundamental, like 'buried treasure.' Tell him, 'I'm going to hide this toy in a box, then we're going to open it, and the toy will still be there.' As we've said over and over, it is senseless to teach an SP 'age-appropriate' behavior when he has missed most, if not all, of the earlier social stages which allow for normal behavior development. As Dr Bryna Siegal recently said, 'You can lock me in a room for three weeks with some mathematicians and force me to learn calculus, and I will learn some, but by the end of the three weeks, I'll become hostile and resistant to your efforts.'

Once you've simplified your SP's life sufficiently so that he realizes that life can be pleasant, he will start wanting to experience more things. And he will begin to trust you. When he trusts you, he will listen to you. And eventually he will have the courage to trust other people.

68

Disagreeing with Other People*

Problem

When an NP develops, he shares the same opinions as other NPs. He thinks an artwork or picture is beautiful if another NP thinks it's beautiful, even though sometimes an NP disagrees. But when the NP does disagree, it is because he is doing what he thinks is right, like all NPs do.

But when an SP develops, since he does not behave and does not develop like an NP, he always disagrees with everything an NP says. (For example, when my mom wanted to show something to my dad that was beautiful, he would tell my mother, 'I doubt it.' He is an SP.) So whenever the SP is shown a beautiful picture, as we've discussed in Chapter 62: Saying the Opposite, the SP may say, 'It's rotten!' The mother and the person who showed the beautiful picture to the SP are now very embarrassed because of what the SP did to them. The mother may come up to the SP, hit him on the back, and scream at him, 'Why can't you say things are beautiful when they are beautiful, like everybody ELSE!'

When an SP develops some judgment, there is still a mystery: When an NP disagrees, that is seen as his right. When the SP disagrees, he's called weird. Is that fair? Why do you think that happens? I think it's because NPs only understand NPs, and they don't think they have to understand SPs.

Also, when the mother is trying to teach the SP a new skill, that is a change to him (see Chapter 9: Change), and the mother may want to teach him her own way, while the SP wants to learn the skill HIS own way (if the SP's way is a different way), and the mother and SP

* By James, age 8

214

will get confused on which way they should choose. The mother's or the SP's? So the mother hits the SP on the back and screams at the SP, 'Why can't you agree with other people's ways of doing things, like everybody ELSE!'

Solution

This is also a tough one! Start by telling your SP there is no need to disagree on little things and that he shouldn't. Also, whenever you want to teach your SP a new skill, do it his own way, because then one of his fears of learning a skill is reduced.

[By Mom]: There are certain situations and certain people that immediately cause James's behavior to deteriorate. One minute he's fine, and the next he's chanting and marching and acting like Robin Williams at his most outlandish. When I asked James what was going on, he said that his behavior had become a reflex. He misbehaved in order to annoy me or the other person. He couldn't help himself, the response was automatic, and in fact, he wasn't really aware of what he was doing until he was well into it.

Disagreeing with other people is a person's right, until it becomes a reflex; an immature way of establishing personal boundaries. We all know how a two-year-old disagrees; in an automatic, reflexive way. You say blue, he says green. If you find your SP is communicating in this fashion, analyze this behavior. Is it reflexive, and is he trying to establish some sort of separation from you and the environment? If so, encourage the impulse to be himself, but tell him he needs to find another way. If you have him immersed in some behavioral modification program that was originally intended for rats and pigeons, you should expect reflexive defiance as his nervous system matures. After all, those programs are an insult to a child's intelligence and sense of self and should be used only when there is no other way to get through to a non-verbal child.

Ultimately, James's brief advice above is the best we can offer in this situation. Tell your SP that disagreeing with little things accomplishes nothing, but that if it has become a reflex, you will try to respect him more as a human being and listen to his opinions. And if you're trying to introduce something new to him, listen to his opinions on the matter and try to do things his way as much as possible. Encourage him to give the reasons why he wants to do something a certain way. You'll probably learn something yourself.

69

Carelessness*

.

Problem

When an NP grows up, he learns how to navigate through his world, the NP world. That means that he learns how to balance things (see Chapter 22: Balance Problems), and he learns how not to fall and how not to bump into people and things (see Chapter 19: Space Problems). After a while, he doesn't have to think about what he is doing.

When an SP grows up, his senses are all messed up, so that he doesn't get the right signals from his eyes and ears about the world, which is not set up for SPs. So he is constantly spilling things and breaking things and bumping into things and offending people. When he is walking across a room, he is so concerned with walking correctly, as well as thinking about his own thoughts (see Chapter 34: Thinking Styles) that he often does not notice that there is a person or a thing that he could bump into. He is not being careless; he just doesn't see what is ahead. So he rams into someone in his way, spills his milk, or pours out too much, because it is impossible for him to control the bottle. His mother hits him on the back and screams, 'How can you be so clumsy? Didn't you see that person?' When the SP says, 'No, I didn't see him,' the mother hits him on the back and screeches, 'How could you not see him??? He was right next to you!!!'

This makes the SP very sad and confused. How can he look harder at something that he didn't see at all?

The SP tries to be careful, but this puts him under an intense amount of stress, and he is so worried about being careful that he

* By James, age 8

forgets what he is doing and spills his milk or walks on someone's foot, or he manages to do one thing right, but is so stressed that he does something else wrong.

Solution

Try to anticipate problems the SP will have. Don't give him a huge glass of milk and then tell him not to spill it. He will be so worried about spilling it that he will forget where he is going, and knock over the glass.

70

Being Lonely and Making Friends

Problem

Because NPs like each other, they are not lonely very often. When they want to be with someone else, they call up a friend. When one friend moves away, they find another friend. This is how it has always been with NPs.

But SPs can't make friends. For one thing, other people bother them constantly, and no one can stand being around something that bothers them. Second, SPs bother NPs, so the NPs stay away from SPs. Third, SPs lack the social skills to make a friend, keep the friend, and behave properly in a social situation. After he has misbehaved a million times in public, the SP's mother hits him on the back and says, 'I can't take you ANYWHERE!! Why do you always embarrass me?? Why can't you behave like everyone ELSE??' When he gets older and wants to make friends, the mother still leaves him at home whenever she goes anywhere. This makes the SP sad and lonely now. He doesn't understand what he has done wrong, and he doesn't know why people always stay away from him. He is a good person and tries very hard to do the right thing.

Solution

Find places where the SP can be with other SPs. Find SP social groups and classes, where everyone is behaving inappropriately. In fact, by seeing inappropriate behavior in other people, the SP will learn how to behave appropriately in contrast. This will help him learn how to make friends and how to avoid inappropriate social behavior. And it will bolster his self-esteem when he sees that other people are worse than he is. Avoid mainstream school completely, it will only add to the SP's loneliness.

[*By James*]: I recently learned two valuable lessons on appropriate speaking, in my SP sports class. A boy named Roger, who has ADD and is an SP, went into the men's room the same time I and another boy did. We had no choice about being private, since there was only one toilet when the first lesson was learned. Roger spied on me and said, 'Your [private part] is smaller than my [private part].' Carol, the teacher, came to find us since we were taking too long. When we came out, Carol was right next to the door. Then Roger announced, 'James's [private part] is smaller than my [private part].' I was embarrassed, but Carol said, 'We don't talk about that in class.'

However, Roger did not learn his lesson. A couple of weeks later, Roger and someone else and I went to the bathroom (and because there were only two bathrooms but three people, Roger and I went to the same bathroom). Even though he couldn't see me, he listened to me peeing and announced, 'You don't pee as fast as my sister.' When I came home, I told my mom that Roger had been rude and inappropriate again.

[*By Mom*]: Seeing Roger's inappropriate behavior made James feel good about himself because James's behavior is so much better. He learned a valuable social lesson, and he now knows that if he wants to make a friend, he should not mention private parts. However, Roger did not learn a lesson, and James does not want to be his friend. (Roger is in mainstream school, by the way, where he is teased and taunted all day long. When Roger's mother came to his defense, that is the reason she gave for his behavior: that other kids had done it to him. So much for learning social skills in a mainstream setting!)

The only NP friends you should invite over to your house are rent-a-friends. When James was four, a teenage girl in the neighborhood offered to play computer games with James. It turned out she was learning disabled and a bit weird herself, but she had a good heart. I paid her $4 an hour [in 1993], and the era of James's rent-a-friends began. Soon I met mothers who had 'nice' kids who could use a little extra money, and by the time he was five, James had four or five rent-a-friend playdates a week. At first, he ignored them all and they couldn't understand him, but they soon found a common interest in computer games and in board games such as Monopoly and chess. Because the rent-a-friends were being paid, it was their job to be nice to James and not tease him. Also, they tended to be altruistic kids in general, who wanted to help.

Rent-a-friends are valuable because they give your SP *positive* social interactions and help him learn to trust the world. He won't learn much in the way of social skills if his social learning centers aren't ready to receive and store any information, but these centers will be stimulated in a *positive* way and this will encourage their development. An early childhood program full of baffling rules about waiting in line, taking turns, and sitting quietly during circle time will stimulate those social centers, too, but provide so many negative experiences that when your SP finally develops some social interest, he will have years of anger and resentment to undo. And as we all know from listening to adult SPs, that childhood rage sometimes plagues them for the rest of their lives. Besides rent-a-friends, you should also limit your SP's social world to *nice* adults. Keep him away from ignorant, condescending relatives, neighbors, and teachers who think that all he needs is more discipline. They will instil in him a lifetime hatred of authority. He does not need to get used to the real world in all its variations right now, or he will simply retreat back into his own realm.

71

Loving Other People

Problem

When an NB looks at his mother, he feels warm and tingly and safe. The mother looks back at him with infinite love in her heart. She will protect and nurture him for the rest of her life, and often when she is with her friends, she will say that her whole life revolves around her child or children and that she would never be happy again if something happened to them. In fact, she and her friends often say things like, 'I'd kill myself if something happened to my kids.' That is how it has always been with NP mothers. Love is something that is all-encompassing to them. The NK feels this love when he is with his mother, and it makes him infinitely content and happy, too.

When an SB is born, he may or may not be normal. If he is normal, then he will look at his mother and feel happy and do all the things that NBs do, until eighteen months. If he displays SB characteristics at birth, or when he reaches eighteen months, here is what happens when his mother is with him:

1.   When she looks at him, he is overwhelmed by the visual image of some giant glaring down on him, and he turns his face away.

2.   When she talks to him, cannon balls reverberate in his head, so he tunes her out. (See Chapter 48: Tuning Out.) Or her voice has the irritating whine of a mosquito in his ear. If he hasn't learned how to tune her out yet, he either screams or starts making funny noises to block her out.

3.   If she gets too close, her smell will overwhelm the SB. (See Chapter 10: Nose Sensitivity.)

4. Finally, and perhaps worst of all, when she touches him, her fingers feel like spikes or fire brands on his skin. He feels strangled and squeezed like he is in the jaws of an anaconda. At first, he might scream or stiffen his body to get away from her, but she might just hold on harder. Then he will let his body go limp, and finally he will fall down out of her grasp and tune out everything. The mother finally gives up and stops trying to hold him. Or she shakes him or (if he's older) hits him on the back and screams, 'What's wrong? Why can't I hold you?' Often she will call up her friends and complain about what a pill he is and how she secretly wished he belonged to another family. The father might overhear this and scream at her, or else he may say something like, 'Just have the adoption papers drawn up, and I'll sign them.'

Eventually, everyone starts leaving the SK alone, and he spends his time watching TV or doing the computer. His body doesn't get the right amount of connectedness with other people. Therefore, his snuggle centers do not develop. He becomes very lonely, and starts to hate other people. However, when he tries to be near other people, they put him under an intense amount of stress by blasting him and flashing images at him (see Chapter 3: Eye Contact, and Chapter 2: Noise Sensitivity) and stinking on him (see Chapter 10: Nose Sensitivity) and burning him with their fingers (see Chapter 7: Touch Sensitivity). He has to run away from them. Other people mean pain to him. How, therefore, can he learn what love is?

Solution

Learning to love is the toughest problem an SP has to face, and many SPs never resolve it. We think that the SP should start with a doll or a stuffed animal (a real dog will probably smell and slobber too much for an SP). He can pick one that is very, very soft, and since it is not alive, it won't change its mind or become different from day to day. Once he learns how to trust a stuffed animal, he might be ready to try loving a living thing.

Maybe he should try loving a baby or a little sister, if he has one. Little sisters are soft and they love you without realizing you are an SP. They are also gentle, and they love to hold things. It is important to tell the sister that her brother has a snuggle problem and that if he is doing the wrong thing (like holding her inappropriately or too hard or too often), she should tell him what he is doing wrong. He is used to people smothering him and used to having things go wrong all the time, so when he reaches out and tries to connect with her (see Chapter 61: Connecting with Other People), he may be overwhelming to her. He does not mean it; he is only doing to her what other people do to him.

Please be patient. After months and months of gentle rubbing and holding and not being overwhelming to the SP, he might begin learning that it is OK and even pleasant to be near another person. After years of learning to be near other people, he may be ready to love. Probably he will love his sister or his mother first, since they love him the most.

But it is worth the effort. Your SP secretly has a lot of love to give someone.

72

Understanding Feelings*

Problem

When an NP grows up, he shares the same feelings as other NPs. He feels sad when somebody dies because other people are sad; he feels happy when he is given a present from somebody else if another NP is happy when he is given a present. So it is easy for an NP to know what people feel, because all NPs feel basically the same way when they are in the same situation.

When an SP grows up, however, since he is a negative thinker (see Chapter 34: Thinking Styles), he may feel mad or upset when he is given a present, since it is a change to him (see Chapter 9: Change), and he may feel happy when somebody dies. It is hard for an SP to know what NPs feel, because an SP does NOT feel the same way when he is in that situation. So when somebody is sad, he may say, 'This person feels happy!' because HE would feel happy when he was in the situation.

Also, an NP cannot understand the feelings an SP has, so why should an SP understand the feelings an NP has? NPs can only understand people who are like them, and SPs can only understand people who are like them.

Unfortunately, after the SP has once more misjudged what other people were feeling, the mother may hit the SP on the back and scream, 'Why did you laugh when that boy got hurt? That was *inappropriate*! Why can't you react properly, like everybody ELSE!'

But since the SP tries to do the right thing, he does not understand or know that he did the wrong thing, but the terror of being hit on the back and being yelled at, and the fear and terror of

* By James, age 8

not knowing how to know what NPs feel, means that he has to deal with two stresses, which puts him under a double-intense stress. He was not telling a lie; he was just saying how he would feel if it had happened to him. And the stress makes it even harder to make the right prediction of an NP's feelings.

But anyway, he was only feeling what he thought were their feelings.

Solution

One way to get your SP to understand feelings is to always tell him how an NP feels in that situation and then he can remember what the mother said about that situation, and can make a right prediction of a person's feelings the next time. You must tell him over and over, because he is a slow learner, especially when he is terrified.

Another way to tell the SP how to understand feelings is to make a face chart, to teach your SP how to predict feelings from the looks on their faces. If he wants, he can carry it around and refer to it.

73

Cooperation

Problem 1

When an NK is first asked to help another NK, he doesn't like it very much. When he is in preschool, he wants to do everything his own way, and he sometimes has a tantrum if he has to compromise. By the time he is five, however, he begins to realize that when people cooperate, everyone benefits. The work goes much faster, and everyone supports everyone else. This is one of the ways NPs have survived throughout the millennia.

When an SK is first asked to cooperate with an NK, he suffers all of the problems that NPs suffer when he is faced with another person. But the SK, who is less mature than NKs his age, has an even worse reaction to other people than an NK. So the idea of cooperation is out of the question. Because ideas hit SKs like tidal waves, it is impossible for him to compromise on anything. He has to do things HIS way, or he will explode. It is not his fault, he is simply overwhelmed by the need to do it his way, not your way. His mother may hit him on the back and say, 'Play nicely. Don't be the boss.' But the SK doesn't know the first thing about playing nicely, and since he cannot connect with other people (see Chapter 61: Connecting with Other People), he has no choice but to be his own boss.

Solution 1

The only way an SP can learn how to cooperate is if the brain center that controls cooperation is ready to receive input. If it is not ready (and in almost all SPs, it isn't ready at age five, as in other kids), then you are trying to socialize a reptile. Don't force cooperation or cooperative play, or compromise, or any of the other higher endeavors on a child who hasn't mastered the basics, who cannot talk (see Chapter 43: The Rules of Language) and cannot tell what is going on in his own body. That is why mainstreaming to teach social skills is useless (see Chapter 39: Going to School) until the child's nervous system is ready to receive such learning.

Problem 2

When an NK is first asked to help another NK, he doesn't want to. He'd rather think only of himself. But eventually he discovers that it is fun to help another person. Giving is fun, and once he experiences the joy of receiving, he naturally wants to pass that good feeling on to others.

An SK, however, never feels good. Gifts are a change, and he hates change. (See Chapter 9: Change.) Furthermore, people bother him all day long, so that he wants to wipe them off the face of the earth. Why would he want to help them?

Solution 2

Again, don't force an SP to help other people. He is like a drowning man clinging to a life raft. He only has energy for himself, not for other swimmers. If you do force an SP to act social, he will simply do so because he is following orders, or will learn how to behave by rote. This teaches his brain negative lessons, because he does not understand what he is doing and ends up resenting the people he is forced to help.

It is far better simply to work on the SP's personal problems first; the social problems will have to wait.

Problem 3

[By James]: When an NK is at the playground or walking down the street, he may see a group of kids playing. Sometimes he may want to be in that group, and since he knows how to be polite (see Chapter 66: Being Polite), he can ask to join the group politely, without bothering the kids in the group.

When an SK is at the playground or walking down the street, he may see a group of kids playing, and he may want to go in the group. But first, since the SK does not want a change to happen (in this context, a game that the group is playing that he has never played before), he first has to watch what the group is doing. If it is a game that is old hat, he may try to join in the group. Often SPs are not allowed in groups, however, since SPs are not polite (see Chapter 66: Being Polite), their way of barging in bothers the NKs in the group, and usually, the NKs reject the SK. After a while, he will not even think of going in a group, because he knows that teasing (see Chapter 40: Teasing) awaits him. So he gives up. You would give up when a person who you wanted to make friends with wasn't nice to you, so the SP does the same too.

So when the mother and the SK take walks together, if they see a group of kids playing, the SK refuses to join in. The mother will hit the SK on the back and scream at him, 'Why can't you play with other kids, like everybody ELSE!'

Solution 3

SKs cannot simply join into groups of NKs. Their mothers need to find nice, accepting, understanding groups for their SKs first. A therapeutic drama group or a special sports class is a good start. The only place an SK can even hope to find acceptance is among other SKs with their own problems. Like everything, true social skills have to wait until more personal skills are acquired.

74

Being Flexible*

Problem 1

When something small changes, an NK learns not to care. For example, he always drinks his 'V8' in a can. What if his parents stop buying cans, and buy big bottles to pour into glasses? The NK does not care. He has enough skills to tell himself that it tastes the same if it is given to him in a different container.

However, an SK cannot think in a flexible manner, or accept change easily (see Chapter 9: Change); therefore, it is impossible for him to behave in a flexible manner. Because he is a visual learner, he has to drink stuff that always looks the same, and will only drink his apple juice in his own glass, and will only drink milk in another glass, not in his own glass like he drinks apple juice with, and must always have his 'V8' in a can and all of his other junk in a can, which he cannot drink in a glass. Because he is a right-hemisphere processor, he learns patterns and global rules, and his brain holds fast to these rules. As a result, it is almost impossible for him to move from an old rule to a new one without feeling as if someone is stabbing him in the heart.

If he is forced to do something differently, he resents the person who is forcing him to do so, and he secretly plots to destroy that person. He wants to do things his way, and he cannot compromise. This makes people hate him, and he hates them in return.

When I (James) was three, I had the same problem with flexibility. I had to go get lollipops every day. It had to be the two most perfect lollipops (a tidy wrapper, and a flavor I liked) in the store. Since we lived in New York City, no one noticed us. One time this happened, it

* By James, age 8

was followed by a big disaster. We once visited my grandmother, who lived in a small town. Well, when we had to get my lollipops (like I had said, I had to get the two perfect ones), it took almost a half-an-hour to do so.

When I was picking my lollipops, everybody in the store was looking at my mom and she felt embarrassed. Then, when my mom was tired of being embarrassed or being spied on, she got mad at me and screamed, 'These are the two lollipops you are getting. It doesn't matter if they are not perfect.' So my mom grabbed two lollipops, paid her dime (which was what two lollipops cost when the story took place), and went out of the store dragging me behind her. I was yelling and screaming and not walking by myself.

But trouble awaited her. There was a parking ticket on our car, because we had stayed too long in the store. I was screaming about having the wrong lollipops, and my mom went into a rage. My mom said, 'If you don't like these, I'm going to throw them in the street.' I echoed, 'Throw them in the street.' However, I had no idea what that meant. So my mom threw them in the street, and a truck came by and we watched as the truck crushed them. I burst into tears, screeched and screamed, and kicked the seat all the way home. Mom was in a huge rage, like Calvin's mom (of *Calvin and Hobbes*) was in a rage when he missed the school bus and she had to drive him to school.

Solution 1

[*By Mom*]: A child with developmental problems cannot be flexible. He does not understand what is going on in the world, so he clings to the few things he does understand. Taking away his habits and rules is like taking off a baby's water wings. The baby will drown. Don't make him do scary new things so he will get used to them; he will become allergic to them.

Problem 2

[*By Mom*]: When an NK develops, he develops in all areas: body, mind, and spirit. His growth is well suited to the expectations of the NP world. In school, he is able to master what is expected of him, grade by grade, because educators are aware of what NKs are capable of year by year.

When an SK develops, as we have often mentioned, he resists change in all areas, including the body. In fact, he is so scared of every aspect of life that he stiffens his muscles in an attempt to block out the world and its demands. They don't get the proper stimulation, and they don't develop. By the time the SK is eight or nine, he is as stiff and inflexible as an old man.

Whenever his personal trainer, his chiropractor or his physical education teachers try to loosen him up, he tightens up even more to tune them out. He experiences them like predators – like enemies trying to hurt and destroy him. In fact, when they try to loosen him up, he feels intense pain, and he screams. They either laugh at him, tell him to shut up, or say stupid things like, 'It doesn't hurt! Why are you lying and causing trouble?' Then they attack him even harder, laughing all the way, or ignoring his screams of agony. Mothers do this, too, and they rub and massage the SK while he screams and squirms. At first, the mother says soothingly, 'Don't be afraid. I won't hurt you,' but finally, when he won't stop screaming, she hits him on the back and screeches, 'SHUT UP! You're driving me crazy! Do you want to end up in a wheelchair by the time you're 21? That's going to happen if you don't learn to use your body!'

The SK may lie still as she scratches and tortures him, and by the end of the rub, he has tuned out his mother and his body, too. (See Chapter 48: Tuning Out.) This makes it even harder for him to be aware of his body the next time.

When the SP goes to school, the gym teachers insist that he exercise two hundred times longer than he is able to (he might be able to exercise for ten seconds, whereas the teachers want the class to exercise for a half hour, which is how long the gym class is). He either learns how to cheat (by not exercising whenever the gym teachers turn their backs and exercising only when they are looking right at him, or by cutting off a huge chunk of the time he is supposed to exercise in by going to the bathroom and taking baby steps there and back). If he can't elude them, he might become a behavior problem (see Chapter 36: Behavior Problems), for example, by throwing his ball against the wall instead of over the net, or by refusing to work with a partner.

Eventually, the SK will slink over to the wall and do nothing. The gym teachers will let him, because at least he is not interfering with the class.

James suffered horribly in gym, even though he liked his teachers. The other kids would not dance with him, and often he would cry and sit on the floor. When he was supposed to throw his volley ball over the net, he would throw it under the net. His knees hurt all the time, so he couldn't run, and he would stop running as soon as the gym teachers turned their backs. He improved only when he started going to a personal trainer and working on private shows for his mom. His trainer, Meghan, is a wonderful person, though she is an NP and the mother of two NKs. Therefore, she only chuckles when James calls her 'sadist' and 'the pain keeper' (i.e., she possesses all the pain, and she throws it out at him).

Solution

Keep working at loosening the SK up. Gym classes are useless, but see if the local Y can start a gym class for SKs. A personal trainer is a great help, too, if she can put up with the abuse heaped on her by the SK. We would like to say that eventually your SK will loosen up, but we are still working on that one. James still complains that the lightest massage is like nails from a nail gun on his back. Creeping and crawling might help, or you can take the SK to a physical therapist.

75

Making Good Decisions*

Problem

When an NK grows up, his senses and his abilities are the same senses and abilities needed to live in the NP world. Therefore, he learns how to make good decisions about his behavior and he learns how to live safely in the NP environment. Furthermore, when he does the right thing, his mother praises him, and this makes him feel good about himself; therefore, he wants to do more of the right thing. As he grows, he learns how to make good decisions. His mother stops watching his every move, because she knows he has good judgment.

When an SP grows, his senses and abilities are impaired, because they are the abilities needed for an SP world. However, because there is no such thing as an SP world, the SP is in big trouble. Everything he does is wrong in the NP world. Every time he takes a step, his mother hits him on the back and screams, 'How could you be so stupid?' Eventually, the SP begins to doubt his ability to make any sort of judgment. And he never learns to make good decisions.

For example, we went to the Children's Museum of Indianapolis yesterday (we took a trip to Indianapolis). When we went up to the 5th floor (there's a runway up to the floors in the museum), I stopped walking when we were just at the 5th floor. I looked at the bright blue bannister and I decided to climb on top of it and walk on it. I had no idea it was so dangerous. From where I was, it didn't look so bad. So I did it. When Dad saw me, he was mad. I said, 'Hi!' to him. He said, 'Get down from there or I am going to yell at you.' I did, and

---

* By James, age 10

he got mad at me. Then he forced me to look at the bright blue bannister again and see the dangerous drop on the right-hand side.

However, I did not see the drop on that side, because the bright blue bannister was as wide as a slide, went down diagonally bit by bit, and had straight edges that came up on each side. It wasn't dangerous on the left-hand side because it was attached to the wall. But I didn't want to tell my dad, because then he would yell at me again. But he still talked to me, like he was a little angry because I didn't make the right decision. But when this happened, I was alone when I made this decision, and there was nobody to warn me until Daddy found out. So when he did find out I was walking on the bannister, he also asked me, 'Can't you ever be safe when you're alone?' Even though it was hard to walk on the bannister, since it didn't go very far edge by edge in the runway, I didn't know how risky it was and how dangerous it could have been.

Solution

Give your SP the chance to make little decisions, which don't involve danger. For example, let him choose which shirt he wants to wear. Praise him a lot if he makes an appropriate choice. Little by little, he will learn that he can make a good decision, and he will be better equipped to make more important decisions.

76

Freedom of Choice

Problem

When one NP wants to be with another NP, the first NP usually says OK, and they both have a good time. NPs like to be with each other. That is how it has always been with NPs. They don't feel imposed upon by each other. When an NP wants to be alone, however, the other NPs generally respect that, too, and they give the NP some solitude.

When an SP wants to be alone, this is regarded as inappropriate and weird and socially disordered. He is not allowed to be alone, so his mother makes all kinds of playdates for him that he does not want to go to. When he retreats into a corner, the SP's mother hits him on the back and shouts, 'Get back here! You're supposed to be playing now. Don't go off by yourself.' The SP often complains out of fear, but he tries to escape in another way, by tuning out or playing frozen. (See Chapter 48: Tuning Out and Chapter 49: Playing Frozen.)

Solution

Let your SP be alone when he wants to be. He will not learn social skills in an imposed social situation. You feel you have the right to choose your social environment – why shouldn't your SP?

Freedom of association is in the *Bill of Rights.*

77

Cleaning Up

Problem 1

When an NP goes into his room and sees a mess, he says to himself, 'I'll clean this up.' Then he starts straightening and fixing and putting things in their correct places, until everything is cleaned up and everything looks good. He might dust and vacuum, too. His mother (or his wife) comes in and praises him for the hard work, then they both admire the neatness and cleanliness of the room.

When an SP goes into his room, he does not care if his room is messy. First of all, he does not see or notice that his room is messy, and cannot do something if he does not notice there is something to be done. Second, although he might know what to do in cleaning up the room, he does not know what to do first. He cannot divide the job into its separate tasks, because he is a holistic thinker. And besides, it is so messy he thinks it is too much for one person to do by himself. Third, he does not know the correct or proper place to put things, and cannot put them away in the right place. But sometimes if he cleans it up, he puts everything in the wrong place. Fourth, he feels it is stupid to clean it up, since it will just get dirty again.

His mother comes in, sees all the disorganized stuff, hits him on the back, and screams, 'Read the labels on the boxes. Stuffed animals should go in the stuffed animal box, not the book box!' Or if the SP has not cleaned it up at all, the mother will hit him on the back and scream, 'Why can't you clean up your room when you look at it and see that it is messy?' The SP looks around at his room, and his eyes go into shock. He cannot process it all (see Chapter 9: Eye Sensitivity). He tries to look at it, but he feels sad and swamped. He might sit on his bed and play frozen (see Chapter 49: Playing Frozen), or he might even cry.

His mother might get disgusted and clean the room herself.

Solution 1

The SP cannot process the entire task and break it down by himself. He has to be given certain jobs, with specific instructions, and he definitely cannot figure out where all the places for things are if he cannot process the labels on his boxes. And he also cannot notice that the room is messy if he has a pair of eyes that don't work normally.

Break up an enormous task into tiny parts, with a definite means of completing each one. Tell your SP to put each pencil in the pencil holder. Then tell him to put each pen in the pen holder. Direct his attention to tiny areas of the room, rather than a whole area. Our good friend Sue suggested that you break the room into the twelve hours on a clock. Then tell your SP to 'clean up 12:00, then 1:00, etc.' That way the room will be divided into 12 small areas, which the SP can focus on, rather than the enormous room.

It would help to limit the number of things in the SP's room, too. That way there are not too many things for him to look at, then have to deal with.

Problem 2

When an NP wakes up, his mother or father will tell him, 'Time to take a shower!' Since he knows about proper health care, he knows that part of it is cleaning your germs off your skin. So he takes a shower to clean up his body and all those germs on his skin. This prevents him from getting a lot of diseases.

When an SP wakes up, when his mother or father tells him, 'Time to take a shower,' since he does not know about proper health care, he does not go in and take the shower. Instead, he falls back to sleep in his bed. First of all, hair washing comes during a shower, which hurts him (see Chapter 7: Touch Sensitivity). Second, he does not like the feeling of the water falling on his body. So his mother wakes him up, hits him on the back and screams, 'Why can't you learn to take showers, like everybody ELSE!'

Solution 2

Tell your SP about proper health care and how it is important to take showers. If the feeling of water and soap is painful on his skin, let him chant or quote or echo or do the other inappropriate things he wants to do but is forbidden to do at other times. This way, he can look forward to something to help him endure the pain.

Another way to help your SP with liking the feeling of cleaning up his body during a shower is to teach your SP how to do it, so he can develop a way to do it less painfully. Check your SP every time he does it, so he can learn the right way to do it.

78

Future Judgment*

Problem

When an NK is about two years old, he is always given commands like, 'Don't go in the street. It's dangerous.' This makes the NK mad at his mother, because he was not able to do something he wanted to do. He may have a temper tantrum, and scream and cry, but his mother tells him to stop.

By the time the NK is an NP, he will understand why his mother didn't let him go out in the street. The mother just wanted him to be safe. Also, when mothers tell their NKs, 'If you're lost in a store, go to a clerk,' the NK will not do it deliberately (if he is seven) just to try it out because he knows what will happen. NKs will understand the context that if he is lost, it is OK to ask a clerk. This is because NKs have future judgment, and know what will happen next.

When an SK is about two years old, the same things happen to him that happen to NKs when they are two. But when the SK is seven, he will still do the same things NKs do at two and have to try them out before he knows they are bad. So when the mother says, 'If you're lost in the store, go to a clerk,' the SK cannot understand the context that IF you are lost, go to a clerk; he just thinks that you HAVE to get lost and you HAVE go to a clerk, and it is OK to go to a clerk at all times. So the SK tries to walk to the service desk, but the mother stops the SK, hits him on the back, and screams, 'Don't walk away from me! Stay here!' Then the SK thinks, 'You just told me to go to the clerk.' Then he says, 'I was only going to the clerk.' The mother hits the SK on the back again and screams, 'I was only telling you IF you got lost to go to the clerk! You are not lost, so you don't

* By James, age 8

240

have to go to the clerk! Why can't you understand?' This puts the SK under intense stress, which makes it harder for him to figure out when it is appropriate to go to the clerk.

This once happened to me when I was at a hotel watching *How the Grinch Stole Christmas* on TV, lying down in bed, drinking an Orange Slice. My mother said, 'If you spill the Slice accidentally, it is OK.' Now I was a lot younger when this happened, and didn't know what 'accidentally' meant. I just thought, 'If Mom said it was OK if my Slice spilled, no harm will be done if I do it on purpose.' So I spilled the Slice on purpose. It was a little spill, but as it touched other parts of the blanket, the stain of the spill got bigger. When Mom checked the blanket, she said, 'James!' I said, 'What?' Mom complained, 'There's a huge spill on the blanket.' I lied and said, 'Well, I didn't know I made a spill,' because I did not want my mom to know I did it on purpose. Mom said in a sigh, 'I know. You weren't careful and didn't see the Slice spilling.' But she was disappointed and annoyed, and that confused me because she had said it was OK.

The SK also gets confused when his mother gives him commands like, 'Don't run in the street. It's dangerous.' The SK has no idea HOW the street is dangerous, because he has never run in the street before, doing the dangerous thing. If she tells him he will be run over by a car, he will not understand that this is dangerous, because cars are safe when he rides in them.

So the SK gets angry at his mother, the same thing an NK would do at the age of two, and the SK tries to go in the street, but the mother pulls him back. Finally the SK stops trying, and tells his mother, 'I didn't know it was dangerous.' The mother hits the SK on the back and screams, 'You will die if you go in the street, and you cannot live anymore. You don't want to die, do you?' The SK now just wants to take this risk, so he lies and says, 'Yes. I want to die. Bye, Mom.' But the mother still won't let the SK die, and the SK still struggles to try out being run over by a car. But finally the struggle gets too stressful and too traumatic, so that the SP just realizes that defying his mother isn't going to do any good, and he gives up. But the stress makes it harder for him to learn that what he was going to do was dangerous. All he remembers it that he is angry at his mother.

Solution

Before an experience like the one told above happens, act out what dangerous things will happen, at home in a safe way. When he is pretending this is happening, the SP will feel like he is going to be run by a car in real life, so he can feel that it is dangerous. Act out every possible dangerous thing that could happen in real life, to teach the SP that it's dangerous. Then talk about every detail of the event, so the SK can process them all.

79

Needing Other People

Problem

When an NB is born, he looks up at this mother and father and in a short time bonds with them. He loves them in his own way because he needs them. They make him feel good all day long and they comfort him when he is crying, so he learns to rely on them for these good feelings.

This is the beginning of his need for other people.

An SB may or may not be normal at birth. If he is normal, he will need his parents the way NBs do. When he turns eighteen months, however, something changes in his life. All of a sudden, his mother's hugs hurt, and her voice is like drilling in his ear canal, and she smells funny, and she is threatening to him. As a result, he starts tuning her out (see Chapter 48: Tuning Out) and then tuning out the rest of the world. He learns that other people hurt him, so he becomes as self-reliant as he can. His main goal in life is NOT to need other people because they are the enemy.

The SK is adamant about consistency and about having people fulfil their promises. However, NPs are always changing their mind and telling you one minute you can do something then saying you can't the next. This drives the SK absolutely nuts, and he withdraws even further. By the time he is eight or nine, the SK doesn't need anybody and wants no friends. He wants to live alone as soon as he is able.

Solution

The first step in needing other people is to learn to trust other people (see Chapter 67: Trusting Other People). This is very tough, since most NPs are not very trustworthy (because they are always changing their minds, and they don't respect the SP's special needs). An SP resents the fact that everybody changes their mind, because that puts him in a huge confusion (see Chapter 41: Verbal Confusion), and he doesn't know which alternative to follow. However, if he can accept the fact that NPs are inconsistent and disorganized, and can overlook their stupidity, he may be able to rely on them a little bit.

The second step is to surround the SK with people who are warm-hearted and accepting. James's Aunt Linda is like that. He takes her out for Italian food once a month, and she listens to him and validates him and makes him feel good. It is OK for James to need Aunt Linda, and hopefully, James will grow up and marry someone as nice as she is.

Needing other people is a difficult step. It makes you vulnerable. It opens you up for tremendous disappointment. But it is also the first step towards learning to love (see Chapter 71: Loving Other People).

80

Mine and Yours*

Problem

When an NK is one year old or so, he becomes fascinated by his and other people's possessions. NKs do not know what *their* possessions are at first, but then they go through a possessive period calling everything *mine mine mine*. During this period, an NK will be able to learn what is his and learn what is not his, so when somebody steals his stuff, he will learn how to get it back and the proper thing he should get back at that moment.

When SKs are one year old or so, they may become fascinated by other people's possessions, but they lack a sense of who they are and what belongs to them, so the SK has no idea what belongs to him or what belongs to somebody else. So he never goes through a possessive period calling everything *mine mine mine*. Because of this, and because of his language problems, he never even learns the word 'mine' (see Chapter 43: The Rules of Language).

This can cause problems when the SK passes a group of NKs who call everything *mine mine mine*. They will try to steal the SK's stuff, by pushing the SK around, and hitting him, and taking his things away. Then the SK gets confused (see Chapter 41: Verbal Confusion), and sad, because he does not know how to get the stolen thing back. So the SK just stands there silently, watching the NKs take his toys. The mother, discovering the SK did not know how to get his toy back, hits the SK on the back, and screams, 'If you want to get something back from somebody else, GET IT BACK! Don't just stand there, DO SOMETHING! Why do I have to tell you over and over again the rules for things?' Finally the mother gives the toy back to the SK,

* By James, age 8

245

feeling mad because the SK didn't do it by himself like an NK would.

This happened to me. When I was learning how to walk and pushing my toy shopping cart, an NK stole it away on the playground. I just stood there, because I did not know what to do to get the cart back. The NK's nanny hit the NK on the head and gave the cart back. Mom said I still stood there, shocked. I never paid any attention to anyone else, so I couldn't believe that someone would swoop down and steal something that I was playing with. I certainly never did that.

SKs also have a problem with sharing, because they do not know the things they can't share and the things they can share, so they let NKs share all of their stuff, because they think that everything can be shared with somebody else. The mother hits the SK on the back and screams, 'Why are you letting people play with all your stuff? It belongs to YOU!'

Solution

Put everything that is the SK's in his own room. Then the SK can know what is his and what is not his because everything that's his is in his room, and everything that is not his is not in his room. If your SK is hyperlexic, label all his stuff with his name.

Most important, keep working on those personal pronouns and help your SK develop a sense of self. As with other social issues, the personal issues have to be resolved first.

81

Doing Things People Want You to Do*

Problem

When an NK goes somewhere, sometimes he, or his brother or sister, wants to do something else after they did the first thing. Nobody minds, since two things are better than one to an NP.

When an SK goes somewhere, he expects to do *only* the thing that was scheduled. If he goes to a movie with his dad and sister, he expects *only* to go to the movie. So when his sister says, 'Let's see Santa,' the SK gets filled with terror and says 'No!'

He hates most things NKs like and enjoy. Also, nobody told him that he had to go visit Santa and now somebody tells him he has to visit Santa, which puts a change (see Chapter 9: Change) into his time schedule, and the SK hates changes. The SK has to know what is going to happen in advance, so it will not be a change. The SK cannot have a change that is 'shoved in his face.' So he complains to his parents, 'NO! I DON'T WANT TO SEE SANTA! I WANT TO GO HOME!' The mother hits him on the back and screams, 'Why don't you like seeing Santa! Anyway, why are you so weird? Let us see Santa! We saw this movie for *you*, and you are going to have to do this for *us*!'

Then the SK gets forced to see Santa, but sometimes he doesn't complain. He knows that he'd better not or the mother will hit him on the back again. But he still doesn't want to go. So the SK often lies down on the floor and refuses to move. The mother screams at the SK (she can't hit him on the back), 'Get up! You can't stay lying down

---

* By James, age 8

for your whole life!' The SK then gets up and goes to see Santa, though he is thrown in a whole bunch of stress. He knows what will happen. He will be forced to have his picture taken, which hurts his eyes (see Chapter 5: Eye Sensitivity), he will be forced to sit on a stranger's lap, which hurts him (see Chapter 7: Touch Sensitivity). It also confuses him (see Chapter 41: Verbal Confusion), because everybody has told him never to talk to or to touch strangers, and Santa is a stranger to him.

Because of that, and because he does not want to do the thing everybody wants him to do, he just wants to get the thing done. He wants everybody to hurry up so he can get it done. So he gets obsessed with the thing he doesn't want to do and doesn't like doing. This always happens when he has to do something he doesn't want to do, getting obsessed with things he doesn't like doing. NKs do this too, but not very often, because they like most of the things other NKs want to do.

Solution

The easiest solution for this one is not to force the SK to do anything. When you get to the thing you want to do, let the SK lie down on the floor or sit on a bench. If he wants to do the thing, though, he'll just have to face the stress and terror of the change (see Chapter 9: Change). But he will be in control of the situation.

82

NPs and SPs Together: Part II

Problem

Since the dawn of civilization, until now, that is, people had to work cooperatively in order to survive. Before supermarkets, cars, condos, washing machines, and other conveniences, people needed help from others in almost every activity needed to sustain life. Therefore, the ability to cooperate is hard-wired into the human brain – at least, the NP brain.

However, as you all know, the SP brain is wired differently. Or perhaps it is only half wired up. Some of the plugs have not been inserted into the proper slots. This is not the SP's fault, but rather the fault of the NPs around him.

When NKs do something social, they get praised, and they feel good about what they do. Therefore, this encourages their brains to keep the social plugs plugged in. On the other hand, when an SP does something social, he is usually criticized, screamed at, teased and reprimanded. When he plugs in a social wire, he gets an electric shock. Therefore, his brain attempts to 'unplug' the social wires. They are like outlets with faulty wiring. After a few electric shocks, the SP tries to avoid those outlets.

The school may force the SP to interact with NPs in small groups, which does nothing but give the NPs a golden opportunity to tease and humiliate someone who is different (see Chapter 39: Going to School). His mother may then send him to a social worker or therapist or put him in a social group, but generally this does nothing. According to James, all the kids in therapeutic social groups avoid each other and interact only with the group leader. And therapists merely force an SP to replug some of those unplugged social wires and learn to endure the shocks.

Therefore, the SP becomes like the child who is 'once burned, twice shy.' That is an NP expression which means that if something bad happens to you, you're afraid to do the same thing the next time. Unfortunately, this saying must only apply to NPs, since SPs are not allowed to be 'twice shy.' When the SP is humiliated or hurt in a social situation (see Chapter 26: Special Occasions) or in school (see Chapter 39: Going to School), he is expected to cope with it, 'get used to it,' and do it over and over. Even though he is not once, but ten thousand times burned, and not just shy, but traumatized and suicidal over having to be forced to be burned over and over. Nevertheless, the NPs tell him he has to 'get used to it.' NPs are not expected to 'get used to it.' NPs avoid pain whenever they can, and this is regarded as healthy. But it is inappropriate for SPs, because the NPs have decided that they know better than the SPs what the SPs is, or should be feeling.

Whenever the SP starts to complain or say that something hurts or is bothering him, everybody laughs at him because it is not bothering the NPs. Is it any wonder that the SPs of the world do NOT learn how to cooperate?

Solution

If you want your SP to join your world, you had better learn more about his world. You will find that he is doing just what you would do on an alien, hostile planet. Also, it helps tremendously to teach your SP social skills in an SP environment, not necessarily through special education, but perhaps in a therapeutic drama class, SP sports class, or social skills class led by a therapist *who knows what he's doing.* Then your SP can have a *true* peer group, and learn social skills without the threat of being humiliated. I (Mom) often think about writing a script for therapists and teachers in which they are continually mocked, yelled at, rejected, humiliated, teased, and tormented. How long do you think a normal person would put up with this without displaying some of the 'weird' defensive behaviors our children use?

83

Reciprocity*

Problem 1

When NKs are three years old or so, they begin to understand the value of cooperation (see Chapter 73: Cooperation). They see adults and older children compromising and doing things efficiently. Then the NKs realize that cooperation is more important than always having your own way. Because of that, they learn social reciprocity or, to be more specific, to give and take in a nice way.

But when SKs are three years old or so, they see meanness and evilness in everybody. This is because NPs don't understand SKs, bother SKs, and don't respect SKs. So SKs do not learn the proper social skills being with NKs, because they go through their lives fearing other people.

When the SK is forced to start a conversation with a person, he insists on doing all the talking because then it doesn't hurt his ears, and NKs hurt his ears. (See Chapter 2: Noise Sensitivity.) Another reason why he wants to do all the talking is because the SK is a late talker, and didn't get the proper talking stimulation when he was two, so he MUST get the stimulation now, and get talking 'out of his system.' So the SK keeps talking and talking, but does NOT realize that you want to talk too, because he does not notice the expression of annoyance on your face. Then the mother hits him on the back and screams, 'Let Max [or whoever] have a chance to talk!'

This starts another problem. When an NK talks to an SK, the SK cannot understand or process the talking in his mind, and this makes him confused (see Chapter 41: Verbal Confusion), still struggling to understand the first word after the NK has spoken fifteen words or

* By James, age 8

251

so. Because of all his confusion and ear pain stress, he tries to get rid of it, so he plays frozen, chants, or makes funny noises. If this doesn't work, he just walks away from the NK who is trying to have a pleasant conversation, or ignores him, and doesn't respond when the NK is done telling him the thing the NK wanted to tell him. Or the SK tells the NK what HE wants to say, never mind if he is using social reciprocity or not, never mind if it stays on the same topic or it switches topics, and the SK tells the NK what he was reminded of when the NK was talking.

But when the SK and NK get so confused (see Chapter 41: Verbal Confusion) with each other, they start having a fight, calling each other bad names, or hitting or kicking each other, and forgetting about trying to make a conversation together. The mother, who loses patience, stops the big fight, hits the SK on the back, and screams at the SK, 'Max [or whoever] wanted to have a good long time talking to you, and all you did was ignore him! Now he wasted a whole bunch of time trying to talk when you ruined his conversation!'

But the SK didn't realize that he was bothering the NK, because he was trying to make a conversation his way, but got hit on the back and yelled at.

Solution 1

Practice having conversations together at home. Then your SP may eventually learn the proper skills of reciprocity without an NK being embarrassed. At first, you can actually write out reciprocal conversations and have your SK read them. Afterward, analyze the dialogue in terms of give and take.

It would also help if you didn't even try to teach him about reciprocity until your SK is ready to join the world.

Problem 2

As we have told you in Chapter 73: Cooperation, NKs want to do things their own way at two, but when they are about three or so, they sometimes like to try other kids' ideas when they are in a group. So when somebody asks an NK, 'May I make a suggestion?' or, 'Do you need any help?' or, 'I'll tell you how to do it,' he will often say 'Yes' to the other NK. He wants to try out new ways instead of his own way, because he is not afraid of change (see Chapter 9: Change). This makes it easy for NKs to compromise with other NKs.

When SKs are two, they act the same way NKs act. But when they are three or so, they do not stop acting like two-year-olds when it comes to cooperation. SKs will still not be able to compromise, because the SK wants to try something his own way. Even when an NK asks him if he needs help, he'll just say no, because he thinks that HE is the only one that is able to make the project perfectly, and that no other NK will be able to make it as perfect as he does it. He also wants it to look the way he wants it to look, no bent or crooked parts in the making of the project.

However, he goes throughout his life failing in his own ways, because he is too young to figure things out, and besides he has no future judgment (see Chapter 78: Future Judgment) and hence cannot visualize or predict how something will turn out. Often NKs know that their ideas wouldn't work if they tried them, but an SK doesn't. This makes him frustrated, because most of his ideas NEVER work. SKs never read the instructions, they often disagree with what the instructions tell them, and have to do it another way.

Then the mother comes into the room, looks at her SK who didn't ask for help, frustrated and out of control because his way didn't work. She gets mad because her son didn't ask for help, and she hits him on the back and screams, 'How can you be so stupid? If you need help, tell somebody that you need help and LET THEM HELP YOU, FOR HEAVEN'S SAKE! WHY do you have to become FRUSTRATED if other people can help you!' When the SK says, 'I want to do it my way! I don't want it to look a different way,' she hits him on the back again and screams, 'WHY DO YOU CARE IF IT LOOKS DIFFERENT FROM THE WAY YOU WANTED IT TO? ANYWAY, WHY CAN'T YOU ACCEPT OTHER PEOPLE'S IDEAS, LIKE EVERYBODY ELSE!'

This puts the SK under intense stress, because he was only trying to put an idea into action, but people didn't let him. Often the SK stops doing his project and walks away. The mother then says, 'Finish the project! But ask for help the next time!' But the SK doesn't obey and still keeps walking, afraid that he'll get hit on the back and yelled at again.

Solution 2

[*By Mom*]: We don't have a good solution for this one! Try not to bring frustrating things into your house. Let your SK play with crayons and Play-Doh, not complicated building kits, unless he has a talent for building, and can manage all the little pieces.

Don't expect any sort of cooperation during his early years, especially if he is non-verbal. Try, instead, to develop an emotional bond with him. Gain his trust, which is no easy task, given that you are always reprimanding him or forcing him to do something he doesn't want to do. Once you gain his trust, you can begin to ask for a little cooperation from him.

James once remarked that he often thinks the world is inhabited by evil witches and monsters out to harm him. I'm sure I'm the head monster [though James, who is reading over my shoulder, just denied it]. At any rate, it took us a long time to establish a tight emotional bond, and I think he trusts me. This book was our most cooperative effort to date. We were *once* even able to clean the house in a cooperative fashion! But this ability had to wait until the other personal issues were resolved first, as we've said repeatedly.

84

Saying Goodbye

Problem

When one NP says goodbye to another NP, he feels several emotions: sadness, because he is parting from his friend; relief, since he is now going back home, where he can do whatever he wants; regret, because he is leaving a pleasant moment; but on other hand, excitement, too, because he is on his way to something new. The NP has said goodbye dozens of times, and he has all the proper words memorized: 'So long,' 'Thanks a lot,' 'Great to see you,' etc. He pulls one of these phrases out spontaneously, and uses it without thinking. Then as he drives home, he reflects upon what a nice day he had, then goes on to the next event in his life.

When an SP has to say goodbye to an NP, a lot of the same horrible feelings he had when saying hello (see Chapter 1: Saying Hello) resurface. First of all, saying goodbye means that a change is about to take place (see Chapter 9: Change), which fills the SP's veins with terror juice [James's term]. Second, he is expected to say something significant to another person, undoubtedly an NP, which makes him forget how to talk. Third, a thoughtless NP might try to touch or hug him (see Chapter 7: Touch Sensitivity), so the SP instinctively withdraws into himself to avoid these multiple horrors of parting. His mother, of course, hits him on the back and says angrily, 'Say goodbye!' By now, the SP knows that he'd better comply, or else his mother will hit him on the back again and launch into her lament about what a difficult child he is.

'Goodbye,' he whispers dutifully, but his mother says, 'Louder.'

'Goodbye,' he booms, with his best smile and his best eye contact, while he pushes down the urge to throw up all over the NP who is looking at him.

His mother then says, '*Shh!* Not so loud! You're yelling again.'

Then, even though the SP has done his best, his mother will still probably murmur some sort of apology to her friend, while the NP friend may whisper to the mom, 'I don't know how you stand it. Isn't there some special boarding school you can send him to?' The NP figures that because the SP always seems so out of it that he can't hear such a comment. However, as you know, the SP hears all such comments, and it makes him feel very bad about himself.

On the way home, the SP sits in the back of the car suffering, reliving all the horrible moments he had to endure at the NP's place, then he dreads returning home, where his mother is going to go through all the mistakes he made at the social gathering and embarrass him all over again.

This makes him hate and fear the next social gathering even more.

Solution

Ideally, let the SP stay home and avoid social events altogether until he expresses some social interest. You are just teaching him to hate and fear leaving the house. However, if he has to come with you, let him get used to the place on his own, then encourage him to participate – when *he* is ready. If he hides behind the table or makes a bee-line for the nearest computer, he is not ready to socialize. Although it is necessary to correct his social mistakes (such as when he starts quoting instead of answering someone's question), try not to heighten his stress level by being mean about his *faux pas*. (This is very hard to do, since his nervousness causes him to make a long string of mistakes, which are bound to annoy you.)

When it is time to say goodbye, put your arm firmly around your SP (if he enjoys such contact), then say, 'So long! We had a good time,' then squeeze your child's shoulder to indicate that the *we* took care of his obligation to say goodbye. Most NPs will make a point of saying goodbye to the SP, thinking this is polite and that he will enjoy it, so after saying goodbye to the host of the event, give the SP your car keys and let him sit in the car while you chat with the other people at the event. If you were wise and brought a stack of puzzles magazines or a hand-held game, the SP can occupy himself with these things, probably in a state of utter relief that he is alone and in an enclosed space (see Chapter 50: Cocooning).

After the event is over, go through everything that happened and point out the SP's mistakes, but also point out the things he did right, if any. I try to give James my theory as to why he did what he did, based on my knowledge of SPs. Sometimes he'll say, 'Oh, yeah! That's why I did it.' I try to acknowledge frequently that he never misbehaves or does the wrong thing on *purpose* (unlike normal kids), but rather, he does things based on SP reasoning. Try to avoid hurtful comments such as, 'How could you have been so stupid?' although we all say this to our SP more often than we should.

As in saying hello, practice saying goodbye over and over until it is a reflex. Practice every morning, if necessary. That will help develop the social centers in your SP's stressed-out mind.

Also, the reason he is talking too loud when you tell him to speak louder is because he is only obeying orders. If you tell him to speak louder, he will speak louder. But it is impossible for him to figure out how *much* louder, so he does the best he can.

Conclusion*
The Final Frontier

When NKs are two years old or so, they begin showing a real interest in playing with other NKs. They enjoy being with each other, and soon they engage in imaginary and cooperative play that is fun for everyone. Playing is something that NKs do naturally and are good at. The mothers of NKs start arranging playdates as soon as their kids can walk. This benefits the mothers, since they do not have to spend as much time with their kids that way. The kids take care of themselves during those playdates.

When SKs are two years old or so, they do not show any interest in NKs, because NKs act mean to SKs. SKs also want to be alone (see Chapter 70: Being Lonely and Making Friends), and do not want to play with other people, just be by themselves. NP mothers think that SKs are lonely and want to have friends, but they really don't. They don't care about friends at all. An SK does not need other people (see Chapter 79: Needing Other People), and people do not need him or care about him, because he does not play with them appropriately.

Because the SK's mother thinks that the SK is really lonely and doesn't want to be weird, she starts making a whole bunch of playdates that the SK does not want to be in. When the kid that came over realizes the SK doesn't want to do anything, and the mother sees the lonely and bored NK sitting around doing nothing, not playing with anybody like the NK was supposed to, and a happy SK sitting around being alone like he wants to, the mother hits the SK and screams, 'Johnny [or whoever] came here to play with you and all

* By James, age 8

258

you want to do is be by yourself and sit around and do nothing! Don't be so *selfish*!'

Then the SK is abruptly removed from being alone where he wanted to be, and is forced to be with an NK. When an SK and an NK try to play with each other, the SK often disagrees (see Chapter 68: Disagreeing with Other People) with what the NK wants to do. You see, the NK would rather play baseball or basketball or wants to play a board game, which the SK hates because somebody has to lose, while the SK wants to play on the computer for the whole time the NK is there. The SK often wins the big fight, and goes on the computer, while the NK is watching the SK, still bored to death, waiting for a turn. The SK cannot give the NK a turn because since he is so busy concentrating on the computer game he is playing, that he immediately forgets about taking turns with the NK, so he ignores the NK. The NK would rather get his body moving instead of sitting next to a computer getting radiated, while the SK wants to play all day on the computer. Finally the NK gets tired of sitting around, so he yells, 'Stop,' which hurts the SK's ears. The mother often goes in the computer room and sees the bored-to-death NK and the SK ignoring the NK and hits the SK on the back and screams, 'Let this person get his body moving! He needs his exercise! He came here to play a game too, and all you're doing is ignoring him! And stop playing computer! You've played enough computer already!'

Then the SK is forced to play a physical game, which exercises him at least, but he gets exhausted after ten seconds, and his knees hurt from 'too much exercise,' which is how the SK feels about all exercise (see Chapter 51: Exercise). Then, when the NK still wants to play and is full of energy, the SK is lying on the floor and resting because he feels tired. The NK keeps waiting for the SK to play with him, but the SK is too tired to play at this moment. The NK again asks the SK to play with him. By this time, the SK has fallen asleep. The mother then goes outside and sees the tired SK who fell asleep, and the bored NK who wants to play with the SK, and wakes up the SK, hits him on the back, and screams, 'Play with this person! He wants to play tag, and all you want to do is lie down!'

Then the SK, tired and rundown, tries to run and chase the NK and play tag. But he gets exhausted, and again he falls asleep. Finally the mother gives up trying to wake the SK up and finally the NK gives up trying to play with the SK. The NK goes home, thinking that trying to play with the SK was a huge waste of time. Then the mother lets the SK be alone, because she finally realizes that is the only way that she can have peace and quiet and have time by herself. But the mother still yells at the SK, because she wanted to have time by herself *during* the playdate, but she couldn't have any time because she had to watch the SK because he was not having a positive social interaction, and not having any fun like the mother wanted him to have.

[*By Mom*]: This is the *Final Frontier*, and most SPs never cross it successfully. Social skills are the last tasks the human brain learns, and it is last rung on the evolutionary ladder. As we have discussed in earlier chapters, true social learning cannot take place until the basic personal skills have been mastered (e.g. speaking comes before communicating; self-awareness before awareness of others; social interest before social ability, etc.).

Although we mothers have all been convinced that we have to put our kids into social situations so they will learn proper social behavior, we all know that our kids didn't learn any social behavior before they were ready. At most, they learned a short list of reflexes, in addition to learning how to hate and avoid other people in numerous and ingenious ways.

If I had to do it all over again, I would have arranged NO playdates (except with rent-a-friends, as discussed in Chapter 70), sent James to NO schools, enrolled him in NO social activities, but interacted with him on a one-on-one basis as much as he could tolerate during the day. In the best of all possible worlds, we would have had no guests, we would have cancelled all holidays and family gatherings, and I would have left him at home 365 days a year. If I had done that, I believe he would have naturally evolved from a content loner to someone who was lonely and needed other people. Then he would have been motivated to learn social interaction without being hampered by dozens of negative memories of being forced to play with this boy or that girl. But I feel he is luckier than most SPs, who may need to get over hundreds of negative interactions before true social learning can take place. Once the personal skills are in place and the social interest emerges, social learning can take place much like with any other child: by trial and error, with firm direction, encouragement, and practice. Reading social stories can help a lot, as can writing scenarios and reading them over.

We are still crossing the Final Frontier, and we welcome your input. So far, we haven't heard a lot of success stories in this area. Almost all the SPs we've heard about are still content, as teenagers, to be alone. Instead of really interacting socially, they have found a place for themselves outside normal society, and others have learned to keep their distance and not cross those boundaries unless invited. Love and intimacy are almost out of the question for these SPs, and this makes us sad.

James has been helped tremendously in his entry into the NP world by the love and loyalty of his sister, Lauren. Although she sometimes pushes him away, her own ability to love him has awakened the great potential for love that he has in his own soul. Hopefully, he can someday transfer the love he feels for her to the woman who will become his wife.

Good luck crossing the frontier! If we should meet you along the way, stop and chat. If our kids turn away from each other, that's okay, but maybe they won't. For each SP, we feel there is at least one potential friend out there, waiting to accept him. Since the time this book was first written, James has found several special friends, including one who lives in Canada, but who remains in touch through the magic of e-mail. This special friend introduced James to the miracle of shared interests (e.g. maps, *Calvin and Hobbes*), they hang out together at conferences, and they even gab on the phone once in a while. *SPs*, we hope you find that special friend. We know he or she is out there waiting to meet you – when you're ready.

Getting Better

It is possible for your SP to 'get better', provided he has meaningful language and reasonable language comprehension (see Appendix III: The Self-Help Guide to Teaching Language). By getting better, we mean that your SP learns to make peace with the NP world and either learns how to be like an NP or learns to find a safe place for himself within the NP world. James thinks that it's better to be like an NP; Mom is not so sure, since she finds that SPs possess a unique brand of honor and integrity that is missing in our amoral NP world, a little like the integrity of a *Forrest Gump*.

Whatever your goal is for your SP (inclusion or peaceful co-existence), you must tackle the problem on many levels. First, you have to embrace the doctrine that your SP is doing the best he can at all times, and that if he 'misbehaves,' he is doing so either un-knowingly or in self-defense. This sounds like an easy concept, but how many times have you thought or said, 'How can he be so stupid?' when your SP makes a mistake. And how many times have you yelled at him for breaking a glass, for example, and not accepted his explanation that his fingers didn't work for a minute, or he lost his power of thinking, or he forgot it was in his hand, or he didn't see it on the counter? If you can just be vigilant, and remind yourself that the SP is not trying to be bad, is not lazy, careless, or stupid, then you have the right frame of mind with which to begin helping him.

Second, it is necessary to get the SP to give you constant feedback. If he breaks the glass, stop what you are doing, sit him down, and ask him to tell you exactly what happened and why. He might say, 'I forgot,' or 'It was an accident,' but using your know-ledge of who he is, ask him specific questions: 'Were you thinking about the 'spicey-meat-a-ball' again?' 'Did you think the glass was in your right hand instead of your left?' 'Were you thinking about the time you broke a glass last week and your hand relived what happened that time?' Your SP will undoubtedly not be able to reflect upon his actions at first. (In fact, he may not even have enough language to say hello and goodbye.) Therefore, in the beginning, YOU give him the words. You say, 'I think the glass slipped out of your hand because you picked up a spoon with your other hand and couldn't hold two things at once.' Don't worry about 'putting words into his mouth' (an NP complaint). You know your SP better than anyone [from James: 'And you know a lot about SPs now that you've read this book.']. If there is no language coming out of his mouth, you be his voice. Keep putting all the possibilities in his mind. Eventually he will have a whole repertoire of human experiences to choose from, and he himself will tell you what happened.

Third, try to spend as much time as you can writing things down for your SP. Says James: 'The SP can understand it better, since he is a right-brained creature, and can translate writing better.' Almost all developmental delays involve some form of auditory processing delay, but hardly anyone with normal eyes has a visual processing delay (at least, we've never heard of anyone). Therefore, take advantage of your SK's visual normalcy (and the visual skills of the right brain), and teach him to read, write and type. We have boxes full of stories that we typed out to give James a sense of his own life. At four, he merely sat next to me as I typed. By his fifth birthday, he was typing on his own, and by seven, he was writing stories as good as any average NP adult could come up with. By eight, of course, he was able to compose (and type) significant portions of this book.

Fourth, keep your eyes and ears open to any new piece of information, any new therapy that anyone has used or tried. Listen to parents. Many mothers of speech-impaired kids are incessant talkers: they've learned how to fill the void. Listen to what they are saying! It is from parents that we have learned about every therapy that helped us. We learned hardly anything from the 'experts,' who told us over and over that we had a hopeless situation on our hands.

Fifth, how many times have you told yourself that you want your SP to be happy. How many times have you screamed (or at least thought), 'Nothing makes you happy!' All those times are in his head, so if you want him to be happy, try very hard to hold in your feelings of anger and despair when talking to your SP.

Sixth, you have to remember that you have to work full-time at helping your SP *before* puberty. It is said that bad wiring cannot be fixed after that time of life, so start right now!

Now, on to some specific resources:

For Problems with Saying Hello

Listen to the audiotape *Jazz Chants*, by Carolyn Graham, available from Oxford University Press. It is a series of 'chants' of everyday English conversation, intended for foreigners, to enable them to understand the rhythm of English. Although these chants are set to musical accompaniment, they are actually spoken, so they stimulate the speech centers in both hemispheres of the brain. Eventually you want all your SP's speech to be stored in the left hemisphere, but if he's still young and echolalic, you need to get language into the brain any way you can. He'll enjoy the chants. The first one is: 'Hi! How are you! I'm fine, how are you?' set to jazz rhythm. Be prepared to listen to your child chant them over and over, but they provide some fundamental conversation. Just tell your child that it isn't appropriate to greet someone by saying, 'You speak English *ve-ry* well' [a later chant]!

For Noise Sensitivity

Try Auditory Integration Training. Call the Georgiana Foundation in the US (call 860-355-1545 or 0208-455-5107 in England) to find a trainer near you. Note: Auditory Integration Training, developed by Dr Guy Berard in France, consists of 20 half-hour sessions (2 per day, with a 3-hour interval between each session) of listening to electronically altered music through headphones. The music is randomly altered so that sounds on various frequencies are either augmented or diminished, to encourage the ears to pay attention to the constant changes in the music. If a person is hypersensitive to a given frequency, that frequency is eliminated or reduced. Conversely, if a person has hearing loss on a given frequency, sounds on that frequency are increased, to encourage the ears to listen to that frequency.

For Eye Contact and Eye Sensitivity

Have your SP's eyes tested by a developmental optometrist, and do vision therapy if necessary. Chances are his eyes (like the two halves of his brain) don't work as a team, and he's receiving contradictory messages. Vision therapy can help.

For Change

Tell the SP in advance if something is about to change. I know this is not always possible, but do your best. And if a change is, to use Temple Grandin's term, 'shoved in his face,' try to remind him about another similar situation which he survived. Keep the house in a state of semi-chaos (usually not a difficult thing to do), so there is no correct place for anything. That will get the SP used to disorder.

For Quoting Urges

If you can stand it, let your SP quote as much as he wants at home. Tell him that quoting is socially unacceptable, and he cannot quote outside the house. Also, tell him that he can quote as much as he wants if no one else is listening. On the brighter side, he will do great in an acting class.

For the Chiropractor

Let your chiropractor know exactly what it means to be a special person, and that when the SP says something hurts, he should believe him! On the other hand, a chiropractor can be a friend and ally for a special person, since chiropractors throughout the years have been teased and rejected by doctors, who think they are superior. Therefore, a chiropractor knows what it is like to be left out and rejected, and can relate to the SP.

For Food Sensitivity

Let the SP take his own food when going out. But better yet, buy lots of different kinds of food and encourage the SP to take a tiny bite. He is afraid of most new foods because they are new and they taste weird *because* they are new. After the initial bite, the food is no longer new, and thus probably tastes better. We have named the initial first bite a 'Temple Grandin,' because she was the same way, and she first explained to us that autistic people don't like new things shoved in their faces. When Mom gives James a new glass or a new kind of food, he comments, 'A Temple Grandin, eh?' But when she says yes, it now relaxes him, since Temple Grandins aren't new to him anymore – they are old hat, and hence, not to be feared.

For Touch Sensitivity

Roll your SP in a blanket, or brush him with a surgical brush. Hug him really tight, and that will be less scary to him than a light touch. Lie on top of him, or play horsey, with him being the horse. Give him a nerf ball or Silly Putty to play with. Toughen his hands, so he doesn't fear touching things.

For Chewing and Swallowing

Try more Temple Grandins on this one. Start slowly, with fun foods.

For Toilet Training and Going to the Bathroom

Keep reminding yourself that the SP doesn't have a clear idea of what he is supposed to do, and he doesn't have a clear idea of his body's signals. Help him understand the difference between having to go or just having a gas pain, for example. If he is good at keeping time, maybe have him ask himself every half hour or so whether he has to go. If he is very young (under age five), in other words, an SK, you might try putting a potty in every room for a while. Then he will have visual cues about having to go.

For Auditory Processing Problems

Try FastForword, which is extremely expensive and involves a speech therapist, or *Earobics*, an inexpensive CD which you can own and which does basically the same thing as FF. To order *Earobics*, call (in the US): 847-328-8199.

For School

Try home schooling, if a special school is not available. Don't make your SK suffer in silence as the alien in residence. Contact the *Calvert School* (105 Tuscany Road, Baltimore, MD 21210, US) for a good home curriculum.

For a Home Therapy Program

Please see the website of *Brain-Net* and the *Institute for Brain-Injured Children* at http://www.btinternet.com/~brain.net. The director, Keith Pennock, is one of those enlightened individuals who believes that incredible healing can occur through ongoing, intense, at-home programs. His organization will test a child in seven areas of sensory and neurological development and plan a home program to correct any and all deficiencies. He and his wife, Val, helped their daughter, Allison, recover from severe brain injuries. Although his home base is in England, Keith makes trips to the United States and European countries to evaluate groups of children.

For Thinking Styles

Try listening to the tapes of the *Silva Method of Mind Control*, and find out that your SP thinks like a genius. Also read Temple Grandin's book *THINKING IN PICTURES*. To stimulate left-hemisphere development, have your SP engage in activities that sort, organize, and line things up. Marching around the house while counting one's steps stimulates the left hemisphere. Reading words off flashcards and doing rows of adding problems also stimulates the left brain. The more mindless and repetitive, the better. Reciting (not singing) the alphabet is a good exercise, too.

For Foot Problems

Try orthotics. Also, test to see whether your SK has a Babinski reflex in his feet. If he doesn't, keep stimulating the outside edge of his foot until he develops one. This will help with balance.

For Other People's Anger

Have the other person see a therapist.

For Communication Problems

Try FastForword, or auditory training, as noted above. The therapists at *LinguiSystems* (1-800-PRO-IDEA), a special-ed publisher, are also very helpful. They have someone manning the phones 24 hours a day, and they'll let you try out their language books and supporting materials with a full refund guarantee if not satisfied. [*By James*]: Also, try my technique by having your SP rehearse the thing he might say under his breath, because then the SP will know what to say. I do that all the time so I also won't forget what to say either. Also, I rehearse what stuff I am going to say in my head. I talk to myself by doing the same thing too.

For Telling Lies and Keeping Secrets

Recognize that the SP has hit an important milestone when he is able to tell a lie or keep a secret. Don't punish him too harshly. Enrol him in a drama class, so he can engage in pretend play, which is what a lie really is, isn't it?

For Exercise

Get as many gadgets as you can, with timers and buttons. Set up a program, which involves measurements and goals. That will make the SP feel safer, and will motivate him to keep track of the numbers. Encourage him to make graphs using *Microsoft Works*.

For Aiming Problems

Get those paper targets for the toilet. Set up a basketball hoop. Have the SP crawl around, which will help with depth perception.

For Waiting Problems

Try to imagine what it is like to have a volcano becoming active in your stomach. However, to practice waiting (and extinguishing the volcano), go to a lot of movies, which involve waiting in line. Take your SP to the store (but not a giant store), and wait in the longest line. Don't worry too much about selecting the 'right' line; whenever you are with a child who can't wait, you will automatically stand in the longest, slowest line.

A Word about Identifying with your Child

As you get increasingly involved in your child's therapy, you may find yourself identifying with his problems. In psychology, this is known as *transference*, and Jung used the term *participation mystique* to describe the interrelationship between a *healer* and his '*patient*.' If your child is forgetful, you may find yourself forgetting things or losing them around the house. If he mixes up letters and pronouns, you may find yourself mixing up pronouns for the first time in your life. You also may find yourself avoiding social situations, or feeling terror in the face of normal social encounters. Mothers often say, 'You know, I just realized that *I* have a lot of the issues that my child has.' It could be that you have been compensating for a learning disability your whole life, or you could simply be identifying with your child and absorbing his problems. This is not necessarily a bad thing; identification helps you better understand what he's going through, and it may help him take on some of *your* characteristics. Also, when you are forced to cope with his issues, you can perhaps come up with strategies that help both of you. The worst thing you can do for yourself and your child is to regard him as 'other,' some alien who is outside your control and who is wrecking your life. Once you go to the therapists and find strategies for managing this 'other,' then you set up a combat situation in which no meaningful healing can take place. He will hate you, and you will grow to hate him. Once this hostility gets established, it is necessary to start from scratch. Go back to that primal connectedness you felt with your newborn (or newly adopted) infant. Hold him in your arms, and reconnect. Give him that unconditional love and acceptance that he needs in order to grow. And if you suddenly can't tell the difference between the pronouns *I* and *you*, then you've made it back to the beginning, and there's hope once more for your child.

The Self-Help Guide
to Teaching Language

Language is the key to becoming a productive human being. Without language, your child may be adorable and lovable, but he will remain a pet, unable to join the human race as a participating member. Because a normal child learns language rapidly and without instruction, whereas most autistic children do not, it is necessary to analyze what steps the normal child goes through naturally to prepare himself for speech, then engineer situations for the autistic child that mimic these natural stages. We have stated repeatedly throughout this book that virtually nothing happens naturally for an autistic child, but that development *can* occur through conscious and continuous effort. We believe that even the complex tasks of speaking (and ultimately socializing) can be taught and learned.

Normal children learn how to speak using their mouths, ears, and speech center (normally in the left hemisphere of the brain). Since many autistic children do not learn to speak, we must first assume that something is wrong with any or all of the above, then fix them as best we can. It may be an impossible task, but at least, we have to try. Fortunately, a young child's brain has a characteristic referred to as *neuroplasticity*, meaning that one area of the brain destined to do one sort of task can actually adapt itself and perform some other task. In a blind child, for example, those brain cells that should have devoted themselves to processing visual information can adapt themselves to process some other kind of information depending on the child's need. We all know about a blind person's frequently heightened musical (or auditory) ability; presumably the visual learning center became an auditory learning center, giving the person an auditory advantage. Recently, the mother of a blind child told me that her son was able to read Braille fluently, but that it was almost impossible for a sighted person to learn Braille by touch alone. We simply don't have the sensitivity in our fingers. Perhaps her son's visual center became part of his tactile centers.

So let's assume that there are problems with all of the senses and brain centers related to speech. What do we do about it? Well, we try to fix them one at a time and in the proper order for speech. We can either encourage them to develop through sensory stimulation, or we can encourage other areas of the brain to take over for these damaged areas, again through sensory stimulation. This is no easy task, but it beats parenting a child who spends the rest of his life trying to get by on grunts, screams, and a handful of words. If your infant shows *any* signs of delay, get him to a neurologist for an evaluation, then start a home program. (In our case, the fact that James didn't mouth objects should have alerted us to future problems.) But whenever you realize there's a problem, even in an older child, it's still not too late to try and fix it.

If you have a child who isn't learning how to speak, the first thing to do is pull him out of day care, pull him out of school, pull him out of his early childhood program, quit your job, and devote all your waking hours to teaching language. Forget about playdates, forget about birthday parties, forget about teaching him to take turns or stand in line, and do nothing but teach language. This is very, very important. An hour a week with an expensive speech therapist will do nothing but force you to remain at your job so you can keep your health insurance to pay the fee. Normal children don't learn how to speak by hearing language an hour a week, and neither will yours. Tutoring will be your life for the next several years, but you could be saving your child from a life time of dependence and frustration.

Don't be seduced by the claims of an early intervention preschool. As long as there are other children in the room requiring assistance, much of your child's day will be wasted. Every moment he spends learning to sit still or wait his turn will be downtime for his brain. Because there is no appropriate place in his brain yet to properly store social information, all the lessons in sharing, turn-taking, etc., will be wasted, or worse, stored in an *in*appropriate part of the brain, dooming him to defective social skills the rest of his life.

So get him out of school, forget about making the beds, drop out of normal life, and begin:

The first step in learning language is developing mouth awareness and exercising the mouth. An infant first learns about the world through his mouth, and he is actually exercising those muscles for later speech. If your child doesn't put things in his mouth, refuses solid food, or displays any other sort of oral hypersensitivity, take your thumb and firmly massage his upper pallet. This will cut down on his sensitivity, similar to the way brushing cuts down on tactile sensitivity. Do this before he eats, and frequently during the day.

If he resists you or gags, encourage him to do it for himself. If that doesn't work, buy him an assortment of pacifiers, mouth toys, and other teething things for babies. If he's older, buy him a toothbrush with his favorite cartoon characters or his name on it to bite on, as well as an assortment of lollipops, candy pacifiers, and all the other oral junk that may rot his teeth (though hopefully, he can pass through this stage without too much damage). If he's sucking on his clothes or licking the walls, keep him out of social situations and let him do as much oral exploration as he chooses. Worry about germs some other time unless he's kissing shoes. In that case, buy some new sneakers for him, and wash them frequently.

If he resists solid food, give him nutritional shakes in a baby bottle. Give him water and juice in his bottle, too. One of the dumbest things that parents are advised to do is take away a baby's bottle as soon as he can handle a cup. Sucking exercises and develops the jaw, but more importantly it promotes serotonin release in the brain. Serotonin calms the brain and promotes social awareness and interaction. Researchers have found that the more serotonin a person has, the more social he is. And given that many of our children end up on serotonin-enhancing drugs such as Prozac, it's important to encourage natural serotonin production.

So let's assume your child is now sucking on an array of bottles, toys, and ring pops. Try to encourage him to make noises while he sucks, since another important step in language learning is to experiment with different sounds. Get your own ring pop and vocalize while you suck on it. We all know how wonderful it is to hear a baby babbling. He is actually experimenting with all the sounds he will later need for speech. Your child needs the same exploration. If he already makes sounds, encourage him to keep doing it. If he can't babble, teach him the letters and encourage him to sing the alphabet song, learn the letters visually, and obsess over them. Take his finger, put it over a letter, and encourage him to say it. Many kids will enjoy this. I bought James a workbook for apraxia and motor planning problems that consisted of exercises in which the child put his finger on various letters and said them out loud. He couldn't babble spontaneously, but he could generate sounds in the form of chanting a certain sound repeatedly or repeating the sounds that others made. One of his favorite things as a toddler was be carried in a backpack chanting, 'Ah-ah-ah-ah-ah' in time to our walking. We were smart enough to join in, and soon chanting 'Ah-ah-ah' became a rudimentary social event for James. Chanting is something that James did for years to calm himself down and block out the environment. We didn't realize until years later that chanting also promotes serotonin release and that monks use it to focus their attention during meditation.

If your child is not sound-sensitive, talk up a storm. Talk, talk, talk. Explain in great detail everything you are doing. Don't play music in the house (it stimulates the wrong side of the brain), but keep talk radio going twenty-four hours a day. Play it quietly in your child's room at night, with the radio positioned so that the talking goes directly into his right ear. (Because of the way the brain is wired, the right ear in connected to the left hemisphere, which contains the centers most naturally wired for speech acquisition.) The more speech a child hears, the more his speech centers will be stimulated. If he likes to be read to, read for hours, always positioning your child on your left so that the sound reaches the right ear first.

If he likes to do something odd while you're reading, such as pacing the floor or jumping on a trampoline, let him do it. Movement often enhances auditory processing. When I was homeschooling James, he'd like to lie on the top of the sofa, then roll downward into the seating part behind my back. This seemed like a distraction, but he was actually paying attention. When I learned, by listening to Temple Grandin speak, that movement enhanced language learning, I let James roll as much as he wanted. To this day, I let him assume unusual positions to read in, since he says he comprehends better. His least favorite position is sitting upright in a chair.

If your child is sound-sensitive, get him Auditory Integration Training, which lasts two weeks and can help normalize your child's hearing. If AIT isn't possible, work with your child in a quiet room, and begin by whispering to him. If you have his attention, gradually increase your volume until he displays signs of auditory distress. Then go back to whispering and gradually increase your volume again. If he has significant sound sensitivities, keep him away from crowds, playgrounds, and other kids. Don't force him to eat dinner at the table (the sounds of the utensils might be driving him nuts) or participate in holiday gatherings. Sound sensitivities tend to go away on their own if you give your child a quiet environment to live in.

I didn't initially know about the difference between speech and music in terms of what it did to the brain, so in those early days, I gave in to James's need to have music on all day long. Even when we were outside and I was pushing his stroller down the sidewalks of New York City, we had the tape player hooked to one of the handles, and we positioned the tape player under the swing as his little body arced back and forth above it, a blank look on his face. I didn't know at the time that he was concentrating only on the music and blocking out the discordance of the environment. When the tape player broke, I had to sing as he sat in his stroller or on the swing. Occasionally someone would come up to me on the street and say, 'I know you. You're that woman who's always singing to her kid.' Although all that music stimulated the right hemisphere of his brain, and I believe James is now a right-hemisphere language processor, it helped get auditory input into the brain, and any input is better than none.

The first actual speech your child produces will probably be echolalia (repeating verbatim what someone says to him). If he does that, rejoice. It means that the auditory centers are working, that language is getting into the brain, and that your child understands a basic rule of conversation; that when someone speaks to you, it's your job to reply. When echolalia starts, it's time to go all out to develop language *processing* capabilities. Anyone who has raised a speech-impaired child knows that there is major difference between reciting words and generating conversation. While you should be thrilled when he echoes you, don't stop there.

When James started echoing, he also began displaying his intense fascination with the alphabet. We were blessed with a child who showed us the key to getting through to him, but even if your child doesn't seem to be interested in visual language, expose him to it anyway. If he is a visual learner who can do puzzles, memorizes the route to Grandma's, and protests every time a chair is out of place (a visual change), bombard him with visual language. Buy him alphabet games, watch *Wheel of Fortune* every night, get *Start to Read* books on video (which have subtitles as well as the *Sesame Street* characters reading beginning books), and start pointing out all the written information in your child's world. Stop at every street sign during your walk, point out the *McDonald's* sign whenever you eat there, and point to each word as you read a book to him. If he starts engaging in so-called 'autistic' behaviors such as reciting house numbers as you pass by or chanting phone numbers, rejoice again. He is attempting to bring some order to language, and these apparently mindless activities are organizing his speech center for speech generation.

As we discussed in the chapters on language learning, buy simple flashcards and teach your child the words. Don't worry about comprehension at this point. Buy your child those deadly-dull audio sets such as *Hooked on Phonics* and play them in the car. He may enjoy the repetition of organized sounds and the chanting. If he is starting to 'decode' words, that is, sound out words without any comprehension, don't worry. Comprehension comes later. Don't listen to the experts who say that decoding is a meaningless splinter skill. If that were the case, then babbling is also a meaningless splinter skill. Decoding is a variation on babbling. It is a preparatory skill for deriving meaning out of language.

When your child is chanting, singing *Hooked on Phonics* songs, decoding, and rattling off house numbers, he is ready to take the next step into language comprehension.

I was once told by a speech therapist that James would have to learn English as if it were a foreign language, that his normal speech acquisition centers didn't work right. Although I already knew this latter part, the former idea – that of English as a second language – gave me an idea. I looked through several ESL catalogs and found the Oxford University Press's *Open Sesame* ESL series for kids. The series comes with tapes, workbooks, story books, etc., and assumes no prior knowledge of English! I bought James the first level, and instantly he was hooked. He listened to the tape over and over, and soon graduated to the next tape. Pretty soon the arrival of the next level in the mail became a major event in our house. When we ran out of professionally made tapes, I began making *Mommy* tapes for him, discussing the events of his day. His ability to comprehend language on tape far exceeded his ability to understand it in normal life because he was able to rewind and repeat something over and over.

Along with the home-made audiotapes, we made home videos for him, which he could watch repeatedly. Again, real life whizzed by way too quickly for him to comprehend, but a rewind button allows a child to study an event over and over. We videotaped the few speech therapy sessions we sent him to, and he watched them repeatedly, since I doubt he got anything out of them when they were happening. It was also from these videos that I realized I could do just as well as an expert in language teaching on a basic level. So why spend the money?

James, like most PDD-type kids, was also a computer fanatic (because of the small, visual format), so we allowed him to spend hours doing word- and reading-related games. All of these learning tools – audiotapes, videotapes, and computers – are sometimes regarded as antisocial by the experts, and we parents are told to limit our kids' access to them, but if they are tools for getting language into the brain, they are actually the most valuable socializers you can offer your child at this stage.

Along with decoding, we encouraged James to write, and soon he was writing out lists of things. Car names were his favorite. I began writing out everything I wanted to tell him and putting my finger on each word as I read it to him. Sometimes I put dots under each word to help him focus. We also realized that he comprehended spoken words better when they were spelled (he had a longer time to comprehend the word), so when he didn't listen to us, we spelled out our command. This technique worked like magic.

By the time James was four, I had a child who could echo, spell, decode, and print. He also could answer simple questions. It was at that point that I was told by a social worker not to expect much more, that kids like him 'never become normal.' My furious denial mechanism got activated by that outrageous statement, and I sat down to work out a plan to take James to the next level. *Eventual goal: full normalcy.*

I wanted him to be a self-aware, reflective, complex human being, not a tape recorder. I wanted him to have a sense of self. Since I didn't really have any idea who was inside there, I decided that I would pretend to be him, to get into his head, and 'give him a voice.' What would James say, I wondered, if he had the words to say it?

One day I sat down at the computer with the intention of giving James a voice. We opened up the *Sesame Street Writer*, and I began typing. 'My name is James Williams,' I wrote, 'I am four years old. I live at…' But no, I reasoned, James the human being was more than just a series of names and numbers. I don't remember what it was I actually wrote, but I focused on feelings. 'I don't understand a lot of what's going on, and that makes me feel afraid and scared, and I wish I could tell people what is inside me. I feel so alone.' I have no idea whether James understood a word, but I had his rapt attention. For the next hour, I gave James a voice.

The next day, and the next, I did the same thing for an hour. Each day we printed out our essay, and James carried it around the house. Gradually James started participating. At first, it was simply to decide which muppet character would carry the page number and which typeface to use. Then it was his turn to write the date, then on page 10 of every essay, he would type out a memorized poem. But little by little, he added small variations to the poem, and then he began shooing me away from the keyboard so he could add something. This went on for months, and we amassed several cartons of these stories. Sometimes James would go through the cartons and find a story he particularly liked, and we'd read it like a bedtime story.

In the middle of all this, James received Auditory Integration Training, and he seemed to be better able to comprehend spoken language, although reading, typing, and writing remained his primary means of language acquisition.

Little by little, James took over more and more of the typing of our stories until one day, the phone rang and I went to answer it. While I was talking, our second line rang, and I answered it. When I returned to the computer, to my surprise, James had typed out an entire 14-line poem in which he is complaining that Mommy has left him and is talking on the 'fone.' In the middle of the poem, he wrote, 'Not again. Another fone call,' obviously in response to the second line ringing. I was so shocked and delighted that I kept the poem, reading it to anyone who came over. It was written proof that my son really did have feelings and could even express them!

It wasn't long before James was writing out all his own stories, then poems, then fiction, then letters to other people. Without instruction, he became an accomplished typist who was adept at expressing his feelings on paper. When e-mail came along, he acquired several pen pals.

From ESL materials, we graduated to speech and language materials of increasing difficulty. Although reading comprehension remained a problem, we bought James computer programs such as *Reading Galaxy*, which require comprehension in order to win the game. As his overall knowledge of English increased, so did his reading comprehension. As his comprehension increased, so did his ability to generate speech. Because I kept him out of full-time school until he was ten, I had years to observe how he learned and what he did to enhance learning. At first, he would do annoying things such as speak only when someone else was speaking. When it was his turn, he'd remain mute. It was only later that he told me that hearing someone else speak made it *possible* for him to speak! He said that when he heard someone speak, his mind said, 'I want to do it, too.' Someone else's voice somehow activated his own speech centers. Perhaps that is actually some type of early reflex, and it got me wondering whether babies babble more in a noisy environment. To remedy this problem, we kept the TV on during our lessons to encourage him to speak.

During our homeschooling sessions, James would lie along the top of the back of the couch and roll down to where I was sitting. This was an annoyance until he explained that rolling helped his comprehension. Later on, I read in a sensory integration book that circular movement does improve language comprehension, so speech therapists often put their patients on swings or trapezes.

The rest of the story consists of more exposure to language, more practice, and greater proficiency. James had just turned five when he wrote about 'Mommy talking on the fone,' but by eight, he had co-authored the first version of this *Self-Help Guide*. A miracle? In some ways, yes. But his achievement represented thousands of hours of home speech therapy, more than any school, program, or therapist could ever offer.

As we've said elsewhere in this book, don't wait. Get to work! Your child's future depends on it.

The Self-Help Guide
to Teaching Social Skills

You can't learn social skills without social interest.

James Williams, at age 10

In order to teach social skills properly, you have to go back to the first primal social experiences that a special child missed, and let him experience them one by one in the proper sequence. Trying to teach social skills to an eight-year-old who's been alienated his entire life is like trying to put the roof on a building before the foundation is laid.

Before you even try to socialize your child, you must also think about your goals for him. How important is it to you that he becomes a feeling, caring, emotional person? If you decide that a future of solitude and social aloofness is OK, then teach him self-reliance (how to do his own laundry, shop, etc.) and be content with that. In my case, though, being an emotional, 'feeling' type, I couldn't imagine such a fate for any child of mine. In fact, I refused even to consider raising a cold, eccentric person. No way. I simply wouldn't waste my time on such a creature. So I decided that I would teach James to feel. There wasn't even an 'or else.' And when he was four and given a 'negative' prognosis, I went full-swing into denial and defiance, and I got to work.

So now, here is my advice on how to teach social skills:

If you have normal children, think back on how they first noticed the outside world and other people, and how you responded to them. The first time your SP notices other people, he may have the social awareness of an infant, so treat him like one.

His first and fundamental social bond should be with you. Oh, he may already rely on you to have his needs met and to chauffeur him from appointment to appointment, but has he bonded with you? Does he feel love when he's with you? If not, get to work.

Roll him in a blanket ('swaddling clothes') and watch television with him. Hold him if he likes it. If not, find a distance that's comfortable for him and just hang out together. Then try rubbing and holding. If he has tactile sensitivity, brush him and administer joint compression first, until he will accept your touch. If he likes pressure, sit on him, lie on him, play sandwich, etc., until he looks forward to it. Let your first bond be with touch. All the while, tell him how much you love him, what it feels like to love him, and how special he is to you. Sing love songs to him as if he were your newborn baby.

If he can't bond with you, pull him out of school and other social distractions, and make him totally dependent on you. Limit his environment so that it is *stress-free*, and just treat him like an infant. This is more easily done with a younger child, but you have until puberty to make a real dent in this area. Be in his face all day. If he's playing the computer, sit down next to him. If he's watching television, force him to watch emotional movies and cry your head off at the sad parts. Be as demonstrative and unashamed of your feelings as you can.

As I've written in other portions of the book, I also decided when James was four that I wasn't content to raise a child who could only talk about the alphabet and impersonal things. I wanted a *human being*. When other parents call me and tell me that their child can talk, I ask them, 'Do you feel like you're talking to a human being?' Many times, they admit no, they don't feel as if their child is a human being. They don't know what's going on inside. So in addition to being in his face all day long, I sat him down for an hour a day and gave him a voice, as described above. I did this by pretending to be him and typing out the events of his day. Throughout these essays, I threw in all kinds of feeling statements: 'I wish Mommy wouldn't yell so much. I feel afraid and it hurts my feelings.' I doubt whether James understood a word at first, but I kept typing. And I had his attention. I think at first that he enjoyed watching the letters magically appear on the screen, then (since he was hyperlexic and a spelling fanatic), he enjoyed watching my typos frequently appear. His delight at catching them was his first interaction with me during these sessions. And of course, I threw in some intentional typos to see if he was paying attention.

As I mentioned in the appendix on language, gradually James took over more and more of the typing until he was doing all of it himself. We have boxes full of our essays, and although many of his don't make any sense, he was communicating as best he could.

When I was convinced his relationship with me was solid enough, I started looking for other women for him to bond with. The director of the Kid Zone at the local YMCA is a kind, compassionate, gifted woman, and she befriended him when I left him there. At first, he cocooned under the slide, but Rita coaxed him to come out and play board games with her. One day, he went home and wrote his first love letter to her. One letter turned into a dozen, and although they made little sense, writing to Rita and mailing the letter became a major event of the day. She saved his letters to discuss when they met next. After me, Rita was his first love.

Then his Aunt Linda, also a kind, gifted woman, started taking him out to dinner. Linda has infinite patience and is an excellent listener, and James poured out his heart to her, whether or not it made sense. He and his aunt still have dinner together once a month and this has been going on for over four years now.

Once James developed the ability to bond with another, I thought about how infants take the next step toward social interaction. They don't go to school; they play simple give-and-take games. They play peek-a-boo and hand games, and that's what we did next. One of the major requirements for social interaction is developing an interest and basic understanding of the other person, and peek-a-boo is a simple form of being interested in what the other person is doing. This basic skill evolves into something called 'theory of other minds,' and it is the inability to develop this that seems to be a characteristic of autism. So developing a theory of other minds becomes crucial.

Trying to play with other children is generally a hopeless undertaking for an autistic child, as it was for James at first, but after seeing him interact with adults, I gradually lowered the age of the people he interacted with. I hired a number of rent-a-friends of varying ages, and for several years, his major interaction was with these paid companions. Because this was a job to them, it was their duty to be nice and to figure out meaningful ways to play with James. I didn't care about criticism that this wasn't the 'real world.' The world an autistic child retreats into isn't the real one either.

School was, until recently, a disaster, so I basically homeschooled him until he was ten. We attempted to send him to preschool and mainstream school, but I pulled him out of as many schools as I enrolled him in until the fourth grade. He did have a successful time as a part-time kindergartner at the age of seven, but his gifted teacher wisely let him ignore the other kids and interact only with her. She became the next major female figure in his life, and he still goes to visit her after school.

I could go on and on about the things we did, but you've already read enough about our family. Suffice it say that you should adopt several general principles and stick to them. At first, help your child to bond and trust other people. Then, help him understand his own feelings. Finally, help him to understand the feelings of others and develop that elusive but all-important 'theory of mind.' Our game 'What is Mommy feeling?' helped James a lot in this area. Writing scripts that gave him emotional experience helped as well. Imaginative play was very difficult for James, but reading scripts was easy. The important aspect of play-acting is not that it must be improvised but that the participant gets into another's role. If your child is playing the king, then he is learning how to be someone else, and that helps develop his theory of mind. It doesn't matter if he is simply reading lines.

Don't listen to any criticism from ignorant people who have never raised a special child. Don't worry about squelching his independence. For heaven's sake, your child was born independent and that's his major problem! True independence is light-years away from the alienation your child suffers from.

Only when your child has acquired a sense of basic trust, meaningful language, a rudimentary theory of other minds, *and* social interest can he *begin* to learn real social skills. But even these acquisitions give him only the capacity to learn. When he first sallies forth into the real world, he will be like *Pinocchio* — a little wooden boy who is eager to learn but is prey to all sorts of mistakes, misjudgments, and mischievous people. To become real, so to speak, he needs wisdom and constant feedback. He needs his own form of *Jiminy Cricket* to tell him what's right and wrong *all* the time. I tried to convince the school system that someone like James needed a social aide to instruct him in proper behavior every minute of the day. That was the only way he would acquire enough social learning to become *normal*. Unfortunately aides are provided only to curb inappropriate behaviors, not to teach good ones, and they are provided for the benefit of the other people, not the SP. Neurological normalcy, and what it takes to get there, is never a goal for an SP in a mainstream setting.

So once again I became his tutor, trying to give him the feedback he needed and to dissect and analyze all his social interactions. On his first full day of school, he asked repeatedly if he could call me up for advice, and he was scandalized at being forbidden to do so. He simply couldn't understand a world in which a child wasn't allowed to speak to his mother.

Although James is now a successful fifth grader with no special education support, he's still working towards gaining his 'real boy' status. He has a number of good friends who share his interests in roadmaps, ice skating, and *Pokemon*. But I am still half-Mom, half-Cricket, watching over my shoulder for all the 'Honest John' types who seek to dupe him when my back is turned. One of the things we are both learning is that so-called 'normal' people may have normal social skills but they often lack the higher qualities of compassion, empathy, and honesty, especially when dealing with special-needs people. Although my original goal for James was normalcy, I have now set my sights a lot higher. James will grow up to be an honorable man, who treats everyone with kindness and respect. In that regard, he will truly be special.

The Self-Help Guide
for Special Teachers

It's a new school year, and you've just found out that you're going to have Johnny the SP in your mainstream classroom. You've been handed a thick stack of articles and tip sheets about 'integrating' and 'including' him in a normal educational setting, and you may even have attended a planning meeting in which the special education coordinator talked in glowing terms about the benefits of 'full inclusion' for a child like him. You've also heard from your colleagues, however, about what a problem he was in *their* classes. You may even have been warned that his parents are worse than he is – pushing, argumentative, and unreasonable; bombarding his teachers with notes, phone calls, and complaints – and that you are in for a miserable year. What can you do?

First of all, admit to yourself that 'integration', 'inclusion', and 'mainstreaming' are impossible unless a child is interested, willing, and able to participate in a group educational setting. If his eyes go out of focus every time someone speaks to him, or if he sits at his desk humming and rocking with a scowl on his face, you will not be able to integrate him into your classroom community no matter how hard you try. And don't kid yourself about it. Forcing a child to sit in a room all day with other kids does not mean you have mainstreamed him. You may have mainstreamed his body, but his mind, his brain, and his soul are on another planet.

As you know from reading this book, we believe that mainstreaming an autistic-spectrum child can be destructive to everyone concerned, especially the child. If his brain is not ready to store social information, he will regard the people around him as intruders and invaders and will work on blocking them out. Pretty soon, he will reject other people as a reflex, and his brain will have created negative, antisocial patterns that may be impossible to undo later. Furthermore, without social skills, almost every one of his encounters with his peers will lead to some form of rejection or humiliation, further convincing him that other people are his enemies.

On the other hand, there are some things you can do to make life much easier for everyone in your classroom. Our advice, of course, is for handling a high-functioning, verbal child who has rudimentary social awareness but underdeveloped social skills. A non-verbal, classically autistic child generally has a good time in a mainstream classroom, since he is oblivious to what's going on around him, and people tend to treat him with the compassion afforded a pet or mascot. The kids may see his hand-flapping and immature behavior as cute, and they may try to include him in their games the way they'd include a baby brother. He'll probably also have a full-time aide, who'll protect him from any negative encounters with his classmates.

A high-functioning, verbal SP faces a whole set of problems. If he is academically normal or advanced, he will not deserve an aide, and so you will have to deal with him unassisted. This is no easy task.

From our personal experience, and from the experiences of other families, we have come up with our own set of rules for teachers of SPs.

As we mentioned above, realize from the start that full inclusion is impossible for this child unless he wants to be included. If he avoids the other kids and the other kids avoid him, let him work on his own. Let him sit apart from the other kids and work at his own pace. If you can establish a one-on-one rapport with him, you're doing *great*. Let him interact only with you, but if he does establish that single connection, then you have given him a positive social experience upon which he can build future relationships. James's experiences as a seven-year-old part-time kindergartner were the first positive social encounters he had in a school setting. The instinctively brilliant teacher allowed him to ignore the other kids, and they ignored him, which meant that he got through the entire experience without a single episode of teasing, taunting, or victimization. On the other hand, this teacher encouraged him to develop an intense, almost parental relationship with *her*. She gave him extra attention, regarded his obsessions and fixations with the alphabet and numbers as signs of his brilliance, let him talk her ear off, and kept smiling as he came up with his own unique ideas. That was four years ago, but James still goes back and visits his old beloved teacher regularly. Despite his total lack of inclusion with his kindergarten 'peers,' James learned to trust another person besides his mom during that year, and this provided a foundation for later connections.

That wonderful year was in stark contrast to what came next – a short stint with a teacher who had special education background. From the start, this subsequent teacher was determined to 'socialize' James, and she forced him to interact with the other kids, recite their names aloud (see the Preface), and sit at a desk that was jammed up against his neighbor's. It was during that year that he started humming to block out the noise, picking his nose to bother the other kids, and defying the teacher reflexively. When he came home, he'd lie facedown on his bed dragging his fingers along the carpet. If I hadn't pulled him out of school at Christmas break, I may have lost my son altogether. I kept him out of school for a year and a half, during which time we worked on personal issues such as eye teaming, physical coordination and strength, and language skills. We also wrote the first edition of this book, to help clarify for ourselves just how eight-year-old James experienced the world.

It took me a while to undo the damage done by that teacher and her 'special education' experience, but I did so by re-establishing the intense one-on-one relationship that I and the kindergarten teacher had had with him. I also made sure that his other social encounters were limited to positive, one-on-one interactions with sympathetic adults and rent-a-friends. I got him a personal trainer at the YMCA, every month he took his compassionate Aunt Linda out to dinner to learn manners and social skills, and he went to school only to meet privately with the empathetic social worker, the speech therapist, and this beloved kindergarten teacher after school.

James was ten years old before he was ready for real mainstreaming. He had mastered the normal personal skills, and was showing signs of social interest. He became envious of my daughter's multitude of playdates and friends, and he decided for himself that he wanted to go back to school. I knew that he lacked the social skills to succeed with other kids, but he informed me that I had sheltered him too long. 'Doesn't life include both good and bad experiences?' he asked. When I said yes, he continued, 'So if I have a bad time at school, isn't that still a part of life?'

How could I argue with that? So James became a full-time student at that age of ten, but it was his own decision, and he was interested and motivated to learn how to be a part of his peer group. I believe that was a crucial first step toward real inclusion.

During that year, he was blessed with another gifted teacher, who regarded herself as an SP and therefore was tolerant of James's quirks. She praised his ideas openly in class, and she allowed him to work by himself when unsupervised, as small-group activities proved to be too stressful. She let him sit in the back of the room slightly apart from the other kids, and that added greatly to this physical comfort.

His desire to be in school did not mean that other kids accepted him at first. Far from it. By the second day of school, the bullies were lining up, ready to tease him. Remember that James's entire social experience consisted of interactions with sympathetic adults or hired friends, so he had no self-defense skills or ability to deal with teasing, taunting, and entrapment. In this area, his fourth-grade teacher as well as the social worker were of little help. The kids would tease James, but when he'd complain about them, the kids would deny wrongdoing, profess undying love for James, and James would be told that the teasing was his 'misinterpretation.' James established no meaningful relationships with peers that year, primarily because the adults were unable to see what the other kids were doing to him. So our next piece of advice is to believe the SP when he complains that he is being bothered. Even if it is his 'perception' of the situation, *every* human experience is as it is perceived. If your student is feeling distress, his distress is real. If the other student complains that he was just trying to be friendly, then have the students re-enact the scene for you, and analyze it. You may even decide to have a class meeting every week in which various troublesome encounters are re-enacted in front of the class, so that the kids can all comment on the problems and work on improving them.

This year James has a male teacher, who runs a much tighter ship. He allows no teasing, and James's complaints are taken seriously. Even his 'misperceptions' are listened to, and other kids have been asked to explain their behavior. This teacher has applied gentle but consistent pressure on James to interact with the other kids, especially in small-group activities, but any problem or ganging up against him is resolved immediately. James has actually earned a modest amount of respect and acceptance in the classroom, and he has a few real friends. And now that he is *interested* in truly fitting in, he is *motivated* to learn appropriate social behavior. At eleven, he is learning social skills that should have been learned at age six, but at least he is learning them.

In summary, you will have a much easier year with your SP if you give him the experience he wants and is ready for. If he craves social isolation, let him have it. Forget about teaching him complex social skills; he won't learn them because he can't. He'll have to learn by rote how to wait in line, take his turn, control his impulses to blurt out his thoughts, and suppress his anger at being confined in an uncomfortable situation, but give him as much freedom as the situation allows. Remember that he is under a lot of stress just from the environment, so don't add to his stress by forcing him to work with the other kids.

Try to learn as much as you can about autism and neurological disorders, then try to imagine what it would be like to *be* autistic. Imagine the worst kind of terror and stress (e.g. hanging upside down in a stalled, malfunctioning roller coaster at Great America), then think about having to deal with that kind of terror every day for hours at a time. Also imagine a world in which you had no friends, in which on one understood you or shared your interests, and in which you lived in constant fear of doing the wrong thing. You'll be able to see how important it is for you to reduce your SP's stress level.

Finally, try to validate your SP's talents and interests, and to praise his originality. James not only had a kindergarten and fourth-grade teacher who openly admired his talents, but he has had the good fortune to have a brilliant music teacher at school who has consistently encouraged him to explore and create. This teacher gave him a major role in the recent fifth-grade show, as 'Father Time welcoming in the New Millennium' and everyone who saw the show remembers James dressed in a white bathrobe thumping his cane across the stage as he chased Dick Clark (but didn't catch him, because Dick Clark never ages!).

Just follow your instincts, put yourself in the child's shoes, and you'll do fine. When you're stumped, read over the following bits of advice:

1. Recognize from the outset that real mainstreaming and inclusion are only possible if a child wants to be mainstreamed.

2. Allow a child to work independently if that's what he needs and is all he can handle. Don't make him participate in circle time, small-group activities, or peer interactions if he avoids them or behaves inappropriately.

3. Encourage the child to establish an intense, one-on-one relationship with you to help him develop a sense of basic trust. Do this even is it means giving him more attention than the other kids. He needs it!

4. Try to reduce the SP's stress level whenever possible. Let him skip field trips and special performances and events if they cause him too much anxiety.

5. Allow the SP to work on things that interest him and praise his originality. If you don't understand what he's doing, ask him to explain it to you, and keep trying to understand. The logic will eventually become apparent to you.

6. Make physical and other accommodations to reduce the SP's anxiety and sensory overload. Allow him to sit apart from the other kids. When James revealed that the monthly fire drills were causing him ongoing anxiety because they were unannounced, the principal of his school personally warned him right before each one occurred. This was

bending the official rules, but it saved him from having to worry *every day* whether today would be the day the noise shot through him like a cannon.

7. Take the SP's complaints of teasing seriously. Even if it only his 'perception', that is how he experienced the interaction. You may want to alert the students at the beginning of the year that the SP has special problems, though kids find out for themselves pretty quickly. Try to pick one or two empathetic kids to serve as the SP's allies, and praise these kids lavishly for their mature and compassionate behavior. Set them up as examples of good citizenship.

8. Recognize that your instincts are more important than any principles you've been given for handling your SP. Feel free to ignore any rules, including ours, if a situation warrants it. Confer freely with the parents, who are smarter than you think. They've been working at the task of understanding their special child for a long time.

9. Remind yourself that you're doing important work. James's kindergarten teacher once told me that it wasn't often that a teacher could make a profound effect on a student, and she felt proud that she had changed the course of James's life. Remember that you have the potential to redirect a child's future and to give him the chance to be a happy, productive member of society. Any extra effort you give in this task will be worth it.

APPENDIX V

SPs in the New Millennium

An autistic person couldn't have been born into a better era. While *you* are suffering under the oppression of automated phone menus, websites that send you in circles from one screen to another without showing you what you want, heartless computer programs that can't tell the difference between a simple typing error and a real mistake, and work situations in which you are forced to sit isolated at a desk interacting with a machine all day, your SP may recognize these electronic marvels as his friends – his peers, even – since they think the way he does.

A computer does not understand the nuances of language; everything is literal. So while you see this characteristic as a deficit in your child's language, he may feel at home communicating with a machine in ways that you never will. And while you curse and fume when you have to select from sixteen different phone menus to find out a single piece of information, your SP may be soothed by information that is arranged in that fashion. It is my theory that the people who invented these dreadful things are SPs, who simply don't understand how oppressive they are to the rest of us stupid normals.

Once your child learns language and can generate meaningful speech, he is on the way to being a fully employable worker in the computer era. But even if he can't learn language the old-fashioned way, he now has an array of electronic gadgets to help him. If his auditory-processing centers don't work right, he has numerous visual methods of language learning, including computers, videos, closed captions, etc., and he also has language tapes and audiovisual therapies such as *FastForword* and *Earobics*. Electronics make it possible to learn how to speak without social interaction, just as they make it possible to work without social interaction. As scary as the coming millennium may seem to us in terms of social isolation and alienation, it is the reality that we NPs will have to get used to. No longer will the world be just the NP world; the SPs have fashioned it more in their own image.

When James was four and I was listening to a social worker tell me about his PDD, I asked her with trepidation, 'Will my child ever be normal?' She shook her head sadly and said, 'Nope. These kids never become normal. At most, James might become, say, a computer nerd.' As soon as I left her presence, I burst out laughing. Computer nerds, after all, make a *lot* more money than social workers.

So, too, will your child's allergies and sensitivities serve him well in the coming era. As processed food becomes increasingly toxic, your child's allergies will prevent him from ingesting the worst, which is the overly sugared, overly colored junk aimed at children. James's wheat allergies make it impossible for him to eat most junk foods, thereby eliminating the empty calories, preservatives, additives, and what's worst, the trans-fats from his diet. It might be a hassle now to make spelt bread, but over a lifetime, your child's load of carcinogens will be greatly reduced. And his sensitivities to the air, water, etc., may force you to purify his environment, which will give him a brighter future than all those kids who live on normal junk now, but who are destined to have major health problems later on.

At the beginning of this book, I asked you to imagine a normal classroom full of normal kids engaged in normal activities. Now I ask you to imagine the 'normal' classroom of the future. More than half of the students are twitching, tapping their fingers and toes, tilting their heads, rocking their torsos, murmuring to themselves, and daydreaming. Instead of enjoying a mid-morning snack, most of the kids go to the nurse at 11:00 and wait in an enormous line to get their 'meds'. The number of hall monitors needed to keep order has increased dramatically over the past years. More than half the kids have IEPs (individualized educational programs), and most of them go home for lunch, since they are allergic to the cafeteria food. Throughout the day, small groups of kids leave the classroom for their special therapies. Almost everyone has some kind of learning disability.

An exaggeration? Probably not. If those normal kids who harass your child keep up their current life style of too much stress and not enough nourishment, it's their children who will suffer the consequences of environmentally induced PDD and ADD, while your grandchildren, despite their genetic handicap, will probably do just fine. In fact, the teacher of this class full of neurological problems could be someone like James. From time to time, he says that he wants to become a teacher to help kids like himself. It could be that all teachers in the future will need some kind of special education experience.

So in spite of the problems involved in raising your SP, he is also blessed by his 'disability.' All your work and sacrifice will someday pay off. And even if life continues to be more difficult for him, he will benefit from the extra attention and love that you surround him with. The other day, my daughter, Lauren, who is now seven, observed that SPs get more attention and learn more. 'I wish I were an SP,' she said wistfully. I understood her frustrations exactly. She has watched her 'dumb' brother blossom into a leader in his school and in the special-needs community. His accomplishments in writing, in the recent school play, in the school-wide spelling-bee, in the school newspaper, and in the public eye (people e-mail him from all over the world) far eclipse her own normal achievements. She sees it as unfair that he can sit down and type like the wind while she is struggling with the first word. She also resents the fact that he is self-disciplined, needs no reminders to get his homework done, and is impervious to what other people think. He has a sense of security and self-esteem that she may never achieve. She blames me for 'neglecting' her – by this, she means that I let her engage in unlimited playdates and sent her to play groups, preschool, and normal public education. She did all the 'normal' things, and as a result, she lacks the character, confidence, and self-discipline of her homeschooled brother. If *she* has been harmed by normal childhood experiences, how much more damaging will it be to your special-child to be forced into these activities, which are meaningless and stressful to him and which set him up for social failure?

We hope that our book has given you some insights into your child's special needs and that, as a result, you will try to give him a special world in which to safely reside as he struggles to develop into the person he is meant to be.

Good luck in all your efforts. Your child is worth it.

Index